1,000,000 Books

are available to read at

Forgotten Books

www.ForgottenBooks.com

Read online
Download PDF
Purchase in print

ISBN 978-1-331-01123-1
PIBN 10133237

This book is a reproduction of an important historical work. Forgotten Books uses state-of-the-art technology to digitally reconstruct the work, preserving the original format whilst repairing imperfections present in the aged copy. In rare cases, an imperfection in the original, such as a blemish or missing page, may be replicated in our edition. We do, however, repair the vast majority of imperfections successfully; any imperfections that remain are intentionally left to preserve the state of such historical works.

Forgotten Books is a registered trademark of FB &c Ltd.
Copyright © 2018 FB &c Ltd.
FB &c Ltd, Dalton House, 60 Windsor Avenue, London, SW19 2RR.
Company number 08720141. Registered in England and Wales.

For support please visit www.forgottenbooks.com

1 MONTH OF
FREE
READING

at
www.ForgottenBooks.com

By purchasing this book you are eligible for one month membership to ForgottenBooks.com, giving you unlimited access to our entire collection of over 1,000,000 titles via our web site and mobile apps.

To claim your free month visit:
www.forgottenbooks.com/free133237

* Offer is valid for 45 days from date of purchase. Terms and conditions apply.

English
Français
Deutsche
Italiano
Español
Português

www.forgottenbooks.com

Mythology Photography **Fiction** Fishing Christianity **Art** Cooking Essays Buddhism Freemasonry Medicine **Biology** Music **Ancient Egypt** Evolution Carpentry Physics Dance Geology **Mathematics** Fitness Shakespeare **Folklore** Yoga Marketing **Confidence** Immortality Biographies Poetry **Psychology** Witchcraft Electronics Chemistry History **Law** Accounting **Philosophy** Anthropology Alchemy Drama Quantum Mechanics Atheism Sexual Health **Ancient History Entrepreneurship** Languages Sport Paleontology Needlework Islam **Metaphysics** Investment Archaeology Parenting Statistics Criminology **Motivational**

CONTENTS

CHAP.		PAGE
I.	A FAMILY TRUST	1
II.	THE SQUIRE	26
III.	THE GRAND TOUR	58
IV.	HOME	86
V.	THE WELFORD WEDDING	118
VI.	'GENTLEMEN OF THE MILITIA'	153
VII.	LAETITIA	181
VIII.	'MY BARON'	217
IX.	DRESDEN	252
X.	MRS. HOUBLON NEWTON	272
XI.	THE SIXTH JOHN	282
XII.	EARLY VICTORIA	292
	TABLE SHOWING THE DESCENT OF MRS. HOUBLON NEWTON	305
	PARAGRAPH PEDIGREE	309
	SKELETON PEDIGREE	317
	TABLE OF ALLIANCES	321
	INDEX	325

LIST OF ILLUSTRATIONS

HALLINGBURY PLACE, ESSEX, AFTER REBUILDING IN 1772-3 . . . . . . *Frontispiece*

MARY HYNDE COTTON (MRS. HOUBLON, born 1716). From a picture at Hallingbury. . . . . *facing* 34

SIR JOHN HYNDE COTTON, FOURTH BARONET (born 1688) *facing* 51

MARY HYNDE COTTON (wife of Jacob₃ Houblon, Esq.) *facing* 72

JACOB₃ HOUBLON, ESQ. (born 1710). From a picture at Hallingbury . . . . . *facing* 86

LAETITIA₁ HOUBLON (born 1742) . . . *facing* 92

JACOB₄ HOUBLON, ESQ. (born 1736) . . . *facing* 98

REMAINS OF THE 'DOODLE OAK' IN HATFIELD FOREST, ESSEX. From a Photograph . . . *facing* 107

IN THE FOREST OF HATFIELD BROAD OAK. From a Photograph . . . . . *facing* 110

ARMS OF JOHN ARCHER, ESQ., AND LADY MARY, *née* FITZWILLIAM . . . . . . *facing* 118

JOHN ARCHER, ESQ. From a Miniature dated 1771 by Ozias Humphrey, R.A.; LADY MARY ARCHER, AND THEIR DAUGHTERS SUSANNA AND CHARLOTTE . *facing* 129

SUSANNA HOUBLON, *née* ARCHER, AND HER DAUGHTER MARIA. From a Pastel . . . *facing* 156

THE CHILDREN OF WILLIAM AND SUSANNA ARCHER (*née* NEWTON), viz. JOHN ARCHER, MICHAEL ARCHER, afterwards NEWTON, SUSANNA (married Edward Harley, fourth Earl of Oxford), and CATHERINE (married Philip Blundell, Esq.). Picture formerly at Culverthorpe, Lincolnshire, by Jos. Highmore, 1747 . *facing* 161

SUSANNA, AND JACOB₄ HOUBLON, ESQ., 1771. From Miniatures by Ozias Humphrey, R.A. . . *facing* 166

CHARLOTTE ARCHER. From a Silhouette . . . 168

JOHN₆ HOUBLON (afterwards Archer Houblon), only son of Jacob₄ Houblon of Hallingbury (born 1773). Silhouette 171

LAETITIA₂ HOUBLON, second daughter of Jacob₄ Houblon. Silhouette 171

MARIA HOUBLON, elder daughter of Jacob₄ Houblon. Silhouette 173

JOHN₅ HOUBLON, second son of Jacob₃ Houblon of Hallingbury, Esq. From a Pastel . . *facing* 176

'COIFFURE DE GRANDE PARURE' (1786-1788). Copied from Racinet, *Costume Historique*, vol. vi. . . 193

MISS LAETITIA₁ HOUBLON. From a Pastel . . *facing* 204

JOHN₆ HOUBLON (afterwards Archer Houblon), (born 1773). From a Miniature by George Engleheart . *facing* 234

ARMS OF BARON AND BARONESS VON FEILITZSCH . *facing* 252

FASHION PLATE, 1802 . . . . *facing* 261

MARY-ANNE BRAMSTON (born 1777). By G. Engleheart *facing* 262

MODES. From Racinet, *Costume Historique*, vol. vi. *facing* 266

ARMS OF MRS. HOUBLON NEWTON . . . *facing* 272

SIR JOHN NEWTON, THIRD BARONET (born 1651). From a Picture by Sir Godfrey Kneller . . . *facing* 274

ARMS OF CARADOC *alias* NEWTON, as borne by 'Kradog, King of South Wales' (died 1035). From a Pedigree Roll dated 1584 275

SIR ISAAC NEWTON (born 1642). From a Picture formerly at Culverthorpe, Lincolnshire . . . *facing* 277

SALOON IN CULVERTHORPE HALL, LINCOLNSHIRE. From a water-colour Drawing (about 1852) . . *facing* 278

LIST OF ILLUSTRATIONS

SIR MICHAEL NEWTON, KNIGHT OF THE BATH (1725), FOURTH BARONET. From a Picture belonging to W. H. Graves Bagshawe, Esq. . . . . . *facing* 280

HALLINGBURY. A PICNIC. From an Engraving, 1832 *facing* 286

JOHN₆ ARCHER HOUBLON, ESQ. (born 1773). From a Silhouette 291

CULVERTHORPE. NORTH FRONT. From a Photograph *facing* 292

MRS. ARCHER HOUBLON, *née* BRAMSTON (born 1777). Silhouette 294

MARY-ANNE EYRE, *née* POPHAM. From a Drawing by Mary-Anne Houston . . . . . *facing* 297

'LITTLE HARROT,' AGED 80 (Miss Harriet Archer Houblon). From a Drawing by the Author . . . *facing* 298

SHIELDS OF ARMS (from Drawings by the Author)—

    BATE FAMILY 3
    PARKER, LORDS DE MORLEY . . . 16
    COTTON FAMILY 38
    ARCHER ,, ... 129, 273
    EYRE ,, ... 274
    CARADOC OR NEWTON FAMILY . . 275
    BRAMSTON FAMILY 283
    POPHAM ,, ... 295
    ARCHER ,, (Table of descent) . . . 306
    EYRE ,, ,, . . . 306
    NEWTON ,, ,, . . . 306
    SHIELD OF QUARTERINGS OF THE HOUBLON FAMILY (Skeleton Pedigree) 318

THE HOUBLON FAMILY

CHAPTER I

A FAMILY TRUST

'Vous êtes riche ou vous devez l'être ; Dix mille livres de rente, et en fonds de terre, cela est beau, cela est doux !'
Caractères de la Bruyère, 1756.

IN order rightly to understand the nature of the Trust of which we propose to give some account, it will be necessary to go back many years in our narrative.

Jacob[1] the fifth son of old Mr. Houblon, formerly Fellow of Peterhouse, Cambridge, and after the Restoration, Rector of Moreton in Essex, died in 1698, leaving two sons and several daughters, all of whom were born at Moreton. Charles, the eldest son (who took his christian name from his grandfather, Charles Whincop, D.D.), was born on the 15th of December 1664, and was a merchant. Jacob, the younger, born the 12th of February 1666—the year of the great fire—followed the profession of his father, and became a clergyman. He was afterwards Rector of Bubbingworth.[1] Charles Houblon was a Portugal merchant, and apparently a successful one. His London place of business was in Aldersgate Street, and in the year 1708 he purchased the 'lordship of Bubbingworth Hall in Essex,' and the following year

1698

1708

[1] Of the sisters, Anne married Dr. Lilly Butler, Prebendary of Canterbury, and had a son John, and other children. Mary was married to Mr. John Trimmer, and Elizabeth to Thomas Wragge, M.A., and their son Charles became Rector of Great Hallingbury in 1737.

VOL. II.   A

a property adjoining it. He survived the purchase of Bubbingworth Hall but little more than two years, and never made it his home. Charles was married the same year that the purchase was made, 'to Mary Bate, of Barton Court, Abingdon, in Berkshire, with licence, by Dr. Barton.'[1] Mary was the only child of Daniel Bate of the Vintners' Company, and a merchant of London, his own marriage having been solemnised at the same church (St. Mary Magdalen, Old Fish Street) with Mrs. Anne Halcott, on the 3rd of February 1672.[2] The quaint old manor-house of Barton Court on the River is still in existence, and until lately had been but little changed.[3]

The married life of Charles and Mary lasted less than three years, and their second child (who was named Jacob), was born at Stoke Newington on the 31st of July 1710. But Charles$_1$ Houblon died the following March at Watbroke Regis; the elder child surviving him but a short time. Charles appointed his brother Jacob$_2$ his executor, leaving him the guardianship of his young children, while to his wife he bequeathed a third part of his net estate, his horses, coach, plate, jewels, etc. Mr. Bate died in March 1716, and Mrs. Bate then came to live with Mary Houblon at Barton Court, which place had apparently been hers from the time of her marriage with Charles Houblon. One small item in the undertaker's long account of the expenses of Mr. Bate's funeral, viz. 'gloves for little master,' shows his grandchild Jacob$_3$ Houblon (then aged six), to have been present at it, while the account itself is very typical

---

[1] Registers, St. Mary Magdalen, New Fish Street.
[2] Archbishop of Canterbury's Marriage Licences.
[3] Mr. Bate was possessed of considerable property, which descended to his daughter. An estate in Lambeth remained for three generations in the Houblon family. For it 'Two heriots were due to His Grace the Lord Archbishop of Canterbury as Lord of the Manor,' viz. 'Two Coach Geldings.' In 1770 £31 was paid by Jacob Houblon, Esq., great-grandson of Mr. Bate, in lieu of the above.

A FAMILY TRUST

of the costliness and pomp of funerals in those days. A great many documents exist at Hallingbury relating to the property inherited by Mary Houblon from her father, who probably was a member of that branch of the Bate family who came to London from Esley in Yorkshire in the seventeenth century.[1] That Mr. Daniel Bate was Armiger, viz. that he was entitled to armorial bearings, is shown by the fact that a hatchment was provided for erection on his house after his decease.[2]

ARMS OF BATE.

A year later Mrs. Houblon's own death left her son an orphan, when he was taken by his uncle to Bubbingworth, of which manor he was now owner.

1717

```
                        James Houblon.
                              |
          ┌───────────────────┴───────────────────┐
    Elizabeth = Rev. Jacob₁              Abraham = Dorothy
    Wincop     of Moreton.                         Hubert.
          ┌────────────┤                          ┌────┴────┐
    Charles₁ = Mary Bate,  Jacob₂, Rector of   Sir Richard,  Anne, 1st
    d. March   d. 1717.    Bubbingworth,       d. s. p.     Viscountess
    1711.                  d. s. p.                          Palmerston.
          |
       JACOB₃,
     b. 31st July
        1710.
          ↓
```

The Reverend Jacob was fifty-seven when he found himself the sole guardian of the seven-year-old boy of his brother Charles; and that he henceforth made him and his education the chief object in his life is certain, also that the child responded to his kindness by a warm

---

[1] *Visitations of London*, 1687. Their arms were: Sable, a fess engrailed argent below three dexter hands couped bendways or. The crest a stag's head and neck, erased argent, antlered or.

[2] Mr. Bate was not 'properly buried' according to the laws of the College of Arms, or a Herald would have attended at the funeral and taken a certificate.

affection. When he was thirteen, Sir Richard Houblon put into execution a plan which affected Jacob's$_3$ future very considerably. So numerous had been the deaths in this heretofore large family, that the boy now remained the only heir-male of the race. Both his uncle the Reverend Jacob$_2$, and his cousin Sir Richard Houblon, were old bachelors; and in view of this fact the latter, who was possessed of much wealth, was unwilling to allow either the name to become extinct, or the fortune of the family to be dispersed.

In the midst of his ordinary avocations as a merchant, Sir Richard Houblon had long been interested in the management of certain lands he had either purchased or inherited in the counties of Herts and Essex. In the improvements he made in these he was fortunate in having a coadjutor in the Rector of Bubbingworth, a most able and energetic clergyman. For while Sir Richard was keen to experimentalise, and to make improvements on his property with the enthusiasm born of a new hobby, and a strong belief in the return he expected therefrom, he was dependent upon the experience of his cousin in carrying them out, which the Reverend Jacob's residence in Essex enabled him to do with comparative ease. The two, however, do not appear to have met personally for many years. Being now in failing health and unequal to the execution of the plan upon which he had set his heart,[1] and upon the details of which he had agreed with his father, Sir Richard, the year following upon Mr. Houblon's death, turned for help to the cousin who had already frequently assisted him, and wrote as follows:

1723   'COUSIN HOUBLON,—I owne the receipt of your kind letter of the 26 of this month, in which you give mee hopes of seeing you to-morrow. I am sure nothing can give mee a greater satisfaction than such an Interview.

[1] See vol. i. p. 340.

Wee are now the only two old ones left of our family, and I think, considering the little good wee have done as to the generative part of it, wee ought to have a very great esteem for our selves, as I don't know anybody else [who] will mind us. Soe we must make the best of it. Now after this preamble give mee leave to say, it will be the same thing to mee in w^t place wee dine. If you think coming to St. James'[1] will be inconvenient or too fare for you, I 'le meet you at Pontacks. Write mee but two or three words for fear of blunders in Serv^{ts}, and you 'l oblige S^r your humble Servt RICH^D HOUBLON.

'30 *Aprill* 1723.'

The outcome of the meeting thus arranged between the last remaining 'old ones' of the Houblon family was the Trust we have before alluded to; and a correspondence relating to this business commenced from this time between the two men, which in its terms became increasingly friendly and even affectionate in tone. These letters show that the Reverend Jacob$_2$ began at once the prosecution of the Trust, and Sir Richard Houblon in 1724 made the will which gave effect to it, dying soon afterwards.   1724

The terms of the Trust were briefly as follows: He left 'all his real property in Essex and Hertfordshire and elsewhere, in trust unto his cousin Jacob Houblon, son of Charles Houblon, late of London, merchant, deceased, in tail male, and all his personal estate, the rest and residue of what nature or kind soever, after payment of debts and legacies, upon Trust to lay out and invest the same in one or more purchases or purchase of lands and hereditaments of a good Fee Simple in England, and settle and convey the same when purchased to the use of the same Jacob Houblon, and entail the same on his heirs male.' It will thus be seen

[1] His own house in St. James's Place.

that the principal part of the estate was purchased after Sir Richard Houblon's decease by the trustees who carried out his directions. These trustees were: the Reverend Jacob Houblon, Rector of Bubbingworth, in the county of Essex; Henry Temple, Viscount Palmerston, and Mr. Arthur Ingram, of St. James's, Westminster. Of these three, the first alone was previously cognisant of the terms of the will; to the others the formation of the Trust came as a surprise. In the event of the decease of the heir, or the failure of his heirs male, the whole of the property would revert to Anne Viscountess Palmerston, Sir Richard Houblon's only sister. Meanwhile he left her £10,000 in bank stock, and £2000 to each of her three children—the Hon. Henry, Jane, and Elizabeth Temple, all of whom were minors.

For many years before this time, Jacob$_2$ Houblon had been carrying on business as a merchant. How he had found time for this, being at the same time rector of a country parish, can only be explained by the fact that in those days the duties incumbent on a parish priest were scarcely regarded in the light of later times. Not only were the clergy frequently non-resident on their cures, but often possessed several incumbencies, drawing their stipends and spending them elsewhere, while the spiritual welfare of their parishioners was meagrely administered to by ill-paid curates, with occasional visits at long intervals from their pastors. There seems, however, reason to believe that Jacob was regarded as a faithful and kindly parish priest, and that his duties as such were not neglected for his other occupations. He was a man of boundless energy; one of those gifted beings who *do well* whatever they attempt; and it must be due to this fact, as well as to his kindly, unselfish character, that he was the universal referee and adviser, to whom all his acquaintance turned in trouble or necessity. That the prosecution of the arduous work of the Trust gave him much anxious thought, and took up much of his time, there is no doubt; and there is evidence of the unwillingness with which he allowed himself to be drawn from the daily duties of his parish, in order to meet the wishes of his co-trustees. With regard to his mercantile adventures, it would appear that they were almost exclusively undertaken for the benefit of others. As a matter of fact, we find the names of a number of his friends and relations recurring over and over again in his business accounts.

Sir Richard died the 13th of October 1724 at Langley, and on the 4th of December we find the first letter from Lord Palmerston to the Reverend Jacob on the subject of the Trust. 'I shall bee glad to serve you, which I must confess is the chief end I propose in taking any part in the execution of Sir Richard Houblon's will. I have from Mr Ingram Mr Talbot's opinion about the Trust, which makes us no wiser than before.' He adds that the lawyers have been to Langley, that the house (in London) is being disposed of, and that they are awaiting him (Mr. Houblon) in London, which is 'att present the scene of action.' A series of letters from Lord Palmerston, together with occasional rough drafts of the Reverend Jacob's replies have been preserved. These letters extend over the period between 1724, at the formation of the Trust, and 1729, when the purchase of the estate of Hallingbury was completed. They then recommence in 1733 and continue at intervals till 1736, the year following Lady Palmerston's death.

After the proving of Sir Richard's will, and the execution of business at the 'scene of action' with his fellow-trustees, the Reverend Jacob returned to his parish at Bubbingworth, where he appears to have endeavoured to carry on the conflicting duties of a clergyman and a trustee to the best of his ability. Very soon after

1724

this he ceased entirely to engage in any commercial transactions. When obliged to come to town he lodged in Bridgewater Square, at the house of his niece, Mrs. Norris, who at this time appears to have undertaken the charge of young Jacob₃ Houblon during the intervals of his school life, as she received an allowance from the trustees for his maintenance. Mrs. Norris was the daughter of Dr. Lilly Butler, Prebendary of Canterbury, and Mr. Jacob Houblon's sister, Anne.[1]

Lord Palmerston wrote in May 1725 from East Sheen, 'I believe it may be some considerable time before we can invest the cash in land.' Referring to some property in the market, he says : ' The trouble of land is greater than Bank-stock, but I allways thought land to bee preferred on many accounts. It is also as you say, fulfilling the will. As for any contingent interest to my family, I would have you think as little of it as I do.'

The marriage of Lord and Lady Palmerston had been one of happiness and affection, nor was it ever clouded by the fact that she was not made her brother's heir. Whatever he may have felt at the time, Lord Palmerston maintained a dignified silence, although he had perhaps some reason to be mortified by the will of his brother-in-law, with whom he had evidently been on terms of confidence and affection. For not only had Sir Richard given no sign of his intentions, but the terms of the bequest to the sister who had been generally regarded as his heir,[2] was a source of continued annoyance to her husband. While exacting and punctilious with regard to the execution of the Trust in which he had a share of responsibility, it was only after many years had elapsed

---

[1] Appeal was made to Mrs. Norris in 1725 by Lord Palmerston to know where 'two old family (recipe) books' were, which had belonged to Mr. Abraham Houblon, and which Lady Palmerston was anxious to possess. We do not hear if they were found.

[2] *The Political State of Great Britain* contains the following notice : 'Died 13th Oct. 1724 Sir Richard Houblon, who left the bulk of his estate to his sister Lady Palmerston.'

(on an occasion when he was ill with the gout and consequently under the influence of great mental irritation) that Lord Palmerston permitted himself to betray the extent of his early disappointment and chagrin at his wife not having been made heir to 'the great estate which should have been hers.'[1]

In December 1725 we hear of great anxiety respecting young Jacob Houblon—now fifteen years old—and of his serious illness in London. Lady Palmerston and one of her children were also very ill at the same time. Smallpox was very prevalent, and they probably were attacked by it during one of the outbreaks which for so long a time were a terror and a scourge to the whole community. Anne Palmerston was still comparatively young, but what remained of her early loveliness,—judging by the later portraits,—was apparently destroyed by the disease. Lord Palmerston, writing to the Reverend Jacob[2] after having been to Bridgewater Square, informs him that he had waited on Mrs. Norris to inquire about the health of his nephew, and had heard that the great danger was now over. As to his own family he says, 'we have thro' God's mercy escaped what might have been far worse.'

In August 1726 an estate belonging to Lord Haversham was considered as a possible purchase, and another farm in Herts was added to that part of the Trust estate. In 1727 the trustees were in treaty about the estate of Sir John Lumley. In reference to this Lord

---

[1] Though dignity and self-control enabled Lord Palmerston at the time to conceal from the world his mortification, it appears to have for the time soured his always hot and hasty temper. It was not long after Sir Richard Houblon's death that, in a moment of irritation, he wrote a letter to Swift which brought an answer from the brilliant Dean which for stinging sarcasm —not unmixed with pathos—is spoken of as 'as masterly of its kind as any other production of Swift's pen' (see *Works*). Every word betrays the pain caused by this letter from the son of his ancient friend and patron. 'I have found out one secret,' he wrote, 'that although you call me a *great wit* you do not think me so, otherwise you would have been cautious to have writ me such a letter!'

Palmerston seems to have made many difficulties, and finally urged that previous to making so important a purchase with the Trust money, that they should obtain a decree from the Court of Chancery to justify them in laying it out in this manner; which, he adds, 'is absolutely necessary for all our safetys.' This letter nettled the Reverend Jacob[2] who had all the work of the Trust to do, while his colleagues confined themselves to criticism and suggestions, which only added to the labour which they were not prepared to share. In consequence of the creation of these difficulties, Jacob had thrown up Sir J. Lumley's estate, the purchase of which had been contemplated, and Lord Palmerston afterwards expressed surprise at his having done so. But Mr. Houblon now made a sort of ultimatum, sending a message to Lord Palmerston and Mr. Ingram through Mr. Brice, his lawyer, to the effect that he requested them both to empower him by Letter of Attorney to agree for and purchase such estates as he shall think proper, failing which he proposed to free himself altogether from the Trust, and to empower them to act without him. In his answer Lord Palmerston endeavoured to soothe the irritation of his fellow-trustee, but at the same time complained that he never saw him: 'By letters nothing is settled, and by such short stays in town nothing can be agreed on. Had you been to bee seen, you had not given this estate up. Although I know none of those you employ, yett I had rather pin my faith on you than on them. If you will turn the stock into land you must make more journeys than you do.' After this scolding he adds in a postscript—playfully—showing his real regard for his irate friend: 'Well! This Ld Palmerston is a sad man to draw mee from home.'

1733   We find no more letters between the trustees till the year 1733, which leads us to believe that the Reverend

A FAMILY TRUST

Jacob realised the impossibility of doing business satisfactorily from a distance, and acceded to Lord Palmerston's appeal to come more often to town. During this interval the Hallingbury estate was purchased,[1] and from henceforth Mr. Houblon's chief work was in consolidating and improving this part of the Trust estate. Not long after its purchase, its young owner took up his residence there, or more probably passed the vacations there, as he was at this time an undergraduate at Cambridge University. After coming of age, he nominally took the reins into his own hands, although the peculiar nature of the Trust by which the whole of the personal estate in bank stock had to be invested in land, necessitated the intervention of the trustees for much longer than would otherwise have been necessary.

1729

We can imagine young Jacob's first sight of his future home. His uncle had already seen over the estate, which was not more than some sixteen miles from his own parish. But before definitely fixing upon it, we may be certain he consulted his nephew, and that they went there together from Bubbingworth Rectory. In all probability they rode there on horseback, and, if so, their way would have been by Moreton, High Laver, by the village of Matching, and from thence by Hatfield Heath to Great Hallingbury.

Through beautiful wooded country they passed, thick with the great oaks which made Essex famous; stretches of common-land interspersed with scrub and thorns, with occasional shaded fields of arable land;[2] all as yet luxuriant in wasteful profusion, for agriculture had scarcely yet entered upon the golden days of prosperity which the middle of the century was to see, as the result of the new infusion of energy now beginning to stir the

---

[1] Hallingbury Place (pronounced Hollingbury) is in Essex, within three miles of Bishop's Stortford, Herts.

[2] See Kalm, *Visit to England*, 1748, for the beauties of Herts and Essex counties. Trans., Joseph Lucas. Macmillan, 1892.

drowsy country-sides. 'This shire is moste fatt,' wrote John Norden, of Essex, in 1594, 'fruitefull and full of profitable thinges, exceeding, (as far as I can finde) anie other shire for the generall comodities and plentie. It seemeth to deserve the title of the englishe Goshen the fattest of the Lande: comparable to Palestina, that flowed with milke and hunnye.' The Hallingburys, Great and Little, and Wallbury Dells (part of the estate they rode to see), and whose high-crowned earthworks of unknown antiquity,[1] dominating the valley of the Stort, they may have turned aside to explore—were among the county's choicest lands. In the 'comun Rune or Proverbe' of the district, quoted by Norden, 'some especial groundes noted generallie in regard to fertilitie,' comprise lands in the Hallingbury estate.

' Lord Morleyes Baronparke	Is fruitfull and fatt;
In Layr Marney pk	How feild is better than that;
In Wighorn	Copte hall is best of them all;
Parcell of Peldo hall	Yet Hubbledown may wayr the crowne.'[2]

Hallingbury Place, or Hallingbury Morley as it was then called, was greatly altered some forty or fifty years after this time by the second squire of the Houblon name. But when its future young master and his uncle rode up to it on the autumn day in 1729, it was still unchanged. The old place was built of red brick in the Tudor style; the E formation being still traceable. The house was of great length, but of no great depth. Then, as now, it was flanked by square corner towers or turrets, and it had an inner court. The result of their inspection was, that an offer for the purchase of the Hallingbury estate was made by the trustees.

1729

For many hundred years Hallingbury had been the seat of the Lords de Morley, or Morle and Monteagle, but passed out of their hands about 1660, when Sir

1660

---

[1] 'Of one thing we may be sure: whensoever made, this was one of the largest and most important fortresses of these eastern lands.' *Victoria History of the Counties of England*, 'Essex,' vol. i. p. 283. 1903.

[2] *Essex*, by John Norden, 1594, pp. 7-8 (Camden Society).

A FAMILY TRUST

Edward Turner, Knight, Speaker of the House of Commons, Solicitor General, and Lord Chief Baron of England, is said to have 'got the manor' of the last lord, 'and resided there.'[1] Sir Edward was immediately after elected representative for the county of Essex to Parliament. It was from the executors of his grandson, another Sir Edward,[2] that the estate came into the possession of the Houblon trustees. There is so much that is interesting in the history of the ancient owners of Hallingbury that we cannot refrain from giving a slight sketch of the De Morley family, at the risk of the suggestion that it is irrelevant and unnecessary.

The De Morleys came of an ancient and distinguished race, and though possessed of other lands and estates, succeeding generations of them appear to have always resided here. Many were buried in the church, their monuments being still in existence. Through four heiresses, of whom three possessed the Christian name of Hawise, or Harvise, the estates came to them. The first of these maidens was the grand-daughter of William de Langvallei, a great knight and 'person of note,' and also Warden of the Forest of Essex in the days of Richard Cœur de Lion. Both he and his son were successively keepers of the Castle of Colchester in King John's time. With Harvise, the manors of the Great and Little Hallingburys, with many other manors belonging, went to her husband, John de Burgh. The young heiress had been put, by the King, under the wardship of Hubert de Burgh, Earl of Kent and Lord Justice of England, and he of course married her to his son. Harvise died in 1249. Her son John de Burgh had three daughters, to one of whom, named Devorquill, Hallingbury descended, and she married Robert Fitz Walter. They again had three daughters, one of whom (another Harvise) was wife of William le

1660

1249

---

[1] Oldmixon, *History*, i. 502, 515 (*apud* Morant's *Essex*, ii. 196).
[2] He died 1721.

Mareshall, to whom she brought the estates. Their only son having died in 1316, his sister, a third Harvise, became the heiress of Hallingbury, and by her marriage with Robert de Morle, or Morley, brought it to that family.[1] After seven generations from father to son of this family of De Morley, came another heiress, Alianor, whose husband, Sir William Lovell, a son of Lord Lovell, took the title of Lord de Morley in right of his wife, and Hallingbury was now called for the first time Hallingbury Morley. Their son Henry, born
1465 in 1465, married into a great family. Elizabeth, his wife, was daughter of John de la Pole, Earl of Lincoln and Duke of Suffolk, but they had no children, so the estates devolved upon Henry's sister Alice, who was born in 1466 and married Sir William Parker Knight, of London, and their son Henry became Lord Morley through right of his mother. He was one of the Lords who signed the threatening letter to Pope
1529 Clement VII. in 1529, and his wife was another Alice, a daughter of Sir John St. John of Bletso. In her will, dated 1518, the elder Alice, Lady Morley (a very pious dame), bequeathed three pounds 'to the makyng of a pyx for the Sacrament of the Parish Church of Halyngbury Morley,' and this gift is recorded in the parish registers. It is an irony of fate that the same register at a later date notes the destruction of the
1549 said pyx and other altar accessories, as 'popish ornaments,' by the iconoclasts, who were at that time employed in going from parish church to parish church in the county to complete this cleansing process! At the same time a resident enthusiast received for 'bettying downe the auters' (beating down the altars) and 'taking down the particion in ye chancell,' the sum of vs. iiid. Hallingbury Church was 'deformed' in 1549.

Henry Lord Morley and the Lady Alice St. John his

[1] See Morant, *History and Antiquities of Essex*, ii. 190.

wife had a daughter Jane who married George Boleyn, Lord Rochfort, and they were thus related to Queen Elizabeth. Jane's brother Henry, who was born at 'The Place,' succeeded to the Hallingbury and other estates, and after being created Knight of the Bath and being twice married, died there in 1556. This baron is said to have had literary tastes of a poetic order, though but few remains exist from his pen. A fragment is to be found in Nott's works of Lord Surrey.[1] It purports to have been written 'in a chamber where he was wont to be at Hallenbury,' above the door of which, we are informed, he had had inscribed the words: '*Si ita Deo placet, ita fiet.*'[2] His son Sir Henry succeeded him in the barony and estates, and it was in his time that his illustrious relative by marriage[3] visited Hallingbury, for we hear that 'after leaving Lees Priory that Queen Elizabeth in her progress through Essex, Suffolk, and Herts, alighted at Allingbury Morley, where she remained during the 25th and 26th daies of August 1561.'[4] The Queen's hostess on this occasion was a member of the great house of Stanley, Henry Lord Morley having married the daughter and heir of Sir Edward Stanley, Earl of Derby.

Lord and Lady Morley's son Sir Edward, married his cousin Elizabeth, daughter and heir of Sir William Stanley, Lord Monteagle, who was fifth son of Thomas Earl of Derby; and their son, Sir William, assumed the title of Lord Monteagle in right of his mother, in his father (Lord Morley's) lifetime. To him was written, on the 4th of November 1605, the famous letter which disclosed the existence of the Gunpowder Plot. As Lady

---

[1] Vol. i. p. xix. (British Museum).
[2] 'As it so pleaseth God, so let it be done.'
[3] Lord Morley's aunt, Jane Lady Rochfort, was the Queen's aunt by marriage. It is a curious fact that the future owners of Hallingbury were descended from a sister of Lord Rochfort and Anne Boleyn. See I. xiii. 12.
[4] John Nichols, F.S.A., *The Progress and Public Processions of Queen Elizabeth*, i. 99.

THE HOUBLON FAMILY

Monteagle was the daughter of Sir Thomas Tresham (while Francis Tresham was one of the conspirators concerned in the plot), the inference has been that the latter, being desirous of saving the Lady Monteagle the grief and shock of her husband's destruction, wrote the letter which betrayed all.

Sir Henry, twelfth Lord Morley and fifth Monteagle, succeeded his father to the estates and title.[1] He was a Knight of the Bath, and a staunch royalist, apparently making great sacrifices for the royal cause during the civil wars, and thereby greatly embarrassing his estates. Unfortunately for him, he fell into the hands of a neighbour, as stout a Parliamentarian as he was a Royalist, of whom he borrowed a large sum of money on the security of the choicest part of his estate, viz. the forest or chase of Hatfield; he even agreed to sell him the forest upon which his neighbour already held certain rights. But all these plans were frustrated, and both neighbours seriously embarrassed, by the denunciation of Lord Morley by the Parliament, as a 'Malignant guilty of high treason against the state,' while all his possessions were sequestrated. As this sequestration antedated the proposed sale of the forest by Lord Morley, it was never carried out. The son of the unfortunate royalist lord (who died in the greatest poverty) succeeded to a barren title and endless litigation. Finally all lawsuits and litigation between sequestrators, mortgagees, and would-be purchasers, ended in the sale, by act of Parliament, of the Hallingbury estates, including the forest, to Sir Edward Turner, from whose grandson it was ultimately purchased by the Houblon trustees in 1729.

LORDS DE MORLEY—
ARMS OF PARKER.

1729

[1] The Arms of Lord Morley were: Argent, a lion passant gules between two barrs sable, thereon three bezants; in chief as many bucks' heads cabosed of the third. Morant, *Antiquities of Essex*, ii. 573.

A FAMILY TRUST

No engraving or picture, so far as we are aware, is in existence of the old house of Hallingbury Morley, or Hallingbury Place as it is called to this day, and it is not known by whom and when it was built. The park surrounding it has long been much the same size and shape as it is now; in a survey of Queen Elizabeth's reign, its boundaries follow almost the same lines. The beautiful chase or forest of Hatfield Broadoak, which adjoins it, was formerly a royal demesne, and as far back as 1221 there was a park at Hallingbury, for the King informed Richard de Montfichet, his forester, that he had given his trusty and wellbeloved Hugh de Nevill two oak-trees to make palings for his park at Hallingbury, and twenty does to place in that park; and therefore ordered Sir Richard to procure both the oaks and does from Hatfield.[1] That a mansion of considerable importance existed on the site from an early period is evident from brick foundations which have been found, said to be of great age, and so solid that the bricks turned the edge of the picks used to remove them; curiously enough, this brickwork was the foundation of an immense bay window or apse, a new bow having now been built almost on the same spot. Another evidence of antiquity is to be found in a large rectangular piece of water near the house, doubtless originally made for the purpose of preserving fish for use on fast days. It lies some three hundred yards to the south-west of the house. Possibly it may have been done by order of Alice Lady Morley, whose pious gifts to the Church are recorded in the registers. There was a popular tradition that another Lady de Morley haunted the place, the moonbeams glancing on her white dress as she moved along the path under the trees; and in respect of this lady, it has further been said, that she had been guilty of the cruel and false

[1] Patent Roll.

accusation in the court of King Henry the Eighth, which resulted in the execution of Queen Catherine Howard for her supposed intrigue with Lord Rochfort.[1] Judging by the steep banks surrounding the pond, it must originally have been of considerable depth; and of its antiquity there can be no doubt, from the size and age of the great oaks which grow around it on three sides, the fourth being bounded by the sunk-fence which encloses the garden ground round the house. This interesting and beautiful spot goes by the name of Morley Pond to this day.

Meanwhile the acquisition of the estate of Hallingbury relieved Mr. Houblon of a load of anxiety, for the main part of his work was over. He had fulfilled the Trust, and it was but a labour of love to do what more remained.

1732 The good understanding of the trustees was temporarily endangered some ten years after the death of Sir Richard Houblon, by an endeavour on the part of Lord Palmerston to get the terms of his marriage settlement altered by the Court of Chancery, in spite of the trustees, of whom the Reverend Jacob was one; the effort was unsuccessful. Some of Lord Palmerston's letters, written from Bath relating to this business, show signs of the writer being out of temper as well as health.[2] He was ill and suffering severely with the gout at the time, and allowance must be made for the fact. The misunderstanding between the two old friends, who had on the

[1] Lady Rochfort was Lord Morley's sister.
[2] Among the correspondence relating to the Trust there is a packet of letters on this subject. Lady Palmerston's fortune had by the will of her brother remained in the hands of trustees. His aim had been to ensure her separate enjoyment of the income of it, the interest being paid her personally—an unusual provision for those days. As Lady Palmerston's father had made a similar disposition of the property he left his daughter, it would seem as if both he and his son had views relating to married women's property, antedating by more than a century and a half the act of the end of last century.

whole, worked so harmoniously together in the prosecution of the Trust which had been so great a disappointment to the one, and such a labour to the other, was even in danger of becoming serious, when it was cut short by the death of Lady Palmerston. In curious contrast to the heated correspondence above mentioned, we have a letter from her husband, informing the Reverend Jacob of her death. He also informed him 'of a will writt with her own hand (tho' not signed by her), and have proved her handwriting, a copy of which kind Paper I enclose to you.' A kindly, gentle nature speaks in the following words, and we may well believe that the crusty old gentleman had been a kind husband.

1733

'Directed to Lord Palmerston.

'As I have long given you my heart; and my tenderest affection and fondest wishes have been allways yours: so is everything else which I possess; and all that I may call mine being allready yours, I have nothing to give but my heartiest thanks for the care and kindness you have at all time shewed me, either in Sickness or in health; for which God Almighty will I hope reward you in a better world. However, for form sake, I here give and bequeath you as following: 1st, the £10,000 left me by Sr Richard Houblon; the £200 a year annuity left me by my Father; the gold Cup and the two lesser Chocolate Cupps, which I wish you would sometimes look on as a Remembrance of death, as also of the fondest and faithfullest friend you ever had.'

At the bottom of the paper on which she wrote her will, Lord Palmerston added a note to the effect that 'the chocolate cups were made out of burial rings,' which fact explains the thought in her mind which desired to connect the sight of them with 'death.' In a memorandum addressed by his mother to the third Viscount

(the great statesman), she mentions the 'Two gold cups and stand rendered very valuable from the interesting way in which they were bequeathed by Lady Palmerston to her husband — your great-grandfather. Her will I hope I shall find in which this memorial is
1899 specified.' It was, however, not found till 1899 by the Hon. Evelyn Ashley.

In the meantime the work of the Trust had been proceeding. We find record by the trustees of the purchase of farms in both Herts and Essex; one being Stonybury, 'which lyes in the heart of the Trust estate, which he [the owner] is too sensible of by his demands at present. . . . But if I can accomplish it in my lifetime, I shall make the Trust estate the most entire and complete that that county [Herts], or Essex can show.' Stonybury is still part of the family property in Herts,[1] and is near Hormead Hall. Westmill, also in those parts, was purchased in 1735, and another farm called Hottoft. This latter farm, and some others in Hertfordshire, were sold at a later date by John$_5$ Archer Houblon, grandson of young Jacob$_3$.

1736 In May 1736 Lord Palmerston wrote to the Reverend Jacob$_2$, urging very strongly that a history of the Trust, and how it had been executed, together with an account of the sums expended thereupon, should be drawn up — a copy of which statement should be retained by each of the three trustees; and again he insisted upon the necessity for great care, in case their 'action in the matter should bee ever called in question,' etc. The draft of Jacob$_2$'s answer shows all this to have been done, and all his demands already complied with, and he signs himself 'Y^r Ld Sh^{ps} Patient Servant'! Something more was, however, done to satisfy Lord Palmerston's scruples, and he soon afterwards wrote returning 'the Papers

---

[1] It had belonged to Mr. Delawood, who bequeathed it to his nephew Mr. Bownes, from whom it was purchased.

A FAMILY TRUST

executed by your Nephew, who will carry them down to you.'

Lord Palmerston's regard for his fellow-trustee, in spite of occasional differences, was throughout unfeignedly sincere and even affectionate. In his letters we find frequent assertions as to his absolute reliance on him and on his judgment. 'I have said before I would trust my life in your hands,' he wrote in one of his most irate epistles, 'and I say it again now, for I see no reason to change my opinion.' The last of this series of letters on the subject of the Trust—the whole business between the families being now closed by the death of Anne Lady Palmerston, and the handing over of her fortune to her husband by the trustees—evinces a desire on Lord Palmerston's part to show a kindly and appreciative spirit, and possibly a wish to make amends for the somewhat aggressive tone he had at times assumed in the execution of the Trust. He was now most willing to give the Reverend Jacob credit for all that he had done, and ends his letter thus: 'I hope your family (meaning his nephew and his young wife) endeavour to make everything as easie to you as they can, for I am sure they owe that and a great deal more to you. Few such guardians and trustees are to be found as you have been. I should be very glad to see you once more to assure you that I am Sir y^r faithful obedient serv^t Palmerston.'

Lord Palmerston died in November 1757. A letter from his executors, Mr. John Barnard and Lord Berkeley of Stratton, to the Reverend Jacob, with reference to some detail as to the execution of Sir Richard Houblon's will, closes this interesting series of letters.

We believe that his old friend gave Jacob[2] no more than his due in his expressions of regard and esteem. It is certain that he had executed, with but little help from others, a difficult task in an able manner, and at cost of considerable trouble and expense to himself. But while Lord Palmerston left to him the labour attendant on the work, he yet exercised a strict and close scrutiny of the same, and no doubt by his criticism and suggestions contributed largely to the ultimate success which crowned the efforts of him whom he rightly called a 'model guardian and trustee.' As to Mr. Ingram, he appears to have confined his efforts merely to the execution of the deeds he was required to sign.

By the evidence of the handwriting we notice a gradual decline of strength in the Reverend Jacob. At the opening of his 'Journal Book C.' in 1711, the writing is beautifully formed, firm and fine; but after a time a break occurs, and when the keeping of the account is resumed, there is a distinct change, as if the writer had passed through some severe illness or trial. From this time it gradually became larger and less regular, while in his later years it may be called exceedingly bad. The entries in the journal cease in 1731, some two years after the purchase of Hallingbury.

Jacob$_2$ Houblon's life had scarcely been passed in the peaceful, uneventful way usual among the country clergy. A trust such as he undertook would be no very difficult task to a business man in these days of easy travelling and well-organised agencies. But in the early part of the eighteenth century—not far from two hundred years ago—it entailed a labour that it is difficult for us now fully to estimate. Not only had he to find suitable lands, and to travel by coach or on horseback, over almost impassable roads, to see them, but he had to examine the titles of each particular farm or manor; and having done this, came the necessity for consultation with his fellow-trustees, and finally the appeal to the Court of Chancery, which must be satisfied as to all details relative to the property. The greater part of the Trust estate in Essex was purchased in 1729, but much was afterwards done, by the addition of farms and the exchange of others, to improve and consolidate it; while the lands in Herts already owned and left in trust by Sir Richard, were added to and improved in the same way.

Various letters and papers which have come down to us show the Reverend Jacob to have been the most patient and unselfish of relations. As we have seen, all the male members of the Houblon family were now dead; not one of them survived the 'model trustee' but his young nephew at Hallingbury. But his sister's children were many and unfortunate. We find that he sold out at various times funds to the amount of his whole private fortune for their benefit. One of the daughters of Dr. Lilly Butler and Anne Houblon, his wife, was the Mrs. Norris whom we have already noticed. Her husband owned large sugar plantations in Jamaica, but died leaving his estate—a very valuable one—in great confusion. Several thousand pounds were advanced by Jacob$_2$ to his niece Mrs. Norris, to aid her in settling these difficulties, but with little good result. In a pathetic letter to his nephew the Reverend John Butler —written in May 1735, and shortly before his death—he says: 'Your sister [Mrs. Norris] in her straits applys herself to me for money; not one of all your Father's children but have been generously used by me, even to the utmost of my power. I have sold my estate to support every individual of Nephews and Nieces; and I am sorry it is to no purpose. I have an annuity for life which is now my sole support, so do not expect more from me of ready cash, but what comes from Jamaica.' He adds he gives him a gift of £100, and the same to his sister Dorothy, which they can pay themselves from what bonds he holds of their sister's estate. The Reverend Jacob$_2$ included these bad debts in his residuary estate at his death, which he devised equally among his sister's children, Jacob$_3$ Houblon of Hallingbury being

1735

his executor. A series of letters from the Reverend John Butler to the latter at Hallingbury, while acting as executor to his sister Mrs. Norris's will, are very interesting, and show him to have been placed in great difficulties while dealing with agents and trustees in Jamaica and elsewhere, in his efforts to gather in these debts in order to satisfy the claims on her estate. Urged by young Jacob$_3$ of Hallingbury, he appears to have been transformed by this work, from a comfortable country parson and pluralist, into a restless, anxious speculator in sugar, spending months of waiting in London ; the only way in which he could obtain remittances from his sister's estate in Jamaica being in the form of shiploads of so many hogsheads of sugar. His success in obtaining anything at all from the considerable property with which he had to deal from a distance, appears to have been entirely due to the intervention of the family of Beckford, then large and important owners of plantations in Jamaica, whose high character and honest dealing John Butler contrasts with enthusiasm with that of some of the very shady gentlemen with whom he had to do, there and at home. For two consignments of sugars, consisting of fifty hogsheads apiece, the proceeds amounted to above £2000.

To return to our model trustee, now old and infirm ; we think we can trace the existence of a strong affection and esteem between himself and his nephew and namesake, now married and living a useful and happy life as a country gentleman. Here at least he had lived to reap a reward of satisfaction and comfort of his many sacrifices in the carrying out of the family Trust. He was too infirm—shortly before his death as it was—to travel to Hallingbury to be present at the festivities which greeted the birth of another young Jacob$_4$; but we find by an old newspaper of the year 1735, that he stood godfather at the christening, represented as proxy by Sir Thomas Abdy, Baronet; and no doubt the child took his name from the great-uncle who had been so true a friend to his young father.

A few scraps of paper scrawled over in a weak and uncertain hand have escaped destruction, and are all that remain to notice with regard to the Reverend Jacob$_2$ Houblon. They were found among other papers of no value or interest: bills, accounts, and the like. Sick and dying, these are his last directions to the nephew he had loved and worked for; whom he left his sole executor.

'Six clergy for the Pall.'

(Something illegible.)

'Stephen can make a plain Coffin and get a shrowd. . . . Mr Brecknock will help you with . . . Four young men to carry me to Church.'

Then the rough draft of his simple will. 'I leave you my Nephew J. Houblon, my sole Executor.' A few small legacies to his old servants follow; the residue to his sister's children.

Jacob Houblon, M.A., died at Bubbingworth, and was buried there. 1736

CHAPTER II

THE SQUIRE

> 'Tradition said he feather'd his nest
> Through an Agricultural Interest
> In the Golden Age of farming;
> When golden eggs were laid by the geese,
> And Colchian sheep wore a golden fleece.'
>
> *Her Pedigree* (Miss Kilmansegg and her precious Leg).
> TOM HOOD.

ANY one who cares to take up the closing volume of Burnet's *Own Times*, and turn to the last pages, will find his 'dying testament or Conclusions.' These 'Conclusions' are drawn from a long good life of singular opportunities and experience, and much shrewd observation and knowledge of character are to be found in them. After a lengthy disquisition on men of his cloth—by which it would seem that in their virtues and idiosyncrasies they much resembled their successors of this day —the bishop's homilies to 'the Gentry; the Men of trade and business; the Nobility and Parliament Men,' are all wise and thoughtful, and throw much light on existing conditions. Most interesting, too, are his suggestions as to 'the education of young men of birth and expectation'; and in this connection we think we recognise an influence on the future generations of the Houblon family, as they must undoubtedly have had, after their publication, upon many others, who, like the courtly, though cynical, Earl of Chesterfield, controlled the destinies of the youth of the period. The picture he drew of the typical 'country gentleman,' living on his estate, well prepared for the duties, interests, and responsibilities which controlled his time, by a liberal and enlightened education, may well have been held up before the mental vision of our good merchant Sir Richard Houblon, pondering on his big fortune—the memory of his ancestor's strenuous life-work—and the curious isolation in which he now found himself as the last link with that past. We have observed that a strange fatality had swept away one after another, both the men of his own generation, and their children bearing the name; and that a little thirteen-year-old boy—the last of the race—was left, and only he, except the one other old bachelor in Essex! And so it came about that the musings which resulted in the plan which was to transfer this child's person and interests to the country, were also concerned with wise plans for his education, and the moulding of both tastes and character. Over young Jacob's training his two uncles pondered and planned, and we believe they practically followed the course presented in Bishop Burnet's 'Conclusions' as the best possible plan of education for a young man with similar prospects.

1723

There had always been a jealousy between 'Town and Country'; and it would have cost no slight effort on the part of Sir Richard Houblon to determine to sever for good the old ties which had linked the Houblons to their much loved City, the centre of all that was forward, and enlightened, and intelligent. The country had been associated in the minds of City men with rest, almost stagnation; and to the country they had been wont to retire, when stress of work led them to seek change and quiet. Meanwhile, the ordinary country squire had been despised for his rude health, appetite, conservatism, and blundering impulses. Fox-hunting, shooting, fishing, beef, and beer were, in the minds of men about town, inseparable characteristics of the country gentleman; though it was not denied that they were both able and disinterested in their management of county business, and in their magisterial functions. But though political parties were glad to avail themselves of their political power and influence, and the fine gentleman Bolingbroke could speak of the 'landed men as the true owners of our political vessel, the moneyed men being but passengers in it,' it is to be doubted if even his Toryism meant what he said. If the City thought scorn of them, the literary circles and wits and critics who frequented the coffee-houses could speak with equal contempt of the life of which they knew but little. It is probable that there were many country gentlemen who indeed were what they were represented to be by the town; but then, as now, classes in this country were never clearly defined and distinct one from the other, like the French provincial *noblesse* and *bourgeoisie* even to this day. On the contrary, while the greater English gentry and the noble families possessed in common tastes for country sports and other interests, both were also practically on one and the same plane of culture and birth, and in touch with a broader social existence; while the gentry could also trace, link by link, ties of relationship and intercourse to the smallest squire, and till but lately even with the fast disappearing yeoman. This being so, no hard and fast rules could apply to a class whose borders were so far removed in opposite social extremes.[1]

It is a remarkable coincidence that while in the previous centuries the City apprentices were largely drawn from the younger sons of county families, so now the time had come when the descendants of those youths turned once more to the country, and freely spent their wealth and transferred their energies towards

---

[1] 'It is the happiness of a trading nation like ours, that the youngest sons . . . may, by an honest industry, rise to greater estates than those of their elder brothers.' See the *Spectator*, 1775, No. 108, vol. ii. p. 149.

the building up of that great agricultural prosperity which was to be the central economic fact of the eighteenth century. Sir Richard Houblon and his clerical cousin were among the first in this pioneer movement; so while the Reverend Jacob toiled to found his future home and duties, our future young squire went to Harrow—where his name may still be seen cut in the wainscot of the Fourth Form room— then to College, and travelled much abroad, and learnt languages, while at one time he read law. Meanwhile, the opportunities presented by his University career were not neglected, and Jacob₃ left Corpus Christi, his uncle's old College, after having graduated M.A. in 1729.[1]

1729

In the early days of his College life, Jacob probably looked upon himself as a Whig. All his family had been Whigs, and he had as yet probably thought but little of politics or their bearing on his future life. Indeed, to measure the gulf which now separated the whig principles of his forefathers (to whom they had been as meat and drink), from those of the Whigs of the latter-day school of Sir Robert Walpole, needed some degree of character and resolution in so young a man. Moreover, he had influential whig connections; Lord Palmerston was a strong and prominent Whig and supporter of the Walpole administration, and ever ready as he was to push his influence in its favour, he had doubtless used what 'opportunities served, to foster whig sympathies in the mind of his wife's young cousin, whose large property would have rendered his support of use to the party.[2] But in respect of old Mr. Houblon,

---

[1] Graduati Cantabrigiensis sive Catalogus, etc. B.M., 2121 *e*.

[2] Lord Palmerston was at this time in a position to dispense favours with no stinting hand; for not only was he high in favour with the Court (where his wife was lady-in-waiting to Queen Caroline), but also with the all-powerful Minister, Sir Robert Walpole, whose interests it appears he was not above serving in the manner peculiar to the custom and morals of the then whig administration. By Nichol's *Literary Anecdotes* we find that in 1734, 'In the interest of Walpole, he (Lord Palmerston), offered Dr William Webster a crown pension of £300 per

we recognise the wisdom with which he left to the circumstances of his surroundings, the shaping of the political opinions of his nephew: a course which undoubtedly made for the young man's future happiness and welfare.

It is interesting to note the result of these powerful influences upon the life and character of this descendant of a whig race of business men. Transplanted at an early age into the soil which had nourished so many generations of English country gentlemen, Jacob$_3$ Houblon, while retaining much of the capacity for business inherited from his ancestors, gradually assimilated the political opinions, and adopted the prejudices and views of his friends and neighbours. He became a tory squire and a tory member of Parliament, a supporter of the national Church and its privileges, and at the same time imbibed the national jealousy of, and dislike for, France and the French, as entirely as if he had originally sprung from the race which had dwelt for centuries upon the lands which were now his! Living as he did on the extreme Hertfordshire border of the county of Essex, and possessing nearly as much property in the one county as in the other, the sphere of his interests and occupations (after he had left Cambridge and come to settle in his home at Hallingbury) were not confined to Essex, notwithstanding that his country seat was actually situated in that county.

1735-41 Although for a time he sat in Parliament as member for Colchester in Essex, he subsequently represented the
1741-68 county of Hertfordshire in the tory interest for many years; making a total of thirty-three of Parliamentary service. He likewise served in the Herts militia, and sat upon the bench of that county. With Cambridgeshire, too, the wide and far-reaching social inter-

annum, if he would turn the *Weekly Miscellany* into a ministerial paper. Nichol, *Literary Anecdotes*, v. 162.

course in which the county families lived, brought him into near contact, and it was with an old Cambridgeshire family of high standing, that he was to ally himself by marriage.

In the Elizabethan house of Hallingbury, grey with age and memories of a past in which he had no part nor lot, none but his dogs as yet shared with him the lonely hearth in the 'chapel hall,' where the great logs had burned and warmed the past owners of the old Place. But his good temper and buoyant spirits, doubtless soon opened to him the houses and friendship of his neighbours, and, moreover, he was rich and young and a *parti*; he was also tall, well made, and athletic; and, judging by his portrait painted in middle age, was, without being handsome, decidedly pleasing in appearance. He had, in short, both the air and address of what was then called 'a man of parts.' In after years we find his children speaking of the 'family failing' of quick temper, but if he shared in it, we may believe that he was also generous and affectionate, for his letters breathe the kindliest spirit.

It was shortly after his election to Parliament that Jacob Houblon became a suitor for the hand of Mary, the only daughter of Sir John Hynde Cotton, Bart., of Madingley Hall in Cambridgeshire, and it is in great part to his friendship with the young lady's family, that we think we may trace the early source and origin of his opinions and political career. Madingley is near Cambridge; so before he left the University he probably was already acquainted with its owner and his family, while after he had taken up his abode at Hallingbury, he was still welcomed as a friend and not very distant neighbour. Jacob was only twenty-five when he took the step which identified him with the tory party for good and all. The unexpected death of Mr. Rebow (the tory member for Colchester), less than a year after the general election of 1734, had apparently brought momentary embarrassment upon his party. The late election had followed quickly upon the withdrawal by Sir Robert Walpole of the famous Excise Bill, which had excited such violent and unreasoning opposition in the country. In the former Parliament Colchester, in accordance with its traditions, had returned a whig member; but in consequence of the strong feeling which had been aroused, a tory representative was elected in 1734, the whig candidate not venturing to contest the election. But meanwhile the agitation in the country had in part subsided, and on the death of the tory representative (a gentleman of strong influence in the town), the late whig member once more came forward. His doing so roused the whole constituency to a fresh pitch of excitement, partly owing to the conditions under which his former contest had been fought, and partly because he had displeased the electors by his support of the Excise Bill in the last Parliament. It was at this juncture that Jacob Houblon suffered himself to be chosen as the candidate in the tory interest or, as it was called in the political parlance of the day—the Country, *versus* the Court, interest. In Thomas Cromwell's *History of Colchester* we find a contemporary account of this election quoted from the town books:—

'A Poll was taken at Colchester in the County of Essex upon Monday the tenth day of March 1734.5 at a place called the Exchange, before Joseph Duffield Esq Mayor, for the election of a Burgess to serve in Parliament in the room of Isaac Lemyng Rebow Esq decd. The candidates are Jacob Houblon Esq. a person of Great Honour and Integrity, who was sett up by the Country Interest, and Stamp Brooksbank Esq, who was in a former Parliament elected for the said Borough meerly on account of the most notorious Bribery and Corruption; and stood now on the Court Interest, but was out polled by M[r] Houblon 380. The electors expressing their utmost contempt of his former practices, and particularly his Voting in Parliament for bringing in that infamous Bill called the Excise Scheme.'[1] By the *Daily Courant* we find that Mr. Stamp Brooksbank—the 'Court' candidate—was a turkey merchant of Hackney.[2]

In view of the vehemence of the public indignation against bribery which characterised this election, it is probable that there was but little practised on the tory side; but the corruption at elections at this period was notorious, and while on the side of the Whigs it was carried on unblushingly on all occasions, the Tories could hardly have always refrained, or their chances would have been small indeed. Riotous scenes, drunkenness, and disorder were considered as an unavoidable accompaniment of an election, though it was claimed for the one in question that 'it was carried on with the greatest order, a considerable number of constables having been ordered to attend by the worshipful the Mayor to prevent disturbances.'[3] But the young tory candidate had been everywhere announced as 'a gentleman of a very large estate in the county,'[4] and as such he was expected during his canvass to open his purse widely, for the benefit of the Colchester electors.

On the closing of the poll at about six o'clock of the 10th of March 1735 the numbers were:—

'For M[r] Houblon 1085
M[r] Brooksbank 705,'

but the whig party was not satisfied, and so a scrutiny

---

[1] Thomas Cromwell, *History of Colchester*, ii. 290. 1825.
[2] *Daily Courant*, No. 5908, 10 March 1735.
[3] *Ibid.*, No. 5915.
[4] *Ibid.*, No. 5908.

VOL. II.

was demanded and granted, with however no result but that of the addition of one vote to the winning side.'[1]

Darkness was already closing in on the short March day when the final result was announced; but the successful candidate had nevertheless still to undergo the ordeal then considered an indispensable part of his triumph. And so he 'rode in the chair,' carried aloft above the heads of his enthusiastic but doubtless rather unsteady supporters. 'Great rejoicings were made in the town' subsequently,[2] and these were probably carried on far into the night. Any one who is familiar with the wonderful series of 'Election Scenes' painted by the great master Hogarth about this time, can form a vivid picture of the experiences through which our young squire passed, during his canvass and election for Colchester. He took the oath and his seat in Parliament on the 24th of the same month (1735),[3] but at the conclusion of that Parliament he did not again seek the suffrages of the Colchester electors. It appears that by that time the whig and nonconformist borough had recovered from the temporary disorganisation caused by its agitation against the Excise Bill, and in consequence returned to its whig allegiance.[4]

It was some four months following upon the election, that the announcement appeared in the *London Daily Courant*, to the effect 'that a treaty of marriage is on foot and speedily will be consummated, between Jacob Houblon of Hallingbury in Essex, Esqre, Member of Parliament for Colchester, and the daughter of Sir John Hynde Cotton, Bart., of Madingley (Member of Parliament for the town of Cambridge) by his first lady, a

---

[1] *Daily Courant*, No. 4416, 12 March 1735. The majority here given is 381.
[2] *Ibid.*, No. 5920; also the *Daily Journal*, No. 4427, etc.
[3] *Daily Courant*, No. 5920, and *Daily Journal*, No. 4427.
[4] In 1656 the Tory and Royalist, John Evelyn, wrote of the town of Colchester: 'For the rest this is a ragged and factious towne, now swarming with sectaries.' *Diary*, 18 July 1656.

MARY HYNDE COTTON (MRS. HOUBLON).

daughter of Sir Ambrose Crawley, Knight; a very agreeable young lady with a fortune of £20,000.'[1] The wedding was celebrated on the 31st of July the same year at Madingley[2] and the marriage festivities took place there. Mary Hynde Cotton (born in 1716) was now nineteen, and the bridegroom twenty-five. Two portraits of her are at Hallingbury; the earlier showing her as very youthful, with warm, bright colouring and animated expression. The later portrait, though painted when Mrs. Houblon was still young, lacks individuality; the bloom of youth and spirits was over, and the painter represents but a typical specimen of eighteenth-century womanhood in a white gown with aimless hands toying with flowers.

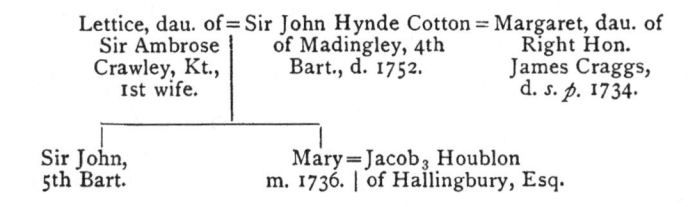

1735

Lettice, dau. of = Sir John Hynde Cotton = Margaret, dau. of
Sir Ambrose   of Madingley, 4th   Right Hon.
Crawley, Kt.,   Bart., d. 1752.   James Craggs,
1st wife.   d. *s. p.* 1734.

Sir John,   Mary = Jacob₃ Houblon
5th Bart.   m. 1736. | of Hallingbury, Esq.

By the young squire's marriage he was admitted into an altogether new society; a wheel within a wheel, as it were, of country life, the intimate circle of which was closed but to those either holding the same views, or connected with each other by ties of blood or near friendship. Not only was Sir John Hynde Cotton a prominent and determined Jacobite, but he was also of strong and interesting personality. Moreover, Jacob now entered a family distinguished for not only much genius, but what was then still rarer, a profound love and reverence for art and literature. It had been a mistake of Sir Robert Walpole, for which he was later made to suffer, that he had failed either to encourage persons of literary talent, or

[1] *Daily Gazette*, No. 17, 18 July 1735. London.
[2] *Gentleman's Magazine*, 1735, p. 500, and many other notices.

apprehend the power for influence they possessed upon others, for or against himself and his administration. As he had slighted men of literary genius and their claims to recognition, it follows that they not only suffered from a neglect which kept them poor, but they hated the minister and his government, and in this dislike they generally included the King and royal family, scornfully contrasting their coarse personality with that of the royal Stuarts. On the other hand, many of the leaders of the Opposition were men of culture and enlightenment, and although they had no lucrative posts to offer, or material advantages to dispose of, their attitude was in many respects the very opposite to that of the Whigs. It thus followed that, while both encouraging and appreciating men of genius, they also profited by the keen wit and satirical powers which exposed to ridicule the weaknesses and vices of their opponents. We have reason to believe Sir John Cotton was one of those who, fully alive to the intellectual enjoyment of the society of such persons, was yet aware of the material advantages to be gained by their support and friendship. When engaged in his investigations at Cambridge for his history, Thomas Carte lodged at Madingley as a guest, and made use of the library and rare collection of pamphlets,[1] and Carte was a Jacobite, and took part in their plots and conspiracies.[2] Dr. William King, Principal of St. Mary's Hall, Oxford, and author of the famous *Anecdotes*, was another visitor, sharing also the political views of his hosts. Hooke, the Roman historian, and Hume Campbell, Lord Registrar of Scotland, are also said to have been welcomed at Madingley (1738), beside Gough and Zachary Grey. William Cole, 'the Cambridge Antiquary,'[3] during many years was likewise a friend and *habitué* of the family home of the Cottons; he

[1] *History of National Biography:* 'Carte.'
[2] Lord Stanhope, *History of England*, iii. 23.
[3] Sir Leslie Stephen, *Ford Lectures*, 1903.

was a high church tory ecclesiastic, an ardent Jacobite, and became the 'antiquarian oracle' on bric-a-brac of his 'ingenious friend Mr. Horace Walpole.'[1] Cole's manuscripts are preserved in the British Museum, another of them is still possessed by the last descendants of the Cottons, viz. 'Gens Cottoniana Cantabrigiensis, or an account of the very ancient family of Cotton of Lanwade and Madingley in the County of Cambridge,' etc.

While the father of Mary Houblon was thus accustomed to gather around him men of varied talents and pursuits, Madingley was adorned with many fine and interesting objects, to say nothing of the rare and valuable library which had been enriched by successive generations of his family. That the name has been intimately connected for centuries with art and literature is well known beyond the circles of historians and antiquarians. The Cottonian Manuscripts, now not the least valuable of the great national treasures in the British Museum, were gathered together and cherished, while still the world had no value for them, by Sir Robert Cotton, a collateral indeed, but originally of the same blood and sharing the same tastes as the Cottons of Lanswade and Madingley. The Cottons were also a warm-hearted and impulsive race, generous to a fault, a characteristic which was to involve future generations of the family (in whom that generosity had degenerated into a weakness) in many troubles and embarrassments. Their devoted adherence to the House of Stuart was in part illustrative of the family character, and had also been traditional from the stormy days of the civil wars. Sir John's grandfather, another Sir John,[2] had striven and fought for King Charles, as his grandson now did in

---
[1] Sir Leslie Stephen, *Ford Lectures*, 1903.
[2] Sir John Cotton of Lanswade, Cambs., born September 1615, died about 1690; married Jane, daughter and heiress of Sir Edward Hynde, Knight, of Madingley, Cambs.

schemes and plots (though not with sword) for his luckless descendants. An unique collection of the earliest newspapers were among the treasures of the library at Madingley. Those extending throughout the whole period of the civil wars were doubtless received weekly by the baronet of the day. Bound up contemporaneously in little stout quarto volumes, the collection now forms part of Lord Crawford's great library at Haigh.[1]

Warmly attached to each other, the Cottons of Madingley adopted Jacob Houblon as a son, and the two families henceforth, to the third and fourth generation, were united by the closest ties, not only of blood, but of mutual interests and tastes. The opening out to Jacob of happy domestic intercourse in his young wife's family, and of her presence in his home, must have been singularly delightful to one who, though possessed of so few of kith and kin, had come of a race which had always been characterised by warm domestic affections.

COTTON ARMS.

The author of an interesting family memoir of the Cottons tells us that Sir John was 'in his prime, one of the handsomest men of his time,' and that when he knew him he was 'one of the tallest, largest, and best-looking of men.'[2] He might have added that he was in later life extremely corpulent! So vast was his size that he had a set of chairs made for his use, strong and wide

---

[1] When an undergraduate at Cambridge the late Lord Lindsay, afterwards twenty-fifth Earl of Crawford, enjoyed the run of Madingley library, and on its dispersal a large number of books were purchased by him and removed to Haigh.

[2] W. Cole, A.M., 'Gens Cottoniana Cantabrigiensis.' Sir John Hynde Cotton, fourth Bart., was fourteenth in male descent from Sir Henry Cotton of Cotton, near Feversham, Kent. He held this manor in 20 Edward III., and he is said to have made the Black Prince a knight. He removed to Lanswade in 1358, on his marriage with its heiress, Alice de Hastinges.

THE SQUIRE

enough for him to sit upon with comfort.[1] His love of good cheer was also proverbial, and he was credited with the power of consuming as large a quantity of wine as any man in England.

'On Monday last, the 9th instant,' the London daily paper announced on the 12th of August 1736, 'the lady of Jacob Houblon, Esq[re], Member of Parliament for Colchester, was brought to bed of a son and heir, to the universal joy of that family, as well as the neighbouring parishes; which was shewn by ringing of bells and other demonstrations of joy.'[2] The child was privately baptized soon afterwards, but, just one month after his birth, viz. on the 9th of September following, the pride of the young father overflowed in hospitality to all his neighbours, gentle and simple. Of these festivities we have a contemporary account. They took place—we gather from the parish registers—on the occasion of the certifying in church of the baptism. After the ceremony, at which the sponsors had assisted, the family party adjourned to Hallingbury Place, where they were joined by the rest of the guests, and the festivities described below took place. The child had been named after his young father's uncle, who at a distance, in his quiet rectory, though now sick and ailing, was doubtless rejoicing in the happiness of the nephew he had loved. Perhaps, knowing what was going forward, and the custom of the day, the words of the wise Burnet in his 'Conclusions' came to his mind: 'Can there be anything more barbarous than for gentlemen to think it is one of the honours of their houses that none of them may go out of them sober? and yet this passes as a character of a noble housekeeper, who entertains his guests kindly!'[3]

1736

[1] Some of these chairs still exist.
[2] *Daily Gazetteer*, No. 352, 12 August 1736. London.
[3] Burnet, *History of his Own Time*, iv. 356.

'On Thursday last,' writes the *Daily Gazetteer*, ' Jacob Houblon, of Hallingbury in Essex, Esq., member of Parliament for Colchester, baptized his new born son with the greatest magnificence imaginable. Most of the gentlemen within 15 or 20 miles of Mr Houblon's seat in Essex were present, and most of the common people within 4 or 5 miles, were made so welcome that they lay in heaps round his house dead drunk. There were three courses of upwards of 200 dishes each, and two tables, at which were 400 persons serv'd all at once, with all sorts of rarities and sweetmeats. Sir John Hynd Cotton and Sir Robert Abdy, Barts., were godfathers, the latter being proxy for Dr Houblon, and the Child was nam'd Jacob. There was a grand Concert of Musick at Dinner, and a noble Ball at night, from which the Company did not break up till the next morning. There were 20 Knights and Baronets, and 150 gentlemen, and about as many ladies. All the stables were taken up some miles about.'[1]

There is no reason to believe that Jacob Houblon himself was otherwise than a moderate drinker, moderate, that is to say, for the time. In comparing his portrait when in middle life with those of many gentlemen of the period, who were, after the fashion of the day, accustomed to drink a great deal, and whose puffy red countenances under their huge wigs betray their love of wine,[2] one is struck by the apparent healthiness of his appearance, which certainly gives no indication of intemperance. But on this occasion circumstances were apparently too much for him. Sir John Hynde Cotton was a deep drinker, and certainly took no inconsiderable part in the hospitality of his son-in-law's house. A decorous veil may then be drawn over the conclusion of the festivities, as was in

---

[1] *Daily Gazetteer*, No. 380, 14 September 1736. London.
[2] See the portraits in the National Portrait Gallery.

fact done by the reporter to the London newspaper, though he was less reticent with regard to the 'common people'! Alas! in those days the latter were not alone in the weakness which disgraced the age; and it is to be feared that after the supper was over, which followed upon the 'noble ball' at the old Place, some at least of the guests remained behind under the supper tables. Though age and infirmity prevented 'Dr Houblon' from giving his blessing in person on this occasion to the child and his young parents, the old man was induced soon after to travel over to Hallingbury, on a less festive occasion than that which has been described, and it is pleasant to think, that in this, the last year of his life (for he died within a few months of this time), he had the satisfaction of witnessing the climax of the happiness and prosperity of his young nephew and ward, in the possession of an heir to the name and family, of which he had been the last remaining.

While the feast we have just described probably took place in the hall of the old Place, the scene of the 'noble ball' would have been in the long gallery usual in Elizabethan houses. In the present instance this gallery ran the length of the north front of the house, and is still traceable in spite of the alterations made later in the century, when the Tudor house was transformed into a Georgian one. It was in these early days panelled throughout with oak wainscot, of the linen-fold pattern of early Tudor time.

When Hallingbury Place passed into the hands of the Houblon family, the furniture, or part of it, was purchased with it, and the inventory of the contents of the house has remained. Scanty in quantity, it yet was probably such as we should now greatly prize; witness some of the Jacobean chairs which adorned the gallery, and which still remain. Thus many of the accessories and furniture of his predecessors had come into the squire's possession, while his young wife had already added what was suitable to her comfort, inspired by the love of beauty which all the Cottons more or less possessed; but the original dining-tables and benches of black oak used by Hallingbury's past owners, together with the four-legged stools belonging to the top and bottom, have remained on through the changing years and many generations, and are still in use in the servants' hall at Hallingbury, one of the tables being a fine specimen and boldly carved; with these is a set of great copper jugs in graduated sizes, for the home-brewed ale; besides a vast number of pewter plates and dishes, some of early date. Some of these are of large size; a huge copper one, measuring 46 by 36 inches in diameter, could have been used only on such occasions of feasting as the coming of age of the heir, or at his birth, when, in accordance with the tradition of the time, the size of the meat served up was supposed to gauge the open-handedness of the hospitality of the hosts. This vast dish was far bigger than needed for a baron of beef, while not great enough for the historical 'ox roasted whole.' It probably bore a leg of beef on the occasion of the christening of the young squire's son in 1736.

As it was now necessary for the squire and his family to reside in London during the sitting of Parliament, he hired or purchased a house in town. For many years we find allusions in bills and letters to this house, which was No. 7 Queen Anne Street.[1] The young couple made many friends during these years, and while Jacob himself had no relations living in town but Lord and Lady Palmerston, who were identified with the whig and court set (Lady Palmerston being a lady-in-waiting to Queen Caroline), they were apparently thrown much more intimately within the circle of

[1] His son in after years occupied No. 14 in the same street.

Mary's relations and connections, and this naturally led to their absorption into a tory and opposition set in society.

London society at this time presented many curious and interesting pictures; but the chief impression conveyed to one's mind by a study of its more fashionable social conditions (especially in respect of the court set) is a strong sense of its unreality, as English and national. It is difficult to believe that the half-century which had elapsed since the days of the 'Merry Monarch' could have so transformed the character and breeding of English people. Charles II. and his court were vicious and dissolute, but never were they either vulgar or common. With all his faults Charles was a gentleman and kind-hearted, and withal he was one of the ablest men of his day; he was also loved by his people.[1] George II. succeeded to the throne in 1727, and he was as much a foreigner, or nearly so, as was his father. Both loved their native Electorate, and made no attempt to conceal their preference for it; in short, they were Germans, with German tastes and characteristics, and these being at that period somewhat plain and vulgar, the court and a large section of general society were influenced accordingly. By humouring their weaknesses and spending much English gold in furthering their schemes on the Continent, Sir Robert Walpole maintained his position and power as supreme minister of the crown for twenty-one years, and after his fall his successors for a while followed the same plan. Walpole understood the necessities of the time. His love of peace led him to make it his chief aim and object throughout his long administration, but his greed of power was no less great, and led to the inauguration of a system of corruption which for the time degraded political life. Every man, he thought, had his price, and

[1] See Bishop Burnet's character of Charles II. in his *History of his Own Time*.

as wish is father to the thought, he was able by this means to carry out his far-reaching plans for consolidating the British power, and establishing the Hanoverian dynasty on a firm basis, that the country, almost unconsciously, was piloted through the troubled waters of a disputed succession without suffering shipwreck. But as years went on, Walpole came to be hated with an intensity only equal to the immensity of the corruption which had secured and maintained his power, and so intimately united was his administration with the King and court in aim and policy in the mind of the country, that the hatred of the minister involved the royal family in his own unpopularity. In view of these conditions in society, it was well that the training and traditions of our young squire were calculated to produce the straightforward honourable gentleman—refined and highly educated—which he proved to be, and to which characteristics we have many references in letters and papers relative to him; perhaps the more flattering from the rarity of the latter qualifications among other country gentlemen of that time. That Jacob held before himself a high ideal of conduct and good manners, and at a later date inculcated the same on his sons, we have clear evidence.

For the Hanoverian royal family it may at least be said, that they were not many degrees worse than were a vast number of their contemporaries, but on the other hand it was chiefly due to the immorality and vulgarity of the court, that the level of morality and manners was lowered and debased for so long a period in English history. That this fact was recognised at the time of which we write, there appears to be no doubt, also that the court resented as a personal affront any attack upon these vicious conditions in society as directly insulting to themselves, and the code of morality they practised and sanctioned in those around them. We believe that at no period in the history of literature as directed on politics and manners, were any two publications received with greater sensation than Dean Swift's strange tale of *Gulliver's Travels*, followed soon afterwards by the no less famous *Beggar's Opera* of the poet Gay.[1] Writing in December 1728 to Swift in his distant Deanery in Ireland, Gay tells him of the anger of the court at his daring work, and pleads that 'I have written nothing that can be legally suppressed, unless the setting vices in general in an odious light, and virtue in an amiable one, may give offence.'[2] A few months later, a letter from Doctor Arbuthnot[3] to Swift speaks of Gay, and how he had become a public person through this wonderful work of wit and satire, in which he had scourged the fashionable sins and corruptions of the day. 'The inoffensive John Gay,' he writes, 'is now become one of the obstructions to the peace of Europe, the terror of ministers.... He is the darling of the City. If he would travel about the country, he would have hecatombs of roasted oxen sacrificed to him.'[4] Again, a little later he writes of Gay, 'He has about twenty lawsuits with booksellers for pirating his book.'[5]

Meanwhile little children were added to the family circle at Hallingbury. Three grew up, while two died in childhood. A picture at Hallingbury represents a pair of little maidens of some five and seven years old attired in velvet dresses reaching to their feet, and having between them a large dog. If we mistake not this animal was an important inmate of the old Place at this time, as two other portraits of him exist, one of which is carved

---

[1] An old caricature printed in colours—possibly brought to Hallingbury at this time—represents the King and his court seated round a huge water tank, in which Gulliver in a pigmy boat is struggling with wind and wave, produced by the efforts of the courtiers, whose crimson cheeks are puffed out with their exertions to create a miniature storm.
[2] *Swift's Letters*, ii. 376.
[3] The author of *John Bull*.
[4] *Swift's Letters*, cclxiv.
[5] The *Beggar's Opera*. See *Swift's Letters*, cclxvi.

in stone. The children accompanied their parents to London for the parliamentary sessions, and here many meetings with the 'cousinhood' of a large circle laid the foundation of future lifelong friendships. Jacob₃ Houblon had not sought to shirk the multitudinous duties of a magistrate and owner of property, while he was generous and liberal in the matter of charity. Periods of extreme poverty and distress were common, and much difficulty was experienced as to meeting the problems presented, for the poor were thriftless, and legislation so faulty as to accentuate the mischief it strove to relieve, and large and indiscriminate charity did harm.[1] Work was what the people wanted, but still more the will to do it.

The Trust had provided the squire with a fine property in what was considered as the choicest county for agricultural purposes, and as beautiful in woodland scenery as any in the home counties. Arthur Young was loud in his praise not only of the land but of the enlightened way in which it was now being worked and improved, according to modern ideas. The young squire inherited these tastes and traditions from his uncles, and continued throughout his life to improve and develop his estates. He built cottages, reclaimed land, and replanted the neglected woods and copses—especially in the area of the beautiful tract of forest land to which we have already alluded. At this period there was but little enclosing of common land, the large amount thus treated in England was mostly accomplished nearer the close of the century.

The special effort of farmers at this time was directed towards the improvement of the methods of cultivating wheat, the growth of which had been greatly stimulated by

[1] 'Jacob Houblon, Esqre, one of the representatives in Parliament for Colchester, has order'd Fifty Pounds to be distributed among the necessitous Families in that Borough who were not standing Collectionists.'—Old newspaper.

THE SQUIRE 47

the act (already noticed) passed in the early years of the
Revolution, which had that object in view, and by which
the Mercantilists had also hoped to encourage its export.[1]
In order to do this, a bounty of 5s. a quarter was given on
exported wheat, so long as the home price did not exceed
48s. Prices were thereby maintained with but slight
fluctuation. Only after the peace of 1763 did the needs
of the growing population cause the price gradually to
rise. Finally, in 1790 this country altogether ceased to
export wheat as a commodity.[2] Although this act was
condemned by the school of Adam Smith, and was bound
to go down under the new conditions which had arisen,
both its success and final doom seem to be fresh proofs
of the theory, that each 'day' as it comes brings its own
needs to be met and dealt with on their own merits.
In his work, the *Growth of English Industry and Commerce*, Dr. Cunningham gives his reasons for the success
of this act of the despised Mercantilists, calling it a
masterly stroke of policy, also his reasons why, when
those conditions under which it was passed were changed,
it became no more an advantage, but a restriction to our
food supply.[3] But thanks to the conditions which
brought about that 'golden age of farming' which prevailed throughout our squire's prosperous and equable
existence, he fulfilled all the hopes and aspirations of
usefulness, serenity, and progress which had presaged
the transference of his race from town to country.

Letters and books of accounts give us many details as
to the Houblon family throughout this century. Jacob
Houblon was a rich man as riches went in those days.
He kept open house, with many retainers within and
without, spent much on his estate of what came to

---

[1] See vol. i. p. 341.
[2] From 1770-80 imports and exports of wheat almost balanced each other. Lecky, *History of England*, vi. 193.
[3] W. Cunningham, *Growth of English Industry and Commerce in Modern Times*, i. 372.

him in rents, subscribed to county and philanthropical institutions, gave away liberally in charity, and yet was able to satisfy his taste and that of his sons for sport, for horse-breeding and racing, while he also kept a pack of beagles for his own diversion. The squire's love for books was also gratified by the purchase of a considerable number year by year. As early as 1731 we find his name on the list of subscribers to Albin's *Birds*, issued that year, and his copy is still at Hallingbury. Between them, he and his two sons, who later co-operated in this work, collected a very complete and interesting eighteenth-century library, more details of which we hope to give later on.

The expenses of a gentleman's wardrobe were considerable in those days. Not only were their clothes quite as elaborate and costly—if not more so—than those of their womenkind, but their wigs alone were no slight item in their personal expenses. From the evidence of his account-books, an abnormal number of wigs were supplied to our squire by his perruquiers, Messieurs Foy et Mattheu. Much wear and tear of these was doubtless unavoidable, and unless a gentleman was oblivious of the disgrace of a tousled head, he was forced to be lavish in new ones. Not only were hats swept off on meeting every acquaintance, whether male or female, but while conversing or walking in the company of a lady in the fashionable resorts of 'Hide Park or the Mall,' it was counted as ill-mannered to remain covered; the three-cornered hat was carried under the arm. No wonder that men were unwilling for so long a period to brave the elements with wigless and unprotected heads, under such circumstances! But the perukes of Jacob Houblon's day were already diminishing in size, and this shrinkage continued till the queue of natural hair finally remained, the last evidence of the long reign of wigs, unless, indeed, it be the clinging to the use of nightcaps, which habit survived till well on in the following century. A 'Tye wig' and two long bob-wigs cost the squire £13, 11s. on one occasion; while dress bag-wigs cost him on an average two guineas. But small bob-wigs, which were worn on 'undress' occasions, and which later took the place of the more ponderous bag-wig, cost no more than thirty-six shillings a piece. After some years we find the purchase noted in the squire's account-book, of wigs for his little boys! They commonly began to wear them, it seems, at about ten years of age, and their large dimensions struck the Swedish traveller Kalm with amusement during his journey in England at this period.

The squire's weekly expenditure for the standing of his horses at livery-stables when in town, shows him to have taken from ten to a dozen horses with him for his own and Mrs. Houblon's use when there. Most of these were coach horses; while we occasionally hear of a favourite 'sorel mare' which frequently carried him when he rode on horseback in town. His excursions to and from Hallingbury, and elsewhere on parliamentary and militia concern, were frequent; and when one considers the then deplorable state of the roads, no less a number of horses would have been sufficient for the work. Thus we find that with a new post-landau purchased in 1760, new sets of harness for six horses to draw it were at the same time supplied to him.

During these years the family went regularly to town for the parliamentary session, living the ordinary life of their class and contemporaries. That Mr. and Mrs. Houblon went out frequently into society is shown by their incidental expenses, such, for instance, as payments for lamp-lighting, the darkness and filth of the streets necessitating the services of men, whose special business it was to carry lanterns before the sedan-chairs of persons being carried in them by their servants at night.

THE HOUBLON FAMILY

These were days of glory for the English stage. David Garrick was already the idol of the London world;[1] while the lively Peg Woffington, Mrs. Clive, Foote, Mrs. Cibber, Quin, Mrs. Abington and others, in turn fascinated playgoers, the gratification of whose taste, though often coarse and unrefined, was then less dependent on the outward circumstances of the *mise en scène*, than on a fine impersonation of parts. It was before the days of Stars, and on the same boards were to be found actors and actresses on the same high plane of excellence. Doubtless rivalries and jealousies abounded, but the keen appreciation of each other's powers gave incentive to exertion in each individual, and together produced a very high standard of performance. The Houblon couple went frequently to the play, and also spent evenings in visiting their friends, and at routs, assemblies, masquerades, Ranelagh, and the Ridotto.[2]

Although we are ignorant how far the squire might go with those who longed to overthrow the existing powers, we do know his wife to have been an ardent Jacobite, and that she inspired her young children with her own enthusiasm. During the first ten years of her married life, the hopes of those she loved were all centred on a successful Jacobite rebellion, and Mary Houblon continually shared their hopes and fears while learning their secrets. All, however, were free to plot and plan without let or hindrance on the part of the Government. The cynical wisdom of Walpole early discovered the secret of knowing, yet not seeming to know of political intrigue, and the safety of allowing the ventilation of discontent. But if both Tories and Jacobites left no stone unturned to expose

---

[1] Lecky says of Garrick, 'His appearance on the stage had a real importance in the history of the English mind.' *History*, i. 546.

[2] Ranelagh, the fashionable resort of the day, was still in the first novelty of its existence. The gardens of Vauxhall, later to become so popular, were opened some years later in the century.

SIR JOHN HYNDE COTTON, FOURTH BART., 1721.

the weakness and foreign characteristics of the royal family, we may well believe the former had not ceased to carry on their campaign of agitation against the great whig ministry, nor the latter to plot and scheme to bring in again the exiled Stuarts; and perhaps, in the words of Lord Stanhope, 'the most active in this work was Sir John Hynde Cotton, member for the county of Cambridge, and a gentleman of old family and large estates.[1] He had sat in Parliament ever since the time of Queen Anne, was not undistinguished as a speaker, and so zealous a Jacobite that he used to make an annual progress throughout England to maintain the spirit of his friends.'[2]

With respect to Jacob Houblon's attitude towards the political creed of his father-in-law, he was always a Tory, though not a narrow one, but if he had been also a Jacobite he would only have been one of the many tory gentlemen who, between this time down to some few years subsequent to the Rebellion of 1745, were also Jacobite, and that not secretly. The great talents and persuasive eloquence of the Jacobite baronet could not fail to have been brought to bear with overwhelming force upon his son-in-law; at least Sir John certainly did not spare himself; for instance, we find him spending the long winter months of 1740 in town, the more easily to act as the channel of communication between 'the King in Rome' and his supporters at home.[3] It was this power of persuasion which rendered Sir John Cotton so formidable, and for which he was hated and feared by the King and the whig party. Lord Stanhope dwells upon his caustic wit and upon his intimate

1740

---

[1] Sir John Cotton had succeeded his father as fourth baronet in 1712, having entered Parliament in 1708. He served as a member of the Board of Trade in the reign of Queen Anne (1713). He sat for Cambridge till 1741, when he was thrown out by the efforts of the whig party, but was elected to Marlborough and sat for that constituency till his death in 1752.
[2] Lord Stanhope, *History of England*, iii. 29. See also Coxe, *Life of Lord Walpole*, p. 276. [3] Lord Stanhope, iii. 30.

52 THE HOUBLON FAMILY

knowledge of the arts of the House and great skill in debate.[1] Though we find from another source that owing to his habit of stammering his speeches were usually brief, they were nevertheless effective, for he knew well on occasion how to make this infirmity serve his purpose.[2]

1741   The quarrel with Spain on the old story of her claims of monopoly in trade in the New World at length broke the spell of Walpole's long rule; for the impetuosity of country and people forced him into war and at length resignation.[3] The miseries and heavy cost of the long struggle that ensued have no part in these memoirs, except in so far that Jacob Houblon was one of the stormy Tories who joined in forcing on the war,[4] as he and his brother-members of Parliament were also responsible for the clamour by which they later forced the successors of Walpole, the colourless Pelhams, to embark on the still greater enterprise of supporting the Queen of Hungary, Maria Theresa, on the Continent.[5]

Jacob Houblon served as Knight of the Shire for the county of Hertford during the Parliament of 1741, and during this part of his parliamentary career we believe was content to follow the footsteps of his brilliant and masterful father-in-law. The election took place in May, and the *Gentleman's Magazine* informs us that both he and Mr. Charles Gore, his colleague, were returned without opposition in the country interest; also, that they were chosen as having voted against the Convention in the former Parliament.[6]

Meanwhile the part taken by Sir John Hynde Cotton in the political crisis was no mean one. Allusions to his activity abound both in histories of the time and in the

[1] Lord Stanhope, *History of England*, iii. 29.
[2] *Gens Cottoniania*, etc.
[3] Mahan, *Influence of Sea Power upon History*, p. 250. Also Coxe, *Pelham Administration*, i. 15.
[4] *Ibid.*, i. 53.   [5] *Ibid.*, i. 48.
[6] *Gentleman's Magazine*, May 1741, pp. 227-229.

records of the House of Commons. So great was his personal influence, and so powerful was he in debate, that we find the whole Opposition, composite as it was, clamouring for a recognition of the baronet's claims to office, and making his inclusion in the Government of what was afterwards called the Broad-bottomed Administration, the condition of their support and assistance in carrying on the government: and loudest in this demand was the Duke of Argyll. As the Government was in urgent need of support at this time—owing to the general discontent in the country with respect of the conduct of the war, and its supposed acquiescence in the King's Hanoverian policy—the ministers were only too anxious to comply with the demand, the only obstacle being the antipathy of the King to such a course.[1]

Party government was then still uncrystallised into sides, and the coalition which resulted in the Broad-bottomed government, was destined to stultify and efface the vitality of the Opposition altogether for the time; for the so-called disaffected Whigs, admitted to power as the result of the compromise, were soon absorbed into the body politic which already reigned, while the tory leaders, likewise included, were altogether swamped by their colleagues. The result was, that the Opposition lost their chief leaders, and were none the better for their accession to office. That Pitt remained outside, and the rest, who like Sir John Cotton were so distinctively Jacobite that nothing would induce the King to admit them to office, was well both for the party and for its future independence of action. It was only in 1744 on the reconstruction of the Cabinet, due to the strength of the feeling in the country,[2] that the situation forced the King to yield, and Sir John Cotton was appointed to a post, though only in the Household. A

---

[1] Stanhope, *History of England*, iii. 114, 115.
[2] Coxe, *Pelham Administration*, iii. 26.

contemporary rare print represents the tory party intently engaged upon forcing the immense form of the Jacobite leader down the throat of the indignant King![1]

The failure of the 'Rising of 45,' as had been the case in 1715, was once more to bring accession of strength to the whig party, and in so far as the Jacobite baronet was concerned, it was immediately followed by his dismissal and of that of the other statesmen who, like him, had been admitted to office so unwillingly.

1745

The story of the Jacobite rising in 1745 is one of deep and pathetic interest. It was the long-awaited climax to hopes and fears, which had risen and fallen through years of patient effort. Passionate loyalty to the royal family, whose claims were so strong that the name of Stuart was said to be a word of magic power felt even by the ministers of the Georgian kings,[2] was perhaps a sufficient incentive to action in some instances; but now Jacobite sympathies were quickened by a dislike to the King, and jealousy of his determined preference for Hanover and its interests. The battle of Prestonpans showed the spirit in which Prince Charles was supported by his friends and by the gallant Highlanders, but it is also possible that the wonderful success of the rising in the north, and of the unopposed march to Derby, may have been in part due to the fact that he came to claim his father's crown unsupported by any but his own countrymen. No Frenchman backed his claim, and historians unite in their opinion that had he continued his advance, he might well have entered London and claimed the crown, and that without bloodshed.[3] For an incursion from the north, led by the son of

[1] Coxe, *Life of Horace, Lord Walpole*, p. 276. The engraving is in the Print Room of the British Museum (Satirical Prints, No. 2613). It is called 'A Very Extraordinary Motion, Dec. 1744.'
[2] Coxe, *Pelham Administration*, iii. 32.
[3] Stanhope, *History of England*, iii. 276.

their ancient kings, caused but little alarm to the people of this country; nor was but little effort made to oppose the Prince's advance. That the French delayed was due to irresolution. They feared to strike before the party in England was ready to co-operate with them. As a test of this they demanded that Sir John Hynde Cotton should resign the offices in the Government he then held; which step his partisans pleaded, very naturally, would have but one result, viz. his arrest and confinement in the Tower.[1] That this actually happened is probable; many English Jacobites were arrested at this time, and of them all, Sir John Cotton would have been the first the Government would desire to secure.[2]

But if the people were indifferent, and the Jacobites many and eager, it was far otherwise with the whig Government and the King. At the near approach of the Highland army King George contemplated flight, so unready was any opposition to meet it. He had packed up his valuables and disposed them on board one of the royal yachts, which lay at the Tower ready for his use. He had but to step on board, to yield the crown to him whom his minister Pelham hysterically called the 'vagabond Prince who ventured so insolently to claim for his family the rights which *we* had so frequently denied them.'[3] But the City as usual had kept its head; two regiments were quickly raised, and the Train Bands called out; more slowly militia regiments in several counties were embodied; but the time was so short in which to prepare, that, until the arrest of the Prince's advance at Derby, 'the dreadful danger and confusion'[4] which prevailed, made all men believe (as was said

---

[1] See letter taken at Culloden, Stuart Papers, *apud* Stanhope's *History of England*, lxxvi.
[2] There is a tradition that Sir John Hynde Cotton was at one time confined in the Tower.
[3] *Pelham Administration*, i. 144.
[4] Of which Fox wrote. See *Ibid.*, i. 264.

by Marshal Wade), that 'England is for the first comer.'[1]

The alarm and apprehension of the Whigs at the near approach to success of the Prince's invasion, led to a terrible vengeance being taken upon the unfortunate Highlanders in the north, who alone had taken active measures towards the realisation of the Jacobite dream of restoring the royal family. In the south wiser counsels prevailed, inspired by a wholesome respect for the power of both Tories and Jacobites; and no attempt was made by the whig Government to prosecute for treason.[2] The Scottish chief—the famous Simon, Lord Lovat—however, provided a useful and edifying example for the benefit of future rebels. Jacob Houblon's Bluebook, retailing the whole long story of his trial by his peers and condemnation to death, still has its place in the 'Evidence Room' at Hallingbury. In reading its crabbed print we can picture the emotion with which the story of the 'badger's baiting' was read there. Old and sick, half blind and deaf, allowed no counsel,—for seven days old Lovat fought for his life—and lost it. It was not worth much, for he was neither true nor honest, but he 'suffered' for the Cause. His execution, with all its horrid details of hanging, disembowelling, and quartering, helped to establish firmly the present royal family on the throne, and we may be grateful with the old lord himself, who in his dying speech remarked, half impudently, half in earnest, 'I must say that since your Lordships and the Nation in general thought fit to have a King from Germany, you could not have chose one from a more illustrious House.'[3]

Down in Essex, in old Hallingbury, we find that

---

[1] *Pelham Administration*, i. 264. See also Mahan, *Influence of Sea Power on History*, p. 269.
[2] Stanhope, *History of England*, iii. 320.
[3] Proceedings in the House of Peers, etc., against Simon, Lord Lovat, for high treason, March 1747.

during those anxious months three little children and their young mother, possibly their father also, had been 'watching and waiting for Prince Charlie's success.' In a letter written in the evening of her life to a niece and namesake,—the little Laetitia, Jacob₃ Houblon's daughter, now old, blind, and infirm, but young in mind and enthusiastic still, tells of her first reading of *Waverley*, and of the many memories of her childhood the book had brought back to her mind, and of those anxious days. For to those who had imbibed the passionate loyalty which inspired the Jacobites in the '45,' whether man, woman, or child, it was a sentiment which transcended all ordinary emotion, and thrilled them to the end of their lives.

CHAPTER III

THE GRAND TOUR

Ante alios quantum Pegasus ibat equos.
'Therefore in the meane time joyne with me in thy best wishes for happy successe in my future travels; and so I commend thee to him whom I beseech to blesse thee at home, and me abroade.'—
CORYAT, *Crudities*, 1611.

1735-69 THE squire's parliamentary career was a long one. Member for Colchester in 1735, he was elected Knight of the Shire for the county of Herts in 1741; and he sat continuously for this constituency for twenty-eight years. With the failure of the Rebellion of '45' and the subsequent assumption of office by the tory party, some Tories were led to reconsider their position in the light of the past—now closed—and the present situation. For a long period the political reaction to the Walpole administration led to an extreme of toryism well calculated to give pause to the more enlightened among educated men. In the case of Jacob₃ Houblon, it certainly would appear that he reserved to himself an independence of thought and action which lifted him above the herd of narrow, and sometimes very ignorant, squires who represented the tory party in the House of Commons, and whose hatred for Walpole had blinded and warped their political intuitions. Thus we find, in a letter addressed by Henry Fox to Lord Digby in 1754, the writer speaking of 'Houblon who is *rather* a Tory.' This letter was written

1754 a few days after Henry Pelham's death, and the assumption of the chief offices of state by his brother the Duke of

Newcastle. The Duke offered Fox the Secretaryship of State and leadership of the House of Commons. Fox was in office but a short space,[1] but that he had already begun to taste the sweetness of power—so longed for by, and denied to, Pitt by the King's dislike—is evident by this letter.[2] How 'Houblon' came into this scheme of Fox we do not know.

The squire's children received as careful an education as he himself had done. They were all taught by a tutor till the boys went to their preparatory school, after which he continued the education of little Laetitia till her brothers were old enough to go to Harrow, when a governess was engaged for her, named Mrs. Wise. We find by his father's account-book that young Jacob$_4$'s departure for Harrow was prefaced by a visit to the theatre and a substantial tip. We are inclined to wonder if his wigs accompanied him to school, and if so, what became of them during a game of football!

Later, Jacob$_4$ was sent for six months to Paris and Brussels to learn French; he kept a journal, rather like a guide-book, but occasionally amusing, and betraying promise of intelligence. His companion on this occasion was Mr. Thomas Lipyeatt, his father's old friend and tutor; and after his return the young man was entered at St. John's College, Cambridge, as an undergraduate.

In 1757 the squire served as High Sheriff of Herts. His papers and accounts have been preserved, but only two points call for observation, viz. the enormous

1757

---

[1] Stanhope, *History of England*, iv. 36.
[2] 'I am glad,' he wrote, 'Ld Egmont does not come in. I like your thought of Lord Shaftesbury. Moderate Whig enough I am sure. I hear of a Tracy, what objection have the Torys to join him? I hear of Houblon too, who is rather a Tory, and I hope to keep Lord Egmont out. . . . Att all events keep out Egmont and don't say that I (who am now a Minister) said so.' See *Report of the Royal Commission on Historical MSS.*, Report 8, p. 22. MSS. of George Wingfield Digby, Esq. Fox did not return to office till 1755.

amount of port wine consumed by the judge, jury, and guests of the Sheriff, and the gruesome details surrounding the executions he was called upon to superintend during his time of office. But executions were so common in those days that it is to be doubted if they affected anybody even with passing pity!

1758   The following year the squire took council as to the future careers of his sons; the elder, Jacob, was twenty-two, while John was three years his junior. The latter was now sent to Trinity Hall, Cambridge, previous to being called to the Bar, while the same plan as had been arranged for himself in his youth by his uncle, was pursued by the squire in respect of his elder son. Since those days, the habit of sending young men of the upper classes abroad for a course of study, including dancing, riding, fencing, etc., to be followed by what was called the grand tour, had become systematised;[1] indeed all these accomplishments, and many others, were considered indispensable to the education of a 'young man of parts'; while in spite of the old rivalry with the French still existing, it was also necessary to speak the language with ease, and French clothes and fashions were likewise greatly sought after. But though a knowledge of French was considered indispensable, it was not to France that the young men were sent, but to Italy. As a rule, each youth was accompanied by a tutor or governor, as it was usual to call him, often but little older and wiser than himself; though occasionally he was a man of high attainments and character, who undertook the position on account of the opportunities it afforded for travel.

    There were those who professed to believe that no good was to be gained by a sojourn abroad for young men, but only an acquaintance with evil. A publication

---

[1] Sir Leslie Stephen, *English Literature and Society in the Eighteenth Century*, p. 122.

which made a great sensation appeared but shortly before young Jacob's departure for the Continent, called an *Estimate of the Manners and Principles of the Times*. This work took a similar view. Nothing too bad could be said of English society in the author's opinion. 'Vain, luxurious, selfish, effeminate,' was his indictment; while he also insinuates, that 'our young men on the Grand Tour learning foreign vices without enlarging their minds,' was rather due to the degeneracy of the English character than to vicious conditions on the Continent.[1] It would appear that society was thrilled with dismay at the supposed degeneracy of the race,[2] and was inclined to believe that the accusation was in part true! Mr. Brown, the author, also reproached the rising generation with being less hardy than their ancestors, and people might possibly agree as to the luxury which led to men of fashion in town going out to dinner in sedan-chairs instead of on horseback, and for 'dining there on foreign cookery rather than plain English fare'; but in respect of his further disapproval of the taste for the new literature just dawning on an expectant age, it is doubtful if his strictures did not come too late! For after once tasting the joys of fiction, whether in the sentimentalism of Richardson or the vivid realism of Fielding and Smollett, it was too much to hope that the theological and philosophical dissertations which were still studied so earnestly by many minds in the century, would have it all their own way with the coming generations. The invention of the novel was indeed to open a new era in the history of English thought, which needed food for its imagination. Nevertheless Brown's *Estimate* was popular, though he left such solicitous parents as our squire still upon the horns of the dilemma as to a choice

1756

[1] Brown's *Estimate of the Manners and Principles of the Times*, 1756, *apud* Leslie Stephen's *History of Thought in the Eighteenth Century*, i. 21.
[2] *Ibid.*

of evils. It is enough to say, that all having been satisfactorily settled and arranged, and Mr. Lipyeatt's younger brother Jonathan engaged to accompany Jacob₄, the two young men left England on the 12th of June 1758 for Italy, *via* Holland, Germany, and Switzerland.

From this time till his return home in June 1761, Jacob₄ Houblon corresponded regularly with his family at Hallingbury Place, his letters being despatched once a month. He wrote well and easily, though his style, especially when addressing his father, was occasionally sententious and even priggish, in accordance with the fashion of letter-writing in the eighteenth century. His youthful high spirits, however, frequently break through the ordered periods, which are also interspersed with most genuine expressions of affection, and eager questions as to all relating to his home and its surroundings. To his uncle Sir John Cotton he wrote more familiarly;[1] and there is much in these letters relating to the progress of the Seven Years' War, now at its height on the Continent. His uncle, on the other hand, appears to have kept him well informed on home politics and the progress of the war in America.

Shortly before young Jacob's departure, the squire, together with a large number of other English gentlemen, came forward to offer their services in a national militia, a measure for the reorganisation of which had been brought forward by Pitt at the outbreak of war, and the despatch of troops to Germany in support of Frederick the Great of Prussia.

The confidence and patriotism of Pitt at this juncture were greatly appreciated by the nation, humiliated and depressed, as it was, by its sense of the debased tone of public life in the past; and the country turned to him and his leading with enthusiasm. Pitt's power once

---

[1] Sir John, his grandfather, died in 1752. Recording the event, Walpole says: 'Died Sir John Cotton, the last Jacobite of any sensible activity.'

firmly established, and the King's dislike of him overruled by the determination of the country to fight, better conditions shortly came about, and the nation entered on the long and apparently aimless struggle in both continents, with something of the old bull-dog courage of Englishmen sure of success in whatever they undertake. The King fought hard against the spirit which sought to place the gentlemen of England in a position to defend its shores; lists of the best men of each county irrespective of party who had undertaken to serve as militia officers, were sent up time after time by the lord-lieutenants for the royal confirmation, to be repeatedly rejected almost *en bloc*. But in the end George II. was forced to submit, and the militia was officered by the pick of the country gentlemen and nobility.

Arrived at the Hague, the young squire and his companion plunged immediately into the excitement and adventure of their surroundings. Well supplied with letters of introduction, Jacob was greatly pleased and interested during his stay in the capital, where they 'introduced him to all the best Company,' and he was received very kindly at the court by the Prince Stadtholder and his English wife, the Princess Royal. After some delay, owing to their proposed route leading them right through the seat of the war, departure became possible, through a change in the military situation. Unlike most other travellers this year who had preferred to take a different road, the spirit of adventure in the two young men had led them to persevere in their attempt to get to Italy by the usual route, in spite of all warlike impediments. Prince Ferdinand of Brunswick, the gallant young officer whom Pitt had named to the command of the allied forces against the French in Hanover, and later one of Frederick of Prussia's best generals,—brought about the alteration which enabled the travellers to proceed on their journey. 'I have taken the opportunity,' Jacob wrote on the 15th of June 1758, 'of Mr. Delaval' (the English minister at the Hague) 'sending a Packet extraordinary, to acquaint you that we purpose setting off this afternoon in good health and high spirits, on account of Prince Ferdinand having yesterday offer'd the French Battle. For that purpose he marched his whole Army in order of Battle within musket shot of the Enemy, who were entrenched in a Wood, and who, with all their courage, did not fire a shot, but on the contrary, as soon as some Hanoverian Cannon were brought up, took to their Heels. Our Friends have taken a great deal of Baggage and are still in Persuite.' This was the battle of Crefeld in Rhenish Prussia.

From the Hague, Jacob and his companion went, *via* Utrecht, Maestricht, Aix-la-Chapelle, and Bonn, to Cologne, from which place we have an interesting letter describing their adventures on the journey thither, the country being full of troops. Lord Brougham was at Aix, and urged them to remain some days with him, but as 'the Armies were so near, they did not venture to postpone their journey, fearing not to get through.' Accordingly on the 20th of June they 'followed a Commissary for Ammunition for the French army,' travelling to Juliers. This proved of service when they overtook large numbers of baggage-wagons blocking the road, the which were peremptorily ordered by Monsieur le Commissaire to draw aside out of his way, the carriage of the young Englishmen passing by also, as part of his suite. After travelling continuously for two days and a night, during which time they got nothing to eat but some dry bread, Jacob and his companion were happy to find themselves at last beyond the risk of further delay by the movements of the troops.

After reaching Lausanne the travellers continued the

journey to Geneva, at which place they were detained for three weeks, the roads being impassable in consequence of heavy floods. Alpine expeditions occupied the time until they were able to proceed, enthusiastic accounts of which Jacob wrote home to Sir John Cotton. While at Chamounix they enjoyed the hospitality of the prior and monks of a community living at the foot of the glacier, and from the monastery they made their expeditions with guides, the prior providing them with 'clean straw beds and tythe fowls in abundance, while in return he drank two bottles of our wine every day. He told us, he had made a vow never to drink water!' After his experiences among the Alps, Mont Cénis was a 'molehill' to Jacob, and the dangers of the journey to Turin trifling. Across the Pass itself they rode on mules, for although they had ridden on horseback over many more dangerous routes in Jacob's opinion, mules only might be used on which to ride up, while 'Porters only might carry one down.' As this was the month of July, one would infer from these precautions that those concerned in the transit of travellers across the Pass, were not unwilling to magnify the difficulties of the way!

Arrived at Turin, Lord Bristol, the English minister, received the young men kindly, and presented Jacob at court, this being the necessary preliminary to his being admitted to the Royal Academy as a student. They accordingly were entered on the 8th of August and took up their residence there, it being nearly three months since their departure from England. 'Here,' writes Jacob to his uncle, 'we live very well, are well lodged, and have good masters. The manège and horses are very good. They generally put me on the horses that rear and kick most; I like it the better. Our dancing master is reckoned one of the best in Europe. The Academists are well received at the Assemblies here,' and he adds that he goes every night either to the

1758

French or Spanish ambassador's. Of public entertainments for the present there were none, though they were promised many in the future. Meanwhile amusement was to be found on the ramparts of the town, where every holy-day the handsome bourgeoises were to be seen. 'Out of long Rows of Beauties set down on the grass,' he wrote to his uncle, 'one may pick out twenty as fine Women as any in Europe. C'est le veritable.' To his father, soon after this, he laments over possible changes in the rules relating to the academists, which he complains 'may do well enough for children or for their own people, but not for the English. Yet their reason for making them is to have more English here.' His father at any rate had given him a pretty free hand as to his movements; for Jacob informs him that he shall certainly not remain in the Academy should he not be allowed to go out without leave of the governor except on feast-days, and then to be in at supper at eight o'clock! But his chief regret in leaving would be on account of the 'good acquaintance' he had made in the society of Turin, but especially in respect of two ladies, who throughout his stay in Italy were invariably kind and hospitable to the young Englishman. Of these two, viz. the Marchesa Corregues and Madame la Comtesse de St. Gilles, the latter retained Jacob's warmest admiration and affection throughout his life. Among the Englishmen then in Turin, wrote Jacob, were 'Lrd Garlies, son of Lord Galloway, with Mr Smith,[1] who are returning home from their travels through Italy; Lrd Arundell with Mr Newton (by some said to be a Jesuit); and Sir Harry Harpur with Colonel de Cronsay. These four last being in the Academy.'

For six months our young squire and his companion, Jonathan Lipyeatt, remained at the Accademia Reale at Turin, the time being broken by one or two short

---
[1] His governor.

excursions during the vacations, in company with some of the academists. The circle of young Englishmen seems to have been a very happy and harmonious society, all greatly enjoying life and apparently eager to attain proficiency in their work. Skill in both fencing and 'the dance' was considered as essential for men of fashion, but it was the 'manège' in which it was the delight and ambition of Jacob to excel. Beyond these accomplishments, mathematics was the only serious study undertaken at the Academy, although Jacob Houblon worked also at drawing and languages. The manège was in its perfection as taught at Turin in the eighteenth century, and for near two hundred years previously it had had its home in Italy and Spain. Maistre Blundevill, who wrote his book in 1597, gives minute descriptions of the various exercises, which, with the help of a series of charming eighteenth-century engravings in Johann Elias Ridinger's work representing the school in Italy at the very time of Jacob's visit, we are able clearly to understand. Part of the training of the cavaliers consisted in the breaking-in of horses to a graceful performance of the various feats; and it needed both horse and rider to be masters of them all, before either could be considered as proficient in the art. The horses consisted of the 'great horse or war horse' and the 'stiver or pleasure horse,' the latter being a better-bred animal, to whose spirit and frolicsome heels the engravings of Ridinger do ample justice. Pacing, trotting, half-turn, double-turn, curvetting, pirouetting, and courbetting were elementary exercises, besides the 'training to noise,' which consisted in subjecting the horse to the ordeal of a hideous din of drums beaten, and brazen vessels clanged over his head. Then there was the *Capriole* and the *Ballotade*, the *terra-terra* and the *Pesate*. Passing the *Carière* was 'a short course of some score and ten paces, along which one galloped at full speed; stopped, did the *Pesate,* or turned *terra-terra* or with a single turn; and again galloped or passed the *Carière'*; the horse being (in the words of the master of manège) 'forced to run swiftlie and so roundly as he possibly can even to the end, to the intent that he may stop on his buttock.'[1] Young Houblon speaks of the horses kicking; they were taught to strike out thus behind, or 'to yarke,' as it was called; and the yarke and the pesate together made the Capriole or 'Goat's leap.'

His letters home from Turin show Jacob to have gone much into society at night, the threatened change of rules for the academists having in the end turned out quite in keeping with the ideas of British manhood at their time of life, as held by all the young Englishmen. From Lord Bristol's successor, Mr. Stewart Mackenzie, and his wife, Lady Betty, all the young men received real and unfailing kindness, and as both were dear friends of Sir John Hynde Cotton, Jacob had a special claim on their goodness.[2]

The magnificence of the Italian courts at this period was great, and their princes very wealthy. The descriptions sent home by Jacob Houblon of the gala fêtes and balls at the courts of Turin and elsewhere, read almost like fairy-tales, so lavish was their splendour. He soon found it necessary to write to his father with a request for more money; for demands upon his purse for clothes, and other expenses, soon left him very low in funds.[3] This expenditure he explained, apart from the very expensive journey out, had been absolutely necessary, as in order to 'make any figure whatever' he had not only to keep a coach and livery-servants, besides

---

[1] Johann Elias Ridinger, *Le Manège.* Translation.
[2] His letter to Sir John Cotton promising his friendship and protection for Jacob Houblon is at Hallingbury. Lady Betty was *née* Campbell.
[3] 'Take care to be *bien mis,*' wrote Lord Chesterfield to his son at Turin but a few years before this time. *Chesterfield Letters,* letter cl.

his two *laquais de place* whom he had brought with him from England, but to supply himself with 'rich suits of cloaths' suitable for court. For the magnificence of the dress worn, he pleads, is beyond anything at home. 'In my best laced London suit on the first occasion of my appearing at Court, I was by far the least well-drest person present!' When he set about rectifying these deficiencies in his wardrobe, he did it thoroughly, as may be seen by the lists of clothes, the particulars of which are detailed with much unction by his *valet de chambre*. Genoa and figured velvet suits,[1] cloth of silver, embroidery, gold lace, flowered silk *robes de chambre*, lace ruffles sent specially from Flanders, dress swords, etc. etc., show the young man to have made a brave appearance for the honour of old England. The reign of wigs was for him over; his own powdered locks in a queue was all he wore; nor do his books of accounts reveal the purchase of one perruque.

'We have had *Bals Masqués* once or twice a Week,' wrote Jacob to his mother in February 1759; 'no Private Balls, except We may look upon that at Court in that light; for there everybody of the best Fashion is invited, both Dansers and Spectators, in both which Characters I have had the Honor to appear. The Ball is opened by the Duke and Dutchess of Savoy; then the Duke of Chablais and the eldest Princess, and the two youngest and their first Officers dance Minuets. Afterwards eight Couple dance two Country dances. Then the Academists (*i.e.* himself and his friends) and those who have not danced before exhibit their Minuets. Then two Country dances again, and so alternately Minuets and Country dances till ten o'Clock, when the Ball finishes. What makes these Balls the more agreable is that the Royal Family are very gracious; nothing could be more so than the Reception I met with from the King and all of

1759

---

[1] He spent £40 upon Genoa velvet at this time.

them. The day I took Leave at Court I was near a Quarter of an hour in the Duke of Savoy's Chamber; and he talked to me all that time. He certainly is a most accomplished amiable Prince, and very fond of our Nation. He told Mr. Robinson the other day, that Turin had been much obliged to England, and that He should always do what lay in his Power to make it agreable to our Nation. I have dined once with the Prime Minister, Chevalier Orsorio, who is very polite to Strangers. Though they keep good Cooks here, Strangers do not often dine with the People of the Country. Count Viri's Letter has not produced me anything like a dinner; though everybody to whom He recommended me have been very polite.'

England and her aims were now high in favour with Italy, and the French in proportion out of it, while the sympathy with which news of successes in either continent was received by the Italians, appears to have caused the liveliest satisfaction in the little English community. If Jacob's letters from home were full of news, political and military, the squire likewise kept his son well informed as to family and home matters, all such details being eagerly received by young Jacob. Though much occupied with militia duties and the training of his own company which was mainly drawn from men off his estate, great planting of young trees was being done by the squire in the Forest of Hatfield and elsewhere, and of these improvements the father never failed to keep his son informed.

After describing a gorgeous procession of the Piedmontese court at this time, Jacob[4] goes on to picture to himself in absence, a scene which he would rather have witnessed than that he had just related. He recalled the expeditions 'from old Hallingbury to the Forest' on summer evenings, in which he had so often shared; merry meetings by the lake, in which friends and neighbours took part, and how 'the Coach drawn by the blacks, filled full,—followed by the little cart conducted by my brother Jack in the old fustian frock in charge of the provisions, and with Phillis and Fanny at his heels—went down from the old Place and wended their way across the Forest to the Cottage Pond.' 'We have had our house full of Company this 3 weeks,' wrote his father, 'and spent several fine days at the Cottage with our Neighbours. Altham had good sport with his Hounds here t' other day; and your old horse Saucebox carried your sister very well with them.' William Altham, the young Master of the Essex Hounds, was Jacob's friend, and many are the references to him in letters.

The eighteenth-century landscape gardener, 'Capability Brown'—as he was commonly called—had lately been doing much work at Madingley, and was now engaged in carrying out alterations at Hallingbury. It was probably at this time that the Elizabethan garden was destroyed, the ha-ha made, and pleasure grounds laid out about the house, in the style which the taste of the day substituted in so many instances for the more formal beauty of the past. That the reconstruction of the house was likewise in contemplation by the squire, his son's letters inform us; but this task was not accomplished till Jacob$_4$ reigned in his father's stead.

Many allusions were made in the letters of both Jacobs to their friends and relations. On the Cotton family side these were numerous; but of the Houblon, only one old lady now remained. A correspondence between the squire and his man of business, Mr. Pocklington, refers to this last remaining daughter of the First Governor of the Bank of England, and to a request she had made 'her cousin,' for assistance in a business matter relating to the Almshouses she and her sisters had built and endowed at Richmond;[1] as also to the investment of part of her property in land. Her house and estate on Richmond Hill, and £20,000 left to the squire's second son, besides other landed property to himself, were the outcome of his efforts to ease the cares of age of his ancient kinswoman. A very dear member of Mrs. Houblon's family was now settled at Goldings in Herts 'within convenient distance.' This was her mother's sister Frances, Lady St. John of Bletsoe, whose husband, the tenth lord, had lately left her a widow. Goldings belonged to Humphrey Hall, Esq., to whom Lady St. John's daughter Jane was married. With all the members of the St. John family the closest relations existed. Two others of 'my handsome cousins,' as Jacob$_4$ calls them—were later married, the one to the Hon. Robert Cotton Trefusis, afterwards seventeenth Baron Clinton,[2] the other (Barbara), to Lord Coventry.[3] Affectionate inquiries as to my 'Aunt Fanny at Goldings,' and for 'my Woodstock Street aunts'—two maiden ladies, Mistresses Philippa and Anne Walton, frequently occur in Jacob's letters.

The squire occasionally amused his son by the gossip of the day as to their own neighbours, and of society in general. From London he wrote in February 1759: 'The Dutchess of Hamilton is married to Mr Campbell, son of General Campbell, who is to be Duke of Argyll when the present Duke dies, and it's thought will be his heir. Lord Weymouth is soon to have the Duke of Portland's daughter. Her fortune is £30,000, wch will be of great use to him, as he has lost most of his by gaming, which he has promised now to leave off. Our friends in the country were

---

[1] See vol. i. pp. 330-331.
[2] We hear of the 'pretty Mary St. John,' and of a 'petit pièce' written upon her before her marriage. See Journal of a visit into Berkshire by Rev. T. Stotherd Abdy, 1769, p. 146.
[3] Jacob$_4$ was trustee to their marriage settlement.

MARY HYNDE COTTON.
m. JACOB₃ HOUBLON, ESQ.

all very well t'other day. Altham is going to take in a couple of Partners to help keep his Hounds; vizt Lord Masham and Mr Archer of Coopersale. He promised to write to you about a month ago, and as I imagined he would acquaint you with our welfare . . . I postponed my letter till now. Lord Bruce is very well. His brother is lately married to Miss Bishop, sister to Lady Maynard. As your mother desires I will leave her some room, I shall add no more, than to say we are all well.'

Later this same year the squire announced that Altham had given up the hounds; while the 'Knight of Hadham' (that is to say, Sir Richard Chase of Hadham) 'had acquired Wright's Hounds.' It would appear that after a time Altham once more became Master, some of the Hunt having subscribed to enable him to do so. Bantering his brother Jack in one of his letters on his having been 'flung off,' Jacob remarks that 'It has happened to Kings! His Sardinian Majesty was t'other day over head and ears in a wet ditch, and told Mr. Mackenzie (the English minister) next day that he had taken the Bath *à l'Angloise!* Most of the Hunt was too good courtiers not to follow the royal example.' To another cousin and neighbour we have frequent allusions; this was Jack Wogan. Jacob$_4$ was a broad, strongly built man with a certain fear in the back of his mind as to what he might *ride* in the dim future of middle age. Jack was as 'lean' as he well could be. A letter from young Jacob to his uncle at Madingley at Christmas time calls to remembrance the jovial times both had spent at that hospitable mansion, and the great incursions they were wont to make upon the sirloins of good English beef;—fare he had not seen for many a day! When Jacob$_4$ came home Jack Wogan was gone. What was his end we can only surmise; a veil of sadness and silence is drawn over this episode of family history which has not been lifted. We do not even know that he died; but he certainly was never again seen at 'old Hallingbury.'

Many of the young squire's letters written after the close of his academical studies, when he, together with Jonathan Lipyeatt, began a systematic set of tours throughout Italy, are worthy of reproduction. They present a graphic picture of the places, habits, tastes and customs of the time, in those states where, owing to the kindness of many influential friends, he and his companion found the 'best society' always open to them. Indeed, it would appear that the young Englishmen who now so generally visited Italy, ostensibly to polish their manners and enlarge their minds, were both an attraction and interest to Italian society, which everywhere received them with hospitality.

The kindness received and the many warm friendships made by Jacob$_4$, both among his own countrymen whom he met in his travels, and in the society of the country, are sufficient evidence of his popularity, and even of the affection with which he met in Italy. That he had suffered considerably before his present ease of mind and manners was attained, is betrayed by a letter written after two years had passed, in which he confessed to his mother how greatly he now enjoyed the society in which he was thrown, and which was the more delightful to him from his having for 'so long suffered from a bashfulness which had made going into company a misery to him.' To his present happiness and comfort he attributed the fact of his now being able to converse with ease 'in the Italian as well as in the French.' This fluency in Italian he appears to have owed, in part, to the fact of his having replenished his wardrobe so liberally; an extravagance followed by a period of quiet and retrenchment! The application for more money to his father had resulted in the sending of a letter of credit for £500, and upon its receipt, Jacob and his companion proceeded with a party of other young Englishmen to Rome and Naples for the Carnival, after which, however, they retired to Siena, the quietest of Italian cities then, as it still is. Here 'at poor unpeopled Siena' they 'studied heartily the Italian' for several months; young Rushout, the son of Sir John, and afterwards to be the father of the famous three beauties immortalised by Gainsborough and Plymer, being also of the party.

The following is part of a letter written from Siena by Jacob to his sister Laetitia, which composition forms an amusing contrast to the carefully composed epistles which he inscribed to his parents :—' I am very glad you diverted yourself so well at Xmas, and that old Saucebox was sensible of the honor you did him, and carried you well; tho' I am malicious enough to think that you deserved to be spilt, for the expedition at the Leaping Bar! You see tho' far from being a congurer I know what passes at so many hundred miles off. I desire you next season not to ride the Old Horse so furiously, for you will make him too hot for me. I begin to think that I have lost my Fox-hunting Seat; the more so as I have some merit in the manège. However three or four Falls will set that to rights. (*Tout beau Monsr s'il vous plaît*, take part in a season's hare-hunting!) I believe that will be best, for I shall have fewer oaths from the Squire of Mark Hall than from the Knight of Hadham should I chance to mention throwing a horse upon his Haunches, or the use of the Lunge *pour délier les Epaules !* It is very likely that I may observe that the Hounds run *Allegro*, or at a good hit cry *Bravissimo !* terms not printed in the last edition of the Fox-hunter's dictionary.' . . . Alluding to a 'Romance' mentioned by Laetitia, Jacob begs her to send him an account of 'one of those enchanting Beauties which the Author so easily finds in his imagination, and wch are so

1759

difficult to find anywhere else, especially in Italy where the Fair Sex are confounded Brown. It would be most extraordinary if I was *not* to go away from this place Heartwhole; for there is more beauty to be found in Billingsgate than in this charming town of Sienna where many Englishmen have pined away in the Fetters of Love.[1] However the Ladies are polite and chatty which makes this Place very proper for learning Italian to which I apply very much. We have a pretty good manège, the horses very well drest, but the Saddles are much too forward, and consequently the Seat bad. In July our Races begin, which tho' not quite so brilliant as Newmarket, will have something well worth seeing in them. ... I have spun this stuff out to an unreasonable length. I desire you would write me one like it, tho' I defy you to equall it.'

In this letter one can perhaps read between the lines the reasons for the sending of young men abroad by the more enlightened parents of the time. We hear much of eighteenth-century coarseness and of the 'boorish tastes and manners of the country squires.' In imagination we can even listen to the parental wisdom on these points flowing from the lips of the courtly squire of Hallingbury for the edification of his sons! Young Jacob's high animal spirits and love of sport might have needed turning into more refined channels than those in which the jolly young squires who were his 'very good friends' ran so easily. Some recognition of this fact is perhaps discernible in him after his acquaintance with many people and things had greatly widened the horizon of his experience.

The friends subsequently left Siena for Florence, Lucca, Leghorn, Naples, and Rome, and it was now that the really pleasurable part of his sojourn abroad began, and the young squire discovered—what he wrote

---

[1] This probably alludes to the supposed beauty of Sienese women.

of with delight to his mother, viz. how greatly his studies had improved his mind, and the exercise of fencing, dancing, and the manège his person and address; another advantage derived from the quiet and retirement of secluded Siena having been that of economy. When the squire of Hallingbury sent his son £500, he made him no reproaches beyond the remark, that the amount of his allowance (at the rate of £1200 a year) had been carefully considered by those whose experience and advice had been accepted as a guide,[1] and that they had deemed it adequate; he therefore trusted that though his son had been unable to keep within it the first year of his stay abroad, that he would so arrange as to spend the less by that amount in the next. This hint was taken and acted upon to the letter.

Not least interesting among Jacob's letters is one describing his visit to Leghorn, where three galleys of the Knights of Malta happened to have put into harbour through stress of weather. The famous Knights of St. John, whose mission of keeping the Mediterranean clear of Turkish and Moorish pirates had earned the gratitude of Christendom up to a few years previous to this time, had now begun to decline. While still rich and powerful, their services were no longer needed as the scavengers of the seas, and the Turks had in turn become their prey. They were now guilty of the very crimes they had existed to suppress, and the African coast and Turkish vessels were raided for corn and slaves, while Valetta had become a great slave mart. Though the wonderful fortifications of Malta were still being added to by the Knights, even as late as 1793—misgovernment and oppression had already degraded and disorganised the Order, and but little remained of their knightly traditions but what

[1] Lords Bruce and Templemore.

savoured of the dark ages. Jacob[4] Houblon went on board one of their galleys now lying in the harbour, in company with the General of the Knights in command, and saw there 'such a scene of misery, that nothing shall ever tempt him to go aboard another of them. Figure to yourself,' he wrote, 'six or seven hundred dirty half-naked Turks, in a small vessel, chained to their oars, from which they are not allowed to stir; fed upon nothing but bad biscuit and water, and beat about upon the most trifling occasion by their most inhuman masters—who are certainly more Turks than their slaves, who have no prospect of ever recovering their liberty. And all this cruel treatment because they have been made Prisoners of War!' In this ancient insanitary galley crowded with miserable human beings, Jacob went on to describe how wretched was the accommodation of the Knights, and even of the General of the Order himself. Details follow as to the guns carried by the ships, and their uselessness as fighting vessels, except 'in a dead calm, when they will venture to attack ships of force, and succeed by the vast numbers of men they fling aboard the enemy. But the least bad weather drives him away to the nearest port, for which reason they never venture out in the winter.' The fate of the galley slave was proverbial; chained to his long-oar he plied it, hopeless of change or relief. Whether the vessel engaged with an enemy, whether she perished through fire, or was sunk in a sudden squall, he stayed by her. In the dim darkness within the ribs of the ship, where he and his mates sat day and night in long rows chained, if she went to the bottom, he went too.

A stay of three months was made at Naples, where the côterie of young men, who had been at the Academy of Turin, appear to have lived together, and made expeditions in each other's company. In a letter to Sir John Hynde Cotton dated the 15th of January

1760, Jacob[4] sends him a list of his companions, giving their full designations and those of their fathers. To our modern ideas of informality as among men of his class, this sounds strange; but addressing a father or uncle as 'Honoured Sir,' a mother as 'Madam,' elderly peers as 'Your Lordship,' was then expected, and was only natural and according to the canons of taste. With whatever familiarity a man might speak to and treat his friends on his own plane of existence, they were designated in his letters as 'Lord this or that, Sir so and so that, and Messrs. that and the other.' With many of these youths with whom he was thrown so intimately, our young squire retained a friendship through life. From the time of his leaving Siena he kept a list of such letters as he wrote and received, and if they were all as long and detailed as those to his home circle, he must have been continually writing. He received a large number himself, and with some of his friends he exchanged letters once or even twice a month. After his father, he wrote most frequently to Sir John Cotton; less often to his mother, sister, and brother; frequently to his friend Jack Wogan; occasionally to Jack's father, also to the elder Lipyeatt, rector of Hallingbury, to Lord Bruce, and to Will Altham, the Master of the Essex hounds. Besides these home letters, Jacob corresponded with Mr. Mackenzie, the English minister at Turin, his uncle's friend; with Mr. Langlois, the son of his banker at Leghorn, who afterwards became a lifelong friend, and young Rushout; a Mr. Crespiny, with whom in after years he corresponded occasionally in Italian; Messrs. Belloni, and Lords Grey and Torrington. Other friends were young Robinson, whose father, Sir Thomas, was ambassador at Vienna;[1] ' Sir H. Mainwaring, Sir Thomas Gray, Mess[rs.] Boothby, Grant, Bunbury, White

[1] He was for a short time leader of the House of Commons in 1754. See Stanhope's *History*, iii. 788.

and Willcox; Sir Brook Bridges; Fordwick; Downe (the son of the Earl of Murray), Lord Archibald Hamilton and Sir Harry Harpur.' Of his friends in Italy, Rushout, Lords Torrington and Grey were the most intimate. With Grey he travelled much, and when they separated they wrote regularly to each other.[1]

Flower and vegetable seeds for his mother, cones of the stone pine, pomatum, artificial flowers, a large number of books and maps, together with a vast amount of smart clothes, were sent home from Naples; the parting from his coloured wardrobe being rendered advisable by the fact that the whole English community was now thrown into mourning by the death of George II. Amidst the brilliancy of the Carnival at Rome, to which all the friends now trooped in concert, they went about 'a black Regiment'; but as their sombre garments were plentifully embroidered with gold or silver lace, and were of the richest materials, the group of fresh, wholesome young Englishmen who 'followed the English Ambassador about,' as a sort of bodyguard, probably made a not unpleasing contrast to the swarthy Italians in their gorgeous, many-coloured costumes. An interesting letter describes the Easter ceremonies at Rome, the benediction of the Pope from the balcony on the façade of St. Peter's being specially described. This ceremony was still characterised by the fanaticism of the middle ages, for 'after blessing the Faithful, his Holiness proceeded to pronounce a *malediction* upon all those outside the pale of Rome!' After this, however, the effect of his cursing was removed, before it could take effect, by a final benediction, in which the Pontiff amiably included the whole world in his all-embracing benevolence!

Much travelling occupied the greater part of the year

---

[1] Baron Grey of Groby, eldest son of fourth Earl of Stamford, born 1737, succeeded his father 1768.

1760, most of the tours undertaken being in company with some of the other young men with whom Jacob had been at the Accademia Reale, or whom he had afterwards met in Italy. His stay abroad appears to have been extended for a short time by his own request, tendered through his always fast friend and uncle, Sir John Cotton, though not for as long a time as he had hoped. His easy good temper, however, cheerfully acquiesced in his father's decision, and he started homewards, having playfully observed that 'by the short extra period of absence for the purpose of witnessing the Carnival at Turin, he had done as much as in him lay towards obliterating what last remained in him of the awkward country Squire; though in one respect'—the inevitable eighteenth-century sententiousness impelled him to add—'he hoped he should never change, viz: in the sentiments of an eager desire to serve his country.'

The last of this series of letters were written in March 1761, when convalescent after a serious illness at Stuttgart. Fifteen days of a very severe slow fever, he told his mother, had made him as lean as ever Jack Wogan was, while, in spite of a now ravenous appetite, his physician allows him to eat but very sparingly; while he had also decreed that two months must pass before he would be fit to travel. As he 'had been on his way home this delay was, of course, a great disappointment,' etc. etc. After sending his 'affectionate duty to Colonel Houblon,'[1] who had written to propose he should immediately join the Herts militia on his return home, long directions to his sister follow, with reference to some artificial flowers from Turin, which he was anxious she should forward for him to a certain Lady Caroline, after having ascertained from her where she would be pleased to have them sent.

[1] The squire was now in command of his regiment.

During his long illness and convalescence at Stuttgart, Jacob experienced the greatest kindness from many friends in the town, who vied with each other in lavishing attentions and sympathy on the sick Englishman. While some visited him or offered him their horses to 'ride out' when he was able to do so during his convalescence, the Duke of Würtemberg and his Master of the Horse had fed him with food from the latter's own kitchen, which they sent to his inn during his illness. When he had partly recovered his strength, he writes how he had been over the Grand Duke's stables, and how the Duke had himself had the horses out to show them off. 'The Coach horses,' wrote Jacob, 'are surprisingly fine, sixteen sets of eight and ten, in one stable, of different colours. There is a coachman here that drives sixteen horses in a four-wheel Chaise, without a postillion. I have seen him drive ten. His Highness has, too, a very fine pack of Staghounds, and a Foxhound is Chase Hound.'

By June 1761 Jacob was at home again, having quite recovered from his illness. Immediately after his arrival he was received by the King, to whom he paid his respects 'after his return from his travels,'[1] and was appointed to a company in his father's regiment. Soon after he joined him at Bristol, where the Herts militia was now quartered. February, March, April, May, and June of the following year were spent mostly in town, where the young man probably went much into society. We have some reason to think that he was paying his addresses to a young lady at this time, and that it was the 'Lady Caroline,' for whom he had taken so much pains about the artificial flowers, seems to be probable. Unsuccessful in his suit, it was ten years before the young squire married, and from a letter from a friend in which he mysteriously alludes to 'the subject

[1] *St. James' Chronicle*, No. 31, May 1761.

he had had so greatly at heart,' we may believe that his disappointment was severe.

Jacob's beautiful Italian clothes, which the mourning for George II. had given him but a short time to wear in Italy, had been meanwhile displayed to their best advantage in London society; and a perusal of some lists of them which remain makes one wonder at the obduracy of the fair Caroline when receiving the homage of so gorgeous a cavalier. The foreign tailors were considered greatly superior to the English. Joshua Gee, author of *The Trade and Navigation of Great Britain*, writing in 1738, laments bitterly over the 'folly of Fashion in those, who thought nothing good unless it was dear'; and on account of the 'Luxury and Excess' of the goods brought from abroad 'in consequence of the rage for French fashions which had always prevailed in England.'[1] One article alone, viz. Flanders lace, he declares 'is valued at Five thousand eight hundred pounds brought yearly into this country';[2] while the passion for travel, he complains, is equally disastrous to home industries. 'The money spent by young Noblemen and Gentlemen upon their travels into France, Italy, and Germany,' he computed as nearly £100,000 per annum.[3] As all these frivolities and expenditures abroad had increased during the twenty years since Gee made his moan, the figure in Jacob's day would probably have been much larger. His expenditure alone during the three years of his residence abroad amounted to nearly £4000.

The following list—one of others made at different times by his valet—is taken from a memorandum book in which Jacob wrote down a variety of odds and ends during these years. It may serve as a specimen of the wardrobe of a man of fashion going into society in town in the early days of George III.'s reign.[4]

[1] Joshua Gee, *Trade and Navigation of Great Britain*, p. 205.
[2] *Ibid.*, p. 173.   [3] *Ibid.*, p. 180.
[4] The amount of gold embroidery worn both by men and women on their

CLOATHS LEFT IN LONDON May 17, 1762.

Flower'd silk Suite.	2 pair Breeches.
Flowered Velvet Do.	2 pair ,,
Pompadour Do.	Ditto ditto
Velvet suit à fond d'or.	,, ,,
Silver Tissue Suite.	,, ,,

Light coloured Suit, gold-laced à la Bourgogne.
Purple ditto silver laced.
Blue and gold embroidery. ditto.
A full suit of mourning. 2 pair breeches.
A Suit of Half mourning.
White cloth Suit embroidered gold.
4 Pair Black velvet Breeches.
A Lyons Waistcoat.
1 Pair Silk breeches black knot.
A Hunting Coat.
1 Pair buckskin breeches.
1 Steel mounted Sword & Couteau de Chasse.
2 Hunting Caps, etc. etc.[1]

At Hallingbury a separate set of less elaborate raiment was left at the same time, as follows :—

CLOATHS AT HALLINGBURY.

Red and Blue embroidered Suite.
Blue, with gold button-holes.

---

clothes often amounted to many pounds weight. In a description of Princess Mary's wedding clothes, in a letter from Lady Hertford to Lady Pomfret, she remarks that no one of her 'night-gowns' (meaning full-dress evening ones) was without gold or silver, while on one gown alone was no less than 18 lbs. weight of gold. *Correspondence between the Countesses of Pomfret and Hertford*, 1738-41, i. 251.

[1] By his foreign account-book we find that Jacob paid for velvet at Genoa 931 livres, and to the tailor who made it into a suit, 109. The waistcoat cost 65 livres. At the same time he paid 535 livres for lace, and later another 194. 'A Lyons Coat' later cost him 978 livres, and a draper's bill at the same time, 590. At Florence he bought 'silver stuff' for 40 sequins, and 'paid a taylor 10 for making it'; this would be the 'Silver Tissue' suit in the above list of clothes. When he was ill at Stuttgart he purchased a muff for four ducats, and some fur. 'A Livre Piedmontese is worth 20 sols. Our shilling is not quite equivalent to it.' '15 Livres go to a Louis d'or.' 'A Sequin is worth 10 Livres.' When £15 was due to Mr. Lipyeatt, 30 Sequins was the amount paid. See account-book.

THE GRAND TOUR

Two blue hunting coats.
2 Swanskin waistcoats.
2 Striped ditto.
5 Washing ditto.
A Shooting Frock.
Full Regimentals Herts M., gold lace.
Old Frock Do.
Leather breeches.
Greatcoat.
Scarlet breeches.
Hunting Frock, gold buttons.
Hunting Frock, silver ,,   etc. etc.

CHAPTER IV

HOME

'Diminuez vos rapports avec les hommes, augmentez-les avec les choses; Voilà la sagesse. Les moyens d'y parvenir sont l'étude et la campagne.'—*Maximes, etc.*, par M. LE DUC DE LÉVIS.

1760

THE Herts militia was at Winchester in 1760, and the Houblon family were settled there in a house which the squire had rented in the neighbourhood of the camp, he as well as other men of like position and occupation cheerfully putting up with the inconvenience of being so long away from home, and its duties and occupations. In a letter written to his man of business in July this year, the squire gives him directions as to such matters which 'at this distance he was unable himself to attend to'; one being an inquiry into certain depredations on the Forest of Hatfield by a neighbour, whose rights over it were occasionally exceeded, and whose proceedings later culminated in a lawsuit.[1] Mr. Pocklington, his attorney and agent (who was also a 'very good friend'), lived at Chelmsford. 'As you were so kind,' wrote the squire, 'as to promise some time this summer to take a ride over my estate in Herts and see how my Tenants go on, ... I have enclosed a list of the Farms as they lay in the way. ... We are settled here for some

[1] An exhaustive search for deeds about Hatfield Forest was made at the 'Rolls Chappell' in 1758 by order of Mr. Houblon, and his position established with regard to it. 'On Saturday last,' says a contemporary newspaper, 'came on at Chelmsford in Essex the great Cause between Mr. Houblon and Mr. Barrington (about digging Turf, etc., in the Forest of Teckley [*sic*] in that County, which Mr. Houblon claims as his)—when a Verdict was brought in Favour of the Plaintiff.'

JACOB₃ HOUBLON, ESQ.

time and are much better off than the incampers this late wet stormy weather.'

The duties of the camp were complicated by the fact that a large body of French prisoners of war were confined at Winchester. 'There are 5424 of them,' wrote the squire, 'and we have a good deal of trouble in mounting guard over them at the King's House. I was unexpectedly surprized t' other day with a visit from the Duke of York, who stop'd here on his way to Southampton where he is gone to bathe for six weeks, and came here to see the Prisoners when I was upon duty, without giving me any notice. But by good luck a Friend ran up just time enough to get my guard out, to pay him the proper Compliments. He then went up to see the Camp, which consists of five Regiments of Militia, and Lord Effingham's. His Lordship commands. Our Regiment and the Warickshire do duty in the Town; and our Colonell is the Comanding officer as being the senior, which don't please Lord Denbigh much! But we receive the Parole etc. from Lord Effingham at present. Sir Richard Chase is very well and desires his compliments to you etc.

'Winchester, *July y^e* 13, 1760.'

It will be recollected that Jacob's stay abroad was lengthened by his own request. It would appear from one of his letters that the request included an appeal to his father to be allowed to serve in the allied armies, the English portion of which was now commanded by the Marquis of Granby. Among his many friends, he pleaded, he had sufficient interest—indeed a promise—to procure him a commission, and it only remained for his father to consent. The permission was refused, and the young man had to content himself with the prospect of serving in the Herts militia, in which he had already been a subaltern before leaving

England.[1] The militia, which had been reorganised in February 1756, remained embodied in the Seven Years' War, during the last year of which Jacob Houblon senior took over the command ; meanwhile both his sons joined the regiment at Winchester, where Mrs. Houblon and their sister were staying. The same summer, however, found them at Bristol, and later still at Warley Camp, where the regiment remained till its disembodiment in November 1762. From this time the yearly training was all the duty the force was called upon to perform.

1762

It was perhaps at this moment of national pride and triumph that the squire caused a splendid 'grandfather clock' to be made, in which the twelve letters of his own and his eldest son's name take the place of the usual numerals on the dial. This clock (if allowed) will reiterate with wearisome persistence the alternate strains of 'Britons Strike Home' and 'God save the King' every succeeding hour.[2]

Two Cedars of Lebanon of unusual size near the house at Hallingbury are said to have been grown from cones brought from the Holy Land by Jacob$_4$ Houblon the younger. No trace of this journey remains (among the family papers) other than the evidence of these trees. Another of the same age stands in the rectory garden; and the same tradition records that it was planted there by Jonathan Lipyeatt, who shared Jacob's first journey, and possibly his second also. After the close of the war and the certainty of the fair Caroline's continued obduracy to his suit, this journey to the East, we will hope, restored the young squire's peace of mind. Meanwhile, at the general election of 1761 the squire had

1761

---

[1] Secure in the promise of a commission, Jacob$_4$ Houblon went so far as to equip himself with a uniform ; and in this he was painted shortly after his return to England. A similar dress is given in Racinet's *Costumes Historiques*, vol. v.

[2] In 1765 the family pictures were cleaned and repaired. The squire's account-book shows this to have cost him £18, 12s. For the portraits, see vol. i. p. 177.

again been returned Knight of the Shire for Hertfordshire, in the 'Country' interest,[1] and in November he was placed on the Committee for Privileges and Elections.[2]

The squire's account-book shows evidence of much travelling; in truth his coach was continually on the road. He went frequently to Hallingbury from London and *vice versâ*, while Hertford, Winchester, Bristol, Buckingham, St. Albans, etc., were visited at different and many times. Before these journeys he drew sums of money upon his bankers (Messrs. Child and Co.) for £30, £50, £70, or £100, according to the length of his probable stay,[3] for people in those days carried with them sufficient cash for all their current expenses. For use at his destination several riding-horses frequently accompanied him.

Gladly must the Houblon family have welcomed the peace, and the disembodiment of the militia regiments which followed. We have but few letters of the next eight years, which, except during the parliamentary sessions, were mostly spent at Hallingbury by the family. In 1766 John had been called to the Bar, and had his chambers in Lincoln's Inn, but he also was frequently at home. Many incidental circumstances enable us to form a pretty clear estimate of the characters and idiosyncrasies of this eighteenth-century family. Of the manly character of the squire and his cheerful devotion to duty we have already given some idea, while his wife and children each in their way had something of interest and individuality. Family life in the upper classes would appear to have been but little different in those

---

[1] His colleague, Charles Gore, Esq., was not returned. In *Lloyd's Evening Post* Jacob Houblon's letters to his constituents before the election and his thanks to them after his return are given. See *Lloyd's Evening Post and British Chronicle*, Nos. 579, 580, 582, and 583.

[2] 'To take into consideration all such matters touching Returns, Elections, and Privileges, and to proceed upon Double Returns, etc., and to report to the House thereupon.' *Journals of the House of Commons*, vol. xxix. p. 10, 2 GEO. III.

[3] Mr. Lookes, the barber, frequently cashed his drafts upon Messrs. Child.

days to what it is now, and parents and children were often on terms of confidence and affection. In the case of the Houblons, no restraint or irksome formality formed a barrier between them, as undoubtedly existed two generations later than this time. It is true that a certain etiquette was observed; her children would not have remained seated had their mother approached them, nor would they have interrupted her in conversation. Their father was addressed in their epistolary efforts as 'Honoured Sir,' while they subscribed themselves as his 'dutiful and affectionate humble Servants'! Mrs. Houblon possessed some of the qualities of the *grande dame*, and was treated with a certain ceremony by her family and dependants, but she was nevertheless kind and motherly, and withal, while a stately and somewhat strict mistress, was the friend and tender helper to all in trouble, whether rich or poor. Her children grew up full of life, high animal spirits, and possessing the many-sided tastes and interests which are rarely to be found except where the seed has been sown in young and plastic youth by kindly sympathy and encouragement. The daughter of Sir John Hynde Cotton had suffered many things in her day, and passed through many experiences. Although she had married when only nineteen, she had been mistress of her father's house for some years previously, until a young stepmother came to rule over it, who in her turn had died but a year before her stepdaughter's own marriage. Mary Houblon had inspired her children with her own strong enthusiasm for the Jacobite cause; it must have been no slight pain to watch the dying embers of that cause flicker and wane, and no less painful to witness the flagging energies and bitter grief of the father, whose whole life had been devoted to its furtherance, and whose failure to act, when English action would have meant so much, must have goaded his memory with futile regrets.

Sir John Cotton's friends indeed were too many and powerful for expediency on the part of the Government to touch him,[1] but for some time after the '45 there was doubtless fear and dread of possible imprisonment and attainder and even for life itself. Possibly for these reasons and the chastening they brought, Mary's early enthusiasms were gradually exchanged in later life for the gentle fireside middle-age which indulgently watches and cherishes the young lives and interests around it, while remaining itself detached and apart, except in the reflected joys and sorrows of others.

Meanwhile her daughter, Laetitia, had grown up and developed into a strong and charming personality. Her letters are many and brilliant; her character was generous and impulsive, with warm affections and enthusiastic sympathies. She had withal a keen sense of the ridiculous, and while perfectly good-natured, possessed a fund of wit and humour which made her a delightful companion and friend. But that she could boast of but little beauty—such as it is now esteemed—is evident from her portrait, for she and her brother Jacob were painted about this time. Nevertheless Laetitia was much admired in her day, and far into middle life had many 'adorers.' Her small round face and piquant features corresponded to the new taste of the time as to female charms, when both dress and manners were emerging from the 'straight-laced' *mœurs* and apparel of a past of stiff-bodiced, long-waisted dames, so tightly encased in whalebone as to render any grace or ease of motion impossible as well as 'unseemly.' This reaction in the toilet is said by French writers on costume to have begun immediately after Louis XIV.'s death released the court from the '*influence monacale*' of Madame de Maintenon upon dress. As to Laetitia and her appearance, as Monsieur de Goncourt remarks, ' La mode façonne le visage de

[1] Stanhope, *History of England*, iii. 320.

femme'; and the following might stand for a description of Miss Houblon in her early youth: 'Pour arriver à piquer par la mine, et se faire un visage au dessus du joli, voici les traits qu'elle voulut avoir, et ce qu'elle fut : Des yeux à la chinoise—car les plus beaux yeux du monde sont de grands yeux *qui ne disent mot*; . . .. et le nez fin et noble au plus joli, dans lequel il se passe certain petit jeu imperceptible qui anime la physionomie. . . . La bouche ne dût pas être petite, ni le teint d'une blancheur fade' . . . 'une créature au corps gracieux et fin, à la tête spirituelle.'[1]

We have noticed the many interests and talents which in past generations had distinguished the Cottons of Madingley; but if from her mother's family Laetitia inherited certain of these characteristics of mind—in especial her grandfather's wit—on the other hand, qualities which she also possessed of calm judgment, broad views of life, and kindly interpretation of persons and things, she took from her father and from her father's 'forbears.' Laetitia and her brothers were seventh in direct descent from their 'Confessor' ancestor, and in the eighteenth century the characteristics of the race were still but little changed. The tastes which were manly and intellectual in her brothers were shared in many respects by their sister; and while she possessed—as witnessed by her correspondence—many warm friends both of men and women, to her brothers she was first and foremost a beloved comrade and confidant. She rode to hounds, loved a good horse and dog, was a good walker, and, like the sensible Elizabeth in *Pride and Prejudice*, was not afraid of dirty roads, stiles, and field paths. She was a skilful archer, and the champion shot of the county at the archery gatherings and matches, already so popular in county society. But while she excelled in such accom-

[1] MM. de Goncourt, *Histoire de Costume en France, apud* Racinet.

LÆTITIA HOUBLON.

plishments, Laetitia was not above a feminine love of dress; fancy needlework and decoration, acrostics, novels, romantic poetry, and close and confidential letter-writing. Her dearest female friend was her own first cousin, the daughter of Sir John Hynde Cotton, her mother's only brother. To this uncle the whole family were devotedly attached. Of his kindness, and interest in all their concerns, there are many evidences.

As to the conditions under which these good people lived, Georgian manners and customs undoubtedly partook occasionally of such licence, or what we should now call vulgarity, as must have made society somewhat like a Pandora's box of surprises, varied almost infinitely according to the persons composing it. Gambling belonged to everyday life, while coarseness doubtless was scarcely ever totally absent; but if anywhere was purity and reticence, and such language as brought no blush to young cheeks, it was in the houses of those English gentlemen who, disgusted by the low plane of thought and venality, which was the inevitable outcome of that corruption where every man had his price, did their best to live honestly and cleanly in their generation. Nothing could elevate the whole standard of being like a great effort to meet and conquer a vice which is recognised as degrading and unworthy a great country and people. From the 'patriot' Pitt, the gentlemen of England drew their inspiration of reform; and later again from the still greater Burke, whose fiery utterances literally burnt up the dross and dregs which had clogged and marred the traditions of this wholesome country. In our next chapter, in the daily journal of the clergyman who performed the marriage ceremony for our young squire, we shall find a graphic picture of a country-house party, assembled together for this event, and reminding us irresistibly of some parts of the eighteenth-century Miss

Burney's famous novel *Evelina*. While the life depicted at Welford (the Berkshire home of the Archer family) differed in many respects from that of Hallingbury Place or Madingley, where a somewhat higher standard both of intelligence and 'good breeding' prevailed, we shall nevertheless find it highly typical of the time, and of that class which has claimed from then to now to represent the so-called best society; that is to say, that society which, well born, well dressed, rich, or fashionable, as the case might be, sucks the honey from every flower, laughs, flirts, dresses, gambles, and sins, passing the 'time of day' in the supreme effort to enjoy itself. The picture presented in this journal is the more detailed and amusing, as being drawn by one outside the class and their mode of life, in the midst of which he for the time found himself.

Mr. Houblon had for many years been adding to his library, and several old catalogues, or rather lists of books, show a considerable part of the present collection to have been bought during the lifetime of the elder squire. While absent abroad, Jacob$_4$ purchased a large number of books which he sent home by sea; in his choice, Jonathan Lipyeatt, his 'governor,' possibly assisted him; but Jacob was himself well read and a good classical scholar. On a list of some of his books we find the names of the towns where each was purchased, or where printed; and these are so various that it is evident that, wherever he went, one of his first visits was paid to the bookshops. Many fine classical works were bought, a great number of Italian and French ones, besides many English. It is also interesting to note that he possessed sufficient interest in the country of his ancestors, to buy all the most noted works on its history, such as Bentivoglio, Strada, Brandt, etc. etc. At Rome he invested in many of the best books of the time on art and architecture, besides engravings. On the other hand, the elder squire's plan seems to have been a systematic collection of all that was representative of the current thought of the day, from Locke downwards. His library was essentially up to date in this respect. For instance, the Deist phase of thought was represented by its principal writers, while the *Bangor Controversy* filled rows of his shelves with its ponderous wrangles, including the whole of Hoadley's and Sherlock's works.

Readers of Sir Leslie Stephen's deeply interesting volumes on the *History of English Thought in the Eighteenth Century* might find and study nearly all the works he mentions amongst the mellow-brown volumes in the Hallingbury library.[1] The intolerable wordiness of some of these lead one to marvel how any one could have waded through them, and yet the desire for enlightenment was so great that they were read and pondered in those days, and that not only by thinkers. The *Religion of Nature*, so called, made a deep impression on the thought of the time, and both Houblons, father and son, were more or less influenced by it. Wollaston's dry volume with that title went through many editions; two copies are at Hallingbury, one of which (a first edition) is covered with pencil-marks by the younger Jacob, showing him to have studied it exhaustively when at Cambridge, in connection with Grotius, and Acheson, another dreary writer on the same plane of thought, and exponent of the so-called *Social Compact*. But if the elder squire read the *Religion of Nature* and talked as the pantheists of the time were wont to do of 'the God of Nature,' so did he also study another writer, viz. William Law, whose book the *Serious Call* is said to have affected deeply many

[1] The late Dean Stanley of Westminster was a frequent visitor at Hallingbury, and was well acquainted with the library, in which he passed many hours.

men's lives and thoughts.[1] The copy of Law's book at Hallingbury bears signs of use and many pencil-marks. While the spiritual side of religion, as presented by Law, imbued the thought of his father in his later life, the younger Jacob's tastes led him away from the controversies and speculations of theology and philosophy into the domains of politics, poetry, history, and art, and the *novel*, which had now begun to open out new vistas for imagination and sentiment scarce dreamt of by the past generation, was bought and read eagerly by him and his sister. These works seem to have been regarded by both as altogether apart from the library proper, and the quaint rough-papered early editions of Richardson, Smollett, and Fielding, and later, Mrs. Barbauld and Ann Radcliffe, were carried away by the daughter of the house after the death of her father, though many of them found their way back again to Hallingbury through her will, or as presents to her nieces.

In order to show how various were the purchases made by the two squires in the building up of their library, we take a page at random from one of the lists above mentioned of books added by the elder Jacob: —Bishop Cosin. Baxter and Locke's Works. Shaftesbury's Works. Chesterfield's *Letters* and Works. Chillingworth's Works. Warburton. Sherlock's *Sermons on the Immortality of the Soul*. Bishop Jewell's *Apology*. Of the classics—a long list, needless to enumerate. . . . Wake's *Catechism*. Voltaire's Works, 'exceeding Handsomely bounde,' 40 volumes. Dante (Aldus). Rousseau. Chaucer. Swift's Works. Butler's *Analogy*, and Hume. Pope's Works. The Bishop of Gloucester *On the Doctrine of Grace*. Smollett's *History*. Paley's *Moral and Political Philosophy*. Bolingbroke's Works. Law's *Serious Call*. Bourdaloue's *Sermons*.

[1] See Leslie Stephen, *History of English Thought in the Eighteenth Century*.

Bentham's and Tindal's Works. Lord Halifax's *Miscellanies*. The *Biografia Britannica*, 1766, and Granger's *Biographical History*. The *Winwood Memoirs*. Picard's splendid book on *Religious Ceremonies, in English*, 1731. *Paradise Lost* and *Paradise Regained* (the one a first, the other a second edition).

Again, a few out of an old list of books purchased abroad by the younger squire:—*Libro di bel parlar gentile. In* 104 *Novelle.* Firenze. 1724. Goldoni's *Commedie.* Roustan (abrégé). Bossuet. Metastasio, and the *Orlando Furioso*. Molière's Works[1] and Boccaccio's; also translations of both. *Aventures de Gil Blas.* Plauti. *Comedia* (Elzivir), 1650. Fénelon's Works. Tasso and Petrarca, and the *Lettres de Madame de Maintenon*. Also Coryat's *Crudities*, even in those days rare, but which very possibly may have accompanied the younger Jacob on his travels, and been frequently consulted as to that quaint individual's impressions when on his.

A splendid set of Sir Isaac Newton's Works was subscribed for some years later when, by his marriage with a lady descended from the great man's family, Jacob₄ became personally interested in him; at other times all Archdeacon Coxe's Works were added, including *Walpole's Life*, also Junius; the *Spectator*; Burke, De Foe, Dr. Johnson, Hobbes' Works, Bishop Berkeley, and Hooker's *Ecclesiastical Politie*. During his close connection with Madingley and Jacobite thought, the elder squire purchased Carte's *History*, and his splendid *Life of the Duke of Ormonde* (published by subscription), also Zachary Grey's Works, and Francis Bacon, 1733. Such books as the following were also bought:—Harvey's *Meditations*. Sterne's *Sentimental Journey*. Mackenzie's *Man of Feeling*. Percy's *Reliques*. Macpherson's *Ossian*, and Chatter-

---

[1] Delightfully illustrated.

ton; all of which were much read and thought of in their day, while, as the century proceeded, many fine books were added, topographical, historical, and poetical, besides such good old books as *Fédora*, Rapin, Stowe, and others on London. Scores of other works will occur to any book-lover, as falling in with the thought that made an eighteenth-century library, including many books of earlier days, without counting the large percentage of 'dead men's bones' of the past, in forgotten ephemeral literature. Dreary and dry as these lists—taken at random—sound to the general reader, the books yet met the want and satisfied, or appeared to satisfy, the aspirations of their day. People had much leisure, and read and thought slowly; nor were their tastes and appetites whetted by *sensation*, which, after all, is what both reader and writer aim at in the race of twentieth-century literature and research, even in natural science. Eighteenth-century writers often seem to postpone indefinitely, in an endless verbiage, the point to be reached, till one has almost forgotten the trend of the argument before he gets to the end of it; and so, that aspect of genius, which consists in the 'infinite capacity for taking pains,' being less conspicuous in these days than its concomitant of brilliance,—it follows that to most of us the plodding patience and honest searching for truth of the common-sense century does not appeal.

Books on religion were almost universally studied, and every old library contains a number of volumes of sermons. These were conscientiously read on Sunday, or slept over, by our sabbatarian ancestors, and by many it was considered as wicked to read anything else. As a vast amount of time was spent by the leisured classes then, as now, 'at cards,' and they appear never to have indulged in them on the 'Sabbath,' it follows that when deprived of their Brag, which for them held the same fascination as Bridge

JACOB HOUBLON, ESQ.

now does for its votaries, time hung heavy on their hands. Thus it is conceivable that the soporific effect of the sermon soothed the tired fox-hunter, or calmed in slumber the stings of loss at cards of Saturday night. The account-books of both Jacobs frequently note 'losses at cards,' though we have not come across in their particular the record of any larger sum than from ten to twenty pounds a night. But as careful people usually kept a gambling purse, 'losses at cards' probably represented the balance over and above what it contained at the time. As members of the Cocoa Tree Club, as they both were, the squires doubtless played for high stakes occasionally, and gaming was not considered wrong, except when indulged in recklessly; indeed it was in an ordinary way as much a habit in society as eating and drinking, going to bed or getting up in the morning, and women gambled and loved it, as did the men. As to literature, many ladies were earnestly painstaking in respect of it in those days; they frequently studied the classics and French and Italian books, with translations. We find fine ladies corresponding with each other and discussing their favourite books and authors, while every *précieuse* dabbled a little in poetry and Italian. Mr. Pope provided the model of rhythm and turgid pomposity of style, while, nevertheless, he was often laughed at, by his fair admirers, for his over-high estimate of his own immaculate productions. Lady Hertford, for instance, quotes with some malice the since famous lines which, engraved on the collar of a favourite dog presented by him to the Prince of Wales, was gravely included among his works by Pope :

'I am his Highness' dog at Kew,
Pray, tell me, sir, whose dog are you?'[1]

So far for the collections of the squire of Hallingbury and his elder son. But John₅ Houblon, the squire's

[1] *Correspondence between the Countesses of Hertford and Pomfret*, 1738-41.

younger son, had also his own tastes and idiosyncrasies, and added a considerable number of books to the general collection. John or Jacky, as his father affectionately called him, was an enthusiast on horticulture. He led and fostered in his neighbourhood the prevailing craze, lately developed in countrysides, for garden and vegetable shows. We hear of his 'great knowledge' on such subjects, and find he acted as judge on these occasions. Being fond of these pursuits he naturally collected books upon them, as well as upon birds, another favourite interest. A less ordinary taste led to his collecting all the works on magic, witchcraft, and astrology he could lay his hands on, of which many weird books are to be found at Hallingbury. He also appears to have been a good mathematician. A lawyer he was by profession, but few law-books are to be found beyond Blackstone with his name in them. Poor John$_5$ became a *malade imaginaire*, and devoured physic, which later revenged itself on him by making him an invalid indeed. Among his papers and between leaves of his books, we have come across prescriptions the potency of which are very illustrative of contemporary doctoring; they cost him much too, for his apothecary's bills are frequent and heavy. Ague was a terribly common malady in those days, and he appears to have suffered from it; but this was in after years.

To return to the sequel of events in the life of the family. Jacob senior was made a deputy-lieutenant in Hertfordshire in the 5th of George III., viz. 1764, by Anne Holles, Earl of Essex, then Lord-Lieutenant, and about the same time his son was appointed a trustee for turnpikes in Herts, both father and son being already on the Ongar Turnpike Trust for Essex. Soon after this, in the general election of 1768, Jacob$_4$ stood for Essex county, and was beaten. This general election caused the keenest discontent in the country, on account of the corruption which resulted in the triumph of the court party. The young King, who had succeeded to the throne on the death of his grandfather in 1760, had imbibed as exalted an idea of his own *raison d'être* as ever royal Stuart entertained. But while he held the belief that he was born to govern, he worked at first to that end, not because he had certain objects in view (whether good or bad), but simply because he wanted his own way and to dictate it to his ministers. If the country was angry with the mode taken by the King and court party for securing a majority in the House of Commons, the discontent soon developed into riot, so great was the indignation at the illegal and high-handed proceeding of the House in respect of the famous Wilkes. Wilkes was popular because he opposed the will of the King and the King's 'friends,' as they were called, but he was a man of bad character, and unworthy of being the object of the nation's enthusiasm, though he served as well as another as stalking-horse for the expression of the people's disapproval, both at his own illegal rejection from the House of Commons, and at the corruption practised by the King's partisans at the election. However the rights of Middlesex and its candidates were in due time vindicated, when Pitt (who had been hidden away ill in mind and body when most he was wanted) returned in 1770 to restore justice and order.[1]

Jacob[4] Houblon, junior, was probably mortified at the result of his contest in 1768, and digusted at the corruption practised; and whether for this reason or because the party was no longer the same in aim and policy, when urgently pressed to contest the county again at the next general election, he refused unhesitatingly to do so,[2]

[1] Pitt was created Earl of Chatham this year.
[2] See a letter from the Rev. T. Lipyeatt congratulating him upon his decision.

nor did he ever again seek to enter the House of Commons. Meanwhile more serious mischiefs had been brewing and were now fast developing into troubles little anticipated by George the Third and his friends. The story of the Stamp Act, which, though repealed, was followed by other measures of taxation equally distasteful to the Americans, is familiar to us, and also how a great struggle was entered upon between the mother-country and her great independent child. Unfortunately for both countries, the King, who so far had run counter to the will of his people in most things, had now their sympathy in this his crowning stupidity. But it took some years before the ill-will bred between kith and kin, was to ripen into deadly earnest and into war.

All this time the squire, in common with other English landowners, was occupied in developing and improving his estates and agriculture generally. As he grew older and heavier, a favourite old horse carried him on his rounds overlooking his many undertakings, planting, and the like; this was Saucebox, formerly a hunter of young Jacob's, to whom we have already referred. Cooper, the famous animal painter of the time, painted this horse together with a black pony ridden by Mrs. Houblon, and the dogs 'Phillis and Fanny.'

'I rejoice to hear of my dear mother on horseback,' wrote Jacob[4] from Italy in 1760. Recurring blacksmith's bills, in which the horses' names are enumerated, reveal the fact of the long lives of some of the squire's horses, which may have been partly due to the fact that hounds were not so fast in those days, and the wear and tear less great to man and beast. People were not so universally in a hurry, and but for *port*, lives would in all probability have been longer than they were. As it was, they appear to have been shorter than our own, though the repertoire of diseases was not so complete.

HOME

There was much discontent in the agricultural districts at this time, in spite of the 'plenty' to be seen everywhere. Arthur Young was never tired of praising the beauty and fruitfulness of both country and produce;[1] while the Swedish economist Kalm writes of the places where 'the wheat stood beautiful' during his journeys through the agricultural districts.[2] Nevertheless the industrial development in the towns had attracted many industries away from the slow-paced countrysides, and quickness and cheapness came with machine-made goods. The farmer's womenkind had formerly added their mite to the family earnings, but now their looms and spinning-wheels were idle, while the village blacksmith, shoemaker, and cartwright also had their rivals in the town. The people too were lazy, and morally injured by the old system of parish relief, which had sapped their self-respect, and was a premium on idleness and begging. The unemployed were better off than the hard-working, honest labourer, and the country swarmed with them. It was during the eighteenth century that so many large undertakings, such as levelling of ground, digging of lakes and ponds, etc., were carried out in the parks and grounds of land-owners. They were generally the outcome of a stress of poverty, and the desire on the part of the landlord to employ the many poor or mischievous idlers, who had not yet learnt to flock to the towns. At some such time as this a piece of water in the forest of Hatfield was made by the squire of Hallingbury. A swamp, through which a streamlet ran, was turned into a large and beautiful lake, by the throwing up of a dam or head, where the ground sloped rapidly away on the border of the forest land. The lake is now but half its original size.

This forest was then, as it is now, the chief charm of

---

[1] Arthur Young, *Six Months' Tour through England*, 1770.
[2] Kalm, *Visit to England*, 1748. Translation, J. Lucas.

Hallingbury. Long before Norman times 'this noble Lordship' was a royal demesne, and in Edward the Confessor's day it belonged to his brother-in-law Earl Harold,[1] afterwards King. After the Conquest the office of steward or chief forester to the King was given to a great Norman noble called Robert de Gernon, and his descendants the Montfitchets held the office till their male descendants failed, but the King always retained the ownership of the soil and the manorial rights. Finally, through females, this hereditary stewardship passed to the great family of De Vere, Earls of Oxford, who held it till in turn their heirs-male failed in the twentieth earl. The forest of Hatfield Broad-Oak or Hatfield Regis[2] was, like the other 'out lying forests of Kingswood, Writtle, and Colchester,' originally integral with the great forest of Essex, or Waltham, as it was often called. But while the great forest proper was frequently altered in extent according to the 'Perambulations of Knights' who adjudicated from time to time the borders and limitations of the afforested districts of the county of Essex (occasionally disafforesting portions which the royal greed had annexed), the above royal demesnes were beyond such jurisdiction, 'because they are ancient demesnes of the lord the King.'[3] Thus each one lay, as it were, like an oasis outside of the forest proper, in the midst of the open disafforested districts; and from the days of King Edward I. they were distinctively called 'free Chases and free Warrens' and were ordered to be held as such for the King's own use, 'and all the woods therein also in such manner for ever after as he pleased.'[4]

While Epping forest now alone represents the old

---

[1] See Morant, *History of Essex*, vol. ii.
[2] As the village of Takely lies on the outskirts of Hatfield forest, it is frequently called by that name; but as applied to the forest, the name of Takely is incorrect.
[3] *History of the Forest of Essex*, p. 31.
[4] 33 Edw. I. *Plac. Parl.*, 279. See *Ibid.*, p. 33.

forest of Essex or Waltham, all trace of Kingswood, Writtle, and Colchester forests have likewise long since disappeared; but Hatfield remains, in extent but little less than in the days of Elizabeth, when John Norden's map of Essex (1594) shows it and the park of Hallingbury as practically one.[1] It was the young King Edward VI. who gave away this fair inheritance of the crown, with all its rights manorial and of the soil, and bestowed it on 'Lord Riche and his heirs for ever,' reserving to the crown the insignificant rent of £13, 6s. 8d. Lord Riche, however, sold both forest and rights. As has been said, the park of Hallingbury adjoined the chase, and for this reason, perhaps, the owner of the former would be willing to buy for a larger sum than another. Lord Riche therefore sold it to Lord Morley, and this is how and when the forest of Hatfield came into the hands of the owner of Hallingbury. But while the soil of the forest passed into his hands, the manorial rights did not do so.

1594

Ancient forest laws and customs are very curious and interesting, as also all to do with the various officers in connection with those laws and customs, and their adjudication. They included—as we have said—the steward, a great hereditary officer, and the Lords Justices. But there were also others: foresters, regarders, verderers, and agisters, as also the woodwards of forests.[2] The woodwards were appointed by owners of woods within the bounds of the King's forests; foresters, on the contrary, were officers of the crown, not having specially to do with the woods. The woodwards were sworn to bring under justice all manner of trespasses done to 'vert or venison' within their keeping; they must not keep the wood badly, or permit damage. If they neglected their duties, the woods were

[1] John Norden, *Essex described by*, 1594. See facsimile by the Camden Society, 1840.
[2] Morant, *History of Essex*, ii. 504.

seized into the King's hands. All the manors had woodwards, to preserve their woods in ancient times.[1] There was an hereditary woodward of the forest of Hatfield Regis, and as both soil and manor were the King's own, it follows that the woodward was his officer, and protected his rights as against all encroachment. Thus, when Lord Riche came into possession of those rights, he found also his woodward in possession of certain rights such as to wind-fallen wood, as by ancient custom.[2] Henry the First gave the office of woodward of the forest of Hatfield to Eustace de Barenton, and made it hereditary; it was thus vested in his descendant Sir Thomas Barrington when Edward VI. gave the forest to Lord Riche; Barrington's estate being situated almost as near to it on the one side as that of Hallingbury was on the other. A compromise was therefore effected between the two men, and while the woodward gave up his ancient office and his rights to Lord Riche, the latter now sold him the manorial rights hitherto never separated from those of the soil, which had now passed by purchase to Lord Morley, owner of Great Hallingbury.[3]

It was the grandson of this Lord Morley—the twelfth lord—owner of the estates sequestrated by the Parliament in consequence of his faithful service to the royal cause during the civil wars, whose sad story we have related in a former chapter.[4] It was perhaps not strange that the lord of the manor would fain have possessed the soil also; but it was not so to be, for the royalist's estates were sold, after endless litigation, by Act of Parliament, and passed into the hands of the Speaker of the House of Commons, and two generations later into those of the

---

[1] *History of the Forest of Essex*, p. 173.
[2] A hatchet was formerly the symbol of the woodward, and he delivered it on his knees to the Chief Justice at the justice-seat. *Ibid.*, p. 176.
[3] Morant, *Indentures*, dated 30 January 1576, ii. 509.
[4] See *ante*, p. 16.

Remains of the "Doodle Oak," Hatfield Forest.

Houblons. The forest was thus their most cherished possession, though they shared some of its rights with a neighbour.

There is on the forest of Hatfield the remains of a great tree, said by many to be the actual Domesday oak which is shown on the Survey as standing on that spot. It owns the curious name of Doodle, owing its origin, as some suppose, to a corruption of the word *doom*: the Oak of Doom; because trespassers against the forest laws had in past times paid the penalty of their 'crimes' by hanging on its great branches.[1] If not the actual oak of the Survey, the Doodle Oak is doubtless its descendant, just as the tall, stalwart young tree now standing close beside its huge ruins is undoubtedly the child of its old age, and was grown from one of its acorns. The giant now lies on its side, a mighty wreck, weather-worn and bleached by centuries.[2]

All the rights of the forest of Hatfield did not lie in the hands of our squire, for he shared them with Mr. Francis Barrington, of Barrington Hall, the descendant of the ancient woodwards,[3] and while one was lord of the manor, the other was lord of the soil; and while one herded certain cattle on the open forest, the other owned the deer that fed on its rich pastures. The right of felling timber was also divided between

---

[1] See a poem by Frederick Locker Lampson, entitled the 'Old Oak of Hatfield Broadoak,' for some of the folklore of the tree. *London Lyrics.*

[2] We believe the name of the forest, Hatfield Broad-Oak, more likely to have had its origin in the great size of its trees in general than that it was due to the dimensions of one particular tree, as has been supposed. A great oak sold, standing, in 1819, by Mr. Archer Houblon, the squire of the day, was famous for its size. The following memorandum was made at the time: 'Ap. 20, 1819. The large oak tree on Tukely forest [*sic*], opposite Basingbourn, was taken down this day. There were upwards of 300 people attending to see it fall. It contained 8 loads at 4 feet cube round measure. It was sold for £120 to Mr. Riddington of Harlow, with the top and bark.' The tree was afterwards sold for £200, taken to London, and used for the principal crane-post in St. Catherine's docks.

[3] This old family has been long extinct.

them.[1] The forest was then, as now, divided into 'out lands that lye open,' and copses, or *coppies*, as is the local name; about thirty acres in a copse 'one with another,' and while 'the one lord owned nine copses, the other owned as many.' Copses and out-lands all told comprised above two thousand acres in Morant's day, and he published his *History of Essex* in 1768.[2]

To the unique privileges of the lords who reigned over this ancient royal demesne, both before and after its bestowal by the King upon Lord Riche, we owe its preservation to this day, and also its noble trees. It has been shown that in the days of Edward I. Hatfield was declared to be a free chase, separate from other afforested districts in the county, and afterwards remaining in the midst of disafforested districts, reserved to the use and pleasure of the King. Thus the laws and customs regulating it differed in many respects from those affecting other forests, whether of Essex or elsewhere. Unlike these, the commoners or freemen from the earliest times possessed but scanty privileges in Hatfield, where the woods were the King's own, protected by his woodward, and not subject to the axe of the commoner, whose rights of *lopping* at stated times and seasons are evidenced to this day by the gnarled and pollarded oaks of Epping and the New Forests, and still more by the denuded condition of the former of old trees.[3] In Hatfield the meagre common rights consisted in the hedges and fences which, enclosed for nine years, were laid open for nine years more before felling. These fences, on removal, fell of right to the commoners, and that was all they could claim in the whole domain of forest land.

[1] The woodwards had no right to any but fallen timber, but the compromise which extinguished the office gave the Barrington family rights of felling certain coppices.

[2] Morant, *History of the Antiquities of Essex*, ii. 509.

[3] The lords of all the fifteen forest manors and sub-manors of the forest of Essex also claimed power to lop and cut their own trees, called pollard trees. *History of Essex Forest*, p. 244.

The King having thus reserved to himself the timber, this remained the property of the lord of the soil till the afore-mentioned compromise was effected between Lord Riche and Sir Thomas Barrington, his woodward, by which the right was accorded the latter, of felling certain 'coppies' once in sixteen years.[1]

The whole countryside received presents of venison when in season. The squire's venison-book contains the names of all his 'good neighbours and tenants' who yearly received their buck, half-buck, or haunch, as the case might be. Since the time of King Harold, and many a day before that, there have been deer on Hatfield forest, though in those days they shared the domain with the hogs. Indeed the manors and lordships were assessed, not according to their acreage, but to the number of hogs fed upon them. Hatfield paid the then great sum of £80 yearly, so the hogs must have been numerous.

Every one knows, who has had to do with woods and forests, that the neglect of even one generation will do infinite harm to the commonwealth of trees, lords and commons of timber and underwood, necessitating drastic measures to re-establish the harmony of growth and periodical fall. Whether it was through age and decay, or that a great fall of oaks left a denuded 'coppy,' a fresh plantation of the 'cottage coppy' was made in 1759, and enclosed according to the old custom. That some fine trees were left standing is evident, for some of those still flourishing antedate Jacob₃ Houblon's day by hundreds of years. We must not forget that since this country had become mistress of the seas, the demand for the wherewithal to build her 'wooden walls' raised the price of timber, and thousands of the great oaks of

1759

---

[1] In cutting wood, 'one, standing and resting upon the trunk of a felled oak or other tree, must not see on looking round, five trees cut down.' This was *waste*, and the regarders declared of the owner, his woods *were wasted*. Mat. Paris Chron. Majr. 165 (M.R.S.) apud *History of Essex Forest*, p. 235.

England fell to the axe during the eighteenth century. The oaks of Hatfield forest had not suffered from the lopping and pollarding which had disfigured so many trees in this country, and the giants still remaining evidence by their huge, straight trunks, the ideal English oak, which was thus specially suited to the requirements of the Admiralty during the period of three generations of Houblons, who lived during England's great wars.

A century and a half has passed by since a room was added to the cottage by the lake, having a separate door opening upon stone steps, and facing it. Then and ever since, this room has been kept for the use of the Houblon family and their friends. In the cottage behind it, in the days of the first Jacob, lived a good woman who kept Mrs. Houblon's poultry and peacocks, which were then considered very good eating. Though that taste is past, peacocks still roost in the great oaks, or fly from tree to tree. On a summer evening it would be difficult to conceive a sweeter English scene than is viewed from these stone steps. Here it is always fresh and cool, in the most parched heat; the old trees stand around upon the deep turf. Beyond the gleaming water, wide open ground, broken with old gravel-pits and grouped with feeding deer, stretches away to the left, and in the fading distance, woods and ever more woods, repeat themselves against the clear sky. And meanwhile no sound breaks the deep solitude but the cry of the wild fowl, shrill against the diapason of that murmur, which, rising and falling with the breeze, is the glorious music of any great unbroken tract of woodland. The love of this place has held six generations of the Houblon family in their turn, though the associations attending it have partaken much more frequently of happy light-heartedness than of sentimental musings over its charm of beauty. For on the smooth turf outside, or in the room built in 1759, its members have had many a merry

1759

In the Forest of Hatfield Broad Oak.

meal. Two huge oaks stand on either side of the stone steps, and deep grown into their rugged bark are the wrought-iron stanchions that formerly held the lanterns, which show the family and their guests to have been in no hurry to go home after dining by the lake in summer. Some years ago these lanterns were found in a loft at the cottage,[1] in which 'Sheldrake the forester' and his wife had lived for fifty-three years. As to the room itself, it must not be forgotten, for it was decorated by Laetitia, the squire's daughter, in the days of its first building. Externally it is, in accordance with the contemporary craze for 'grottoes,' encrusted with shells and split flints. Inside, the panelled walls and coved ceiling in the Adam's style, are quaintly decorated, and hung with cases containing shell-work, feathers, moths, butterflies, and seaweeds; some of the more elaborate shell decoration, representing festoons of flowers and leaves, being a marvel of skill and industry.

This 'grotto' was but one of many upon which it pleased the ladies of the eighteenth century to expend their time and taste. Poets condescended to visit these shrines, and composed elegies on them, and on the fair nymphs who adorned them. Be that as it may, solid mahogany dining-tables, sconces for lights, and a number of the quaint china-handled scimitar knives and forks of the day, show good square meals to have been partaken of,—and the old-fashioned wine-glasses, port wine to have been drunk,—either within or on the grass outside.

'Our good neighbours' often came on these occasions; and in the long unthronged days of the eighteenth century they grudged not the many hours given to such social meetings; for they drove many miles to them in their coaches, the men mostly attending the

[1] They are now at the house at Hallingbury, on either side of the front door.

ladies on horseback. These neighbours who met in Hatfield forest would doubtless have included Mr. Conyers, squire of Copped Hall, and Lady Henrietta —now no longer young—and their daughter, 'the charming Juliana.' Will Altham, 'Master of the Essex,' and Sir Richard Chase, keen militiaman both during the Seven Years' War and later during the American. From Thremhall Priory, on the borders of the forest, would have come Mr. John Wogan, formerly of Gaudy Hall in Reddenhall, Norfolk, and Mrs. Wogan, familiarly called 'the Empress' by the young folk—whose son Jack had been young Jacob's friend and cousin. Mrs. Wogan's mother lived likewise at the Priory; she had been Kitty Hynde Cotton in her youth, and was thus aunt to Mrs. Houblon.[1] She had married the nephew of the famous Archbishop Sancroft, who was also his heir; and so this lady formed a link with a far-off past even in those days. Needless to say, Thremhall Priory had long been a 'nest of Jacobites.' Mr. Wogan was now in bad health; but he had come of a race of famous Cavaliers that were never wont to vegetate. The Wogans were neither 'stay at home' nor easy-going squires. Dare-devil and chivalrous Cavaliers in earlier times, their descendants were Jacobites in later, and shared many a grief and hope and fear with their kinsfolk at Madingley during the days of the 'Risings.' Mr. Andrew Lang has discovered more romance in his researches into the careers of some of these picturesque and passionately loyal devotees to the Cause, than is often to be found in family history. Ill-luck generally attended them, whether political or domestic: Mr. Wogan lost half his fortune in the South Sea Bubble, and poor young Jack, as we have seen—lean and

[1] Kitty Hynde Cotton was the youngest of seven sisters. The former hangings of the 'Family Bed' of Madingley (now at Hallingbury) were embroidered by these damsels. Though tattered they still exist, a marvel of Old English stitching.

HOME

eager, impulsive and generous — like many another Wogan—went under! Once again had the fear of invasion thrilled the country in 1759. Without help and encouragement from over the sea, the French would scarcely have seriously contemplated the venture, even in Scotland.[1] Many Jacobites waited anxiously at Havre for the sequel to this supreme effort, and many paid the penalty of arrest, or thenceforth spent their lives in exile on its failure, in the destruction of the Brest fleet by Hawke. 'De vivre et pas vivre est beaucoup plus que de mourir,' wrote the young Chevalier in 1760,[2] and perhaps Jack Wogan had the happier ending.

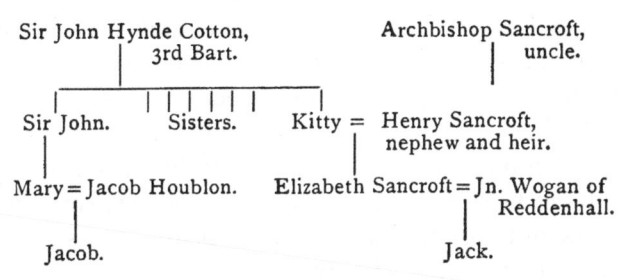

```
        Sir John Hynde Cotton,            Archbishop Sancroft,
             3rd Bart.                          uncle.
    ┌──────────┴────────────┐                    │
 Sir John.   Sisters.    Kitty  =  Henry Sancroft,
    │                                nephew and heir.
    │                                    │
 Mary = Jacob Houblon.   Elizabeth Sancroft = Jn. Wogan of
    │                                         Reddenhall.
    │                                        │
  Jacob.                                    Jack.
```

Others who might have come to the forest were Lord and Lady Maynard from Easton Lodge; Mr. Barrington from Barrington Hall would scarcely have cared to join so merry a throng; he was a bachelor and misanthrope, and none too friendly with his neighbours, poor man. He had loved a fair lady and loved in vain; he is also said to have built and decorated his beautiful house and done other things in hopes of winning her, which had been a strain on his fortune. But still she held him on, though she never took him for her husband, and he died a bachelor and the last of his race. From the beautiful Inigo Jones house of the Ryse or

---

[1] Mahan, *Influence of Sea Power upon History*, p. 300.
[2] Lord Stanhope, *History of England*, Appendix.

Rye[1] would have come the Chamberlaynes; also the neighbours from Down Hall, who had bought it from Robert Harley, Earl of Oxford. Matthew Prior once lived there, and his

        'Down down, derry down,
           Down down'

was written of this much-loved Down Hall. Tradition says that its cut alleys of Hornbeam have the ancient Doodle Oak of Hatfield forest in their line of sight; but as they are many miles apart and Essex is *not flat* thereabouts, we will not vouch for that tale. Lord Bruce might possibly have come. He was not created Lord Ailesbury till some years after this time.[2] Other friends were Mr. Bamber Gascoyne, and Mr. Archer of Coopersale and Lady Mary, and their two daughters, with whom ere long a close connection was to be made. Mr. Archer was a diminutive man with a very bald head. Among the wig-wearers of his generation this must have been regarded as a barbarous self-indulgence! He was notwithstanding a great beau. Last, but not least, there was Mr. Thomas Lipyeatt, rector of Great Hallingbury; though something of a flatterer, a good parish priest and loving friend to squire and people.

    In and out among all these and other neighbours, guests of the Hallingbury family, went a familiar figure. In all the wide forest there are now only three houses, and there were but few more in those days. One of these, on the Barrington side of the forest, was pulled down but a short time ago, and went to the last by the name of the Pest House, having probably served in the days of plague as a sanatorium or place of isolation. In another of these houses, the Forest Lodge,[3]

[1] Afterwards purchased by the great-grandson of Jacob[3] Houblon, and pulled down by him early last century.
[2] The family had a seat at Tottenham.
[3] It was formerly the duty of the forester or keeper to 'keep the lodge of his walk in repair.' *History of the Forest of Essex*, p. 146.

—to this day inhabited by the head keeper,—lived Daniel Gilbey, the honest and worthy ancestor of Sir Walter Gilbey, Baronet, of Elsenham Hall, Essex. Daniel was in fact the more modern representative of the ancient 'Under or Yeoman Forester'[1] of the royal demesne, having for his duties much the same as of yore. Serving the lord of the soil as his 'good man and true' he did so under the same conditions as his predecessors had done, when they took the oath to be 'trew to the game':

> 'You shall trew Liegeman be
> Unto the King's Majestie.
> Unto the beasts of the Forest you shall no hurt do,
> Nor to anything that doth belong thereunto.
>
> . . . .
>
> All these things you shall see done,
> So help you God at His Holy Doom.'[2]

We are told that of old the duties of the underkeepers (who were in fact the chief executive officers of the forests) were 'to take account of all deer killed and which had died, and of all trees felled in the King's demesnes. . . . They were to be stout, strong, and of good courage to take offenders in the forest, . . . not to suffer commoners to put in their cattle, neither in the plain nor in the covert' . . . to permit 'no passing man to have any dog loose or with bows bent, or guns charged. They were to look to the lawing of dogs, and to take guns, nets, axes, etc., of poachers, or off illegal cutters of woods, etc.'[3] From the year 1704 they received for wages £20 per annum, somewhat reduced by the payment of fees; but also, 'in respect of all warrants executed within their charge[4] for the King or any other person,' they had the right to one guinea

---

[1] From 1703 the yeomen foresters were called keepers. *Ibid.*, p. 150.
[2] Manwood, p. 249, edition 1615. *Book of Oaths*, 1649, folio 302, *apud History of Forest of Essex*, p. 75.
[3] *Ibid.*, p. 149.   [4] *i.e.* of deer.

116 THE HOUBLON FAMILY

for every buck, and half a guinea for every doe killed, besides the skin and the 'umbles.'[1]

From a memorandum of the 'Perquisites of my place,' we find that Daniel Gilbey's emoluments varied but little to those of the keepers before him, and that they included the keep of 'a man and a maid, three horses and six cows,' their forage and pasture; besides 'four large Hounds,' used for hunting the deer.[2] Daniel was thus a great man in his way, though he did wear a Lincoln green livery, and leather breeches, and went armed with a long gun and powder-flask. So important was the office of gamekeeper in the eighteenth century, owing to the powers conferred on them by the magistrates' licence, that many landlords were their own gamekeepers, or gave their sons authority to act in that capacity.[3]

1768 The account-book of the squire, which has revealed so many circumstances of his life, shows that when in January of the year 1768 he returned to town for the session, his long parliamentary career had come to an end. At the general election he did not again seek the suffrages of his old constituents of the county of Herts. Moreover, he had been very ill; his handwriting had altered, and it changed still more as the weeks went by. The famous Dr. Heberden, George the Third's 'body physician,' was called in, and big apothecary's bills were paid. Mr. Pocklington died this year, and his death brought to an end a connection of many years' standing between him and the squire. Through a letter from Mr. Bridge, Mr. Pocklington's partner and successor in his business, we find inciden-

[1] The umbles of the deer was the keeper's perquisite from immemorial time. See Shakespeare and Pepys's *Diary*, 13 September 1665.
[2] Papers show the whole question of payments and perquisites of forest keepers to have been gone into in 1758 by Mr. Houblon and Lord Bruce with respect to the two forests of Hatfield and Savernack.
[3] There are several gamekeepers' licences at Hallingbury as held by both Jacob Houblons.

tally that the squire was now greatly changed, though, as he remarks, his condition varied but little from day to day. We have no clue as to what was his complaint, but this failure of strength culminated at last in his death on the 15th of February 1770. It is probable that before this event, his son's marriage was arranged. Jacob junior had not been in a hurry to marry. His early disappointment probably made him unwilling to do so; as also, perhaps, the undoubted happiness of the family circle at Hallingbury. He was nearly thirty-five before he could make up his mind to forget his one and only love, in the Lady Caroline whose surname we have been unable to trace. Marriages were more often than not arranged for the 'contracting parties' in those days. Be that as it may, there are some evidences to show that Jacob's marriage was not a 'love match,' and that with the break-up of the home circle on the good old squire's death, a period, which had lasted many years, of peaceful and harmonious existence, came to an end. 'Old Hallingbury' was shut up for two years during its rebuilding, and when in 1772 the new squire and his wife took possession, not only were its owners changed, but the old place itself was altered to such an extent as would have puzzled its old master to recognise it.

1770

1772

CHAPTER V

THE WELFORD WEDDING

'To my mind there is nothing so illiberal and so ill-bred as audible laughter. I am sure that since I have had the full use of my reason nobody has ever heard *me* laugh.'—LORD CHESTERFIELD, *Letters to his Son*, i. 329.

A Journal of a Visit into Berkshire.

1770 'On Sunday Sept. 9th 1770, as soon as the Evening Service was over, Mrs Abdy & myself[1] set off Post for Saville Row, and came to Sr Anthony's Door[2] there, soon after seven. We amused ourselves with a variety of Books till nine o'clock, & then enjoy'd very comfortably some cold chicken and a bottle of Hock; sliced Tongue & Butter. At about half an hour after ten we retired to bed, in order to rise before six the next morning.

'Monday Sept 10th. We were in the Chaise before seven, & without the shadow of an accident arrived at the Pelican at Newbury, within seven miles of Mr Archer's, before three o'clock. There we dined upon some excellent veal cutlets and a Rabbit, roasted. The wine was good, the people exceedingly civil, the House clean and elegant, and every thing as it should be. We were at Welford between six and seven, and were received with great kindness by the family. Within half an hour after we had seated ourselves in the drawing room, Tea and Coffee and many eatables

[1] The Rev. Stotherd Abdy, Rector of Coopersale, Essex. Died 1773.
[2] Sir Anthony Abdy, Bart., of Aubyns, Essex.

ARMS OF JOHN ARCHER, ESQ., AND LADY MARY. (FITZWILLIAM.

THE WELFORD WEDDING

of the Cake and Bread & Butter kind were brought. We chatted over them for some time, then Cards were called for, & we all sat down to Brag with the most eager desires of winning each others money. At Ten o'clock after I had got rid of some loose shillings (which had travelled with me only seven miles & yet seemed very ready to change their master), there came a summons to supper. Seven very elegant dishes appeared upon the table, and proper comp^{ts} were paid to several of them. We then talked over our Essex Friends, rejoiced that the Bush Fair folks had so fine a day, introduced a Pun or two, laughed not a little, and about twelve, retired to our apartments.

'Tuesday Sep^t 11th. I was out of bed soon after seven. The morning appeared exceedingly wet and dismal. By the help, however, of my comfortable travelling Case & my snuff Box I regarded not the weather. At about half an hour after nine, the Bell invited us to a most elegant Breakfast & so truly good was everything, that I can safely join with Mr Anstey in asserting that: "I never ate a better in all my born days." After this as the weather w^d not allow us the satisfaction of a walk or a ride without doors, we all adjourned into Lady Mary's dressing Room.[1] There we past the chief part of the morning; we rummaged all the book cases, examined the Knicks Knacks upon the Toilet, and set a parcel of shells a dancing in vinegar. Lady Mary and the Miss Archers worked; Mr Houblon[2] gazed with admiration upon his future Bride; Mrs Abdy and Mr Archer were engaged in stamping Crests upon doilys with the new invented composition, and I read to the company a most excellent Chapter out of the *Art of Inventing, addressed to the Patronesses of Humble Com-*

[1] Lady Mary Fitzwilliam, second daughter of John, second Earl Fitzwilliam, married John Archer of Welford and Coopersale, Essex, Esq., in 1751.
[2] Jacob Houblon, Esq. of Hallingbury.

panions. At the usual hour for dressing we all parted, and I staid reading in my Chamber till dinner time. Soon after three we had: Soup, Fish & Venison, and several other elegant dishes, and a desert of Fruit. Over these we chatted with an agreeable mixture of sense & nonsense till the hour for Coffee. At about seven arrived Miss Houblon and her younger Brother;[1] their coming introduced some fresh subjects of conversation: Lord Barrimore's stabbing his servant abroad,— the Preferment vacant by the death of Dr. Jortin; the account of Eastwick Assembly, the state of the Venison upon Takeley Forest,[2] and the deficiency of game everywhere. These were Topicks that lengthened out the time till we sat down to Brag. At this Mrs Abdy was successful: but as for myself since my eyes were hardly ever favoured with the sight either of a red nine or a black Knave in my hand, it may be imagined I did not rise a winner; indeed the gold seemed to be as little inclined to stay quietly in my Purse as the loose silver was to the remaining in my pocket the night before.[3] The Supper was a very good one, and we cracked Crawfish till the Servants I believe were tired with looking at us. The remainder of our Evening was not exceedingly joyous. The intended Bridegroom had just been informed that from some unavoidable cause his happiness which he thought of arriving at on the 13th, must positively be deferred till the 18th inst.; so of course there was a Cloud of no benign aspect upon his Brow. The weight of the air seemed to have a heavy effect upon some

---

[1] Laetitia Houblon, only daughter of the late Jacob$_3$ Houblon of Hallingbury, Esq., and John$_6$, his second son.
[2] Takely or Hatfield Forest.
[3] Mr. Abdy writes as to high play on another occasion at a country house: 'There was a Loo and a Quadrille Table. I beg'd to be at the latter, for I dreaded the thought of sitting down to a game at which I found some of the Party had either won or lost nineteen guineas in a fortnight. . . . The other party laughed and scolded alternately, Mrs Roberts was undone one minute and had a princely fortune the next and the noise and uproar was prodigious.'

THE WELFORD WEDDING

of the company; the loss of Cash did not sit very light upon others; and a bad Headache from the rattling of chaises in the Journey sat upon Miss Houblon. When conversation is forced there can be little room for cheerfulness, so before twelve candles were called for and we retired.

'Wednesday Sep^t 12th. This morning appeared fine. I was at my writing table at the usual hour, and we all appeared at Breakfast the same as the day before. When that was over, Mr Archer and Mr J. Houblon went forth with their dogs and guns threatening amazing destruction to the Partridges. The Ladies, Mr Houblon, Mr Shirley,[1] and myself walked for near two hours. The new kitchen garden, the hot walls, the Steward's House, the menagery, the Still Room, the Trout gliding under the Chinese Bridge, and the shoals of Carp at the edge of the great piece of water, the new serpentine walks in the venerable wood,—all of them in their turns and at different periods, engaged very agreeably different degrees of our attention. We then parted for some time upon various occasions. I chatted a little with Mr Houblon in his chamber, I then turned over a state trial folio for a Qu^r of an hour in Mr Shirley's Room, whilst he was examining a new Bob from Newbury, and bestowing a few gentle reflections upon his Taylor for making Cloaths too tight about the Breast. The next half hour past in Lady Mary's sweet and elegant Dressing Room, & then we retired to dress; the sportsmen appeared at dinner; each man I believe had shot his Bird, and that was all. After a few glasses of wine & the departure of the Ladies into the Drawing Room, I took my Hat & walked round the Ponds & Garden; Tea & cards followed. The whole Party were in high spirits, a thousand good things were said, & all appeared to be in that happy sort of humour that

[1] John Shirley, Esq. He was brother to the Rector of Welford.

the holding up a straw w'd make 'em laugh till their sides aked. This lively disposition continued till twelve o'clock; we laughed so much at Supper that the being choked seemed unavoidable, & the servants could perform their duty but with difficulty.

'Thursday Sept. 13th. This was the morning originally fixed upon for the happy union of the worthy Mr Houblon with the amiable Miss Archer; but, for some Reasons that can't be dispensed with, it was postponed to the real regret I believe of the intended Bridegroom till Tuesday next the 18th inst.

'The day appeared tolerably fine; my plan for the morning was angling at the great Pond. Mr Shirley was so obliging as to prepare every thing necessary for me, & after an elegant Breakfast we sallied forth. Mr Archer & Mr J. Houblon went out to some River at no great distance[1] with the full intention of bringing home an enormous Pike or two. The Ladies walked with Mr Houblon, & now & then paid me a visit whilst I was sitting upon the double Bench " Eying the dancing Cork & bending Reed." The sport was not exceedingly entertaining; Mr Shirley & I shifted our places very often, but all our capture was three little Perch not worth our notice. When we were heartily tired both of our garden seats & the sulky tubs, we honour'd the Ladies with our company, & we found Mr Houblon reading a Newspaper to them as a newspaper should be read; & when he had done with it I took it up and read a line in every Column, wch produced some very laughable nonsense & set the whole dressing Room in an uproar.

'At dinner we had a most noble Pike, but it was not taken by the gentlemen; they return'd home without having engaged a Bite. The rest of the dishes were remarkably good & handsome; but I confined myself

[1] The River Kennet.

THE WELFORD WEDDING

merely to meagre food, & tasted nothing but Fish & pudding. The rest of the day past in a little romping & a great deal of distress at Cards. Heartfelt groans were uttered by the losers, & I, wretched I c'nt help exclaiming

> "Ruin seize thee Ruthless Brag,
> Confusion on th' inventor wait."

I sup'd as well as dined upon Fish after which every body's Fortune was told upon a paper Fire Screen. I was to have four wives & Mrs Abdy two Husbands. How the Fates are to make it out I know not. Mr J. Houblon, happy man! is to suckle five children and marry a Gent.'

Parson Abdy's account of the next day's amusement and the excellent meals he so keenly relished is somewhat lengthy. It included the composition of doggerel verses and much laughter and fun among the young ones of the party, whose high spirits were willing enough to fall in with the kind-hearted, fat parson's desire to make the time pass merrily, and the bridegroom forget the annoyance of the upsetting of his plans and arrangements by the postponing of his wedding; for various papers and letters show him to have been exceedingly busy at this time.

Jacob$_4$ Houblon was now thirty-five. His marriage was one of convenience, arranged previous to his death by the old squire with Mr. Archer of Coopersale; for, as we have already remarked, the Archer family were neighbours in Essex, and well acquainted with the Houblons. Susanna was the elder of Mr. and Lady Mary Archer's two daughters, and was destined to be his heir. The 'fair Charlotte'—of whom we are about to hear panegyrics from Parson Abdy—was destined to a sad and melancholy fate. She was not allowed to marry by her father, who, after her mother's death, neglected and bullied her. While he amused himself at Bath, not always very creditably, he frequently left her alone for months together at Welford, and a large number of letters written from there to her sister remain to this day a witness to her neglected existence. The elder sister, Susanna, was at this time very young, but she was already possessed of a strong individuality, and high-spirited and wilful disposition. Jacob$_4$ Houblon was not in love, though he probably had felt a kindly interest in the girl he had known from a child, and there are some indications of anxiety on the part of his brother John and of Laetitia, as to his chances of happiness with this eager, wilful girl, not unmixed, perchance, with regret at the prospect of the changes her entrance into the family would entail on their own future. During the three weeks of their stay at Welford—the story of which is so graphically told by the worthy parson who had come all the way from the Archers' Essex home to tie the 'knot' in the family of his patron—a certain reserve in Jacob's brother and sister gradually gave place to confidence, and by the time the wedding-party was over, Laetitia, at any rate, had made up her mind that the much-loved brother had a fair prospect of happiness, while the young bride herself had inspired her with that affection which her large and generous heart longed to bestow on her brother's wife. As we shall see, the postponement of the wedding-day, which had annoyed the bridegroom, did not in the end prolong the length of the solid three or four weeks which the two families spent together at Welford. The marriage, it is true, took place some days later, but there was no 'going away' for bride and bridegroom. When Mr. Abdy closed his journal and took his leave, they were still at Welford fulfilling the social duties and ceremonies at home and in the neighbourhood, which the situation demanded and custom prescribed. In the same pocket-

THE WELFORD WEDDING

book in which the good parson inscribed the account of the Welford wedding, is the story of another, for the celebration of which Mr. Abdy travelled down to Derbyshire in 1759, and described as minutely and amusingly as his experiences at Welford.[1]

The exertions of the worthy Mr. Abdy to amuse and entertain the party were amply rewarded, and he flattered himself that all was serene, and harmony in the little party completely restored, for he wrote in the evening of this verse-making day: 'After laughing very heartily over these curious matters we sat down to cards. Mr Houblon was quite himself, Miss Archer look'd angelically, and every body in the height of cheerfulness & good humour. My good Genius attended me this evening in every card I played.

'At Ten o'clock we sat down to Partridges & eight more elegant well drest dishes, & at twelve we took our leaves of each other for the night.

'Saturday Sept. 15th. I was seated with my papers & books before me by half an hour after six. Preparations were making for drawing the great Pond, the water of which had been let down a day or two before. The morning was exceedingly fine, & it was agreed at Breakfast that the Root Benches & double Garden Seats & Chairs shd be placed at the most convenient spot for seeing the best of the diversion; & that the Ladies shd bring their workbags & contribute every thing in their powers to the entertainment of the gentlemen. Soon after ten o'clock we were all at the Pond, & the usual fun upon those occasions (such as throwing mud upon gowns, Coats, & aprons; squealing in Consequence & bawling from one end of the Pond to the other) was

---

[1] This marriage was between Margaret, daughter of Wenham Coke of Longford, in Derbyshire, Esq., and Sir Harry Hunloke of Wingerworth, in Stonechurch, Derby, Bart. Mr. Coke, the bride's father, was first cousin to Mr. Archer. He acted as trustee to the marriage-settlement of Susanna Archer and Mr. Houblon.

sufficiently exerted. The manner of catching most of the fish was very curious. Half a dozen people in the mud carried bottomless Hampers, & stuck them down occasionally where any fish appeared upon the surface. When any were caught worth taking, they were thrown immediately into a flat bottomed Boat upon straw, wch attended the calls of the basket carriers. By two o'clock there was exhibited upon a grass slope, the finest collection of Carp I ever saw! One Brace in particular, measured two feet from Eye to Fork, & upon producing the scales they weighed very near seven pds a fish.

'In the midst of our amusement, a Coach & six of the finest Roan Horses I ever saw, brought Captains Craven & Suckling upon a morning visit; the latter of whom, I believe, is well known to Capt Abdy & is generally esteemed as an agreeable worthy man;—& the former has, (join'd to a large Fortune) all the Cheerfulness, bluntness & sea Humour, of our Neighbour Crabb. I presently got acquainted with both. They seemd in high spirits & as fond of laughable mischief as anybody there.

'I was desired by the Ladies to leave this entertainment, & retire to my chamber, in order to compose a Letter of political & other publick news, to Sir John Cotton's eldest daughter at Madingley. I was very loth to retire from this happy set; but as the Post was to go out the next morning wch was Sunday, & they wdn't suffer my absence from the Drawing Room in the evening, I was forced, as soon as Capt Craven took his leave, to go up stairs, & between that & dinner & dressing included, a Farrago of nonsense was produced from different articles of a Newspaper, filling three sides of Paper, wch upon the reading drew Tears of Laughter from the auditors; & I flatter myself has by this time contributed much to the political emolument of the young Lady to whom it was addressed. As no copy of this curious performance was preserved, I cannot recollect any of the articles of intelligence. The Postcript I remember, informed her it was reported that twenty four Sloops of War found temporary Relief from bathing in the Sea! At dinner we chatted over our Mornings employment, & enjoy'd a Brace of the fine Carp swimming in white sauce. We staid in the eating Parlour till we were summon'd to Tea & Coffee. Then we sat down to Cards, & the Evening was concluded much in the same manner with the preceding ones.

'Sunday Sept. 16th. I put on my sacerdotal habiliaments before breakfast, in order to be ready to perform the whole service in the Church, & every body appeared drest for the day before ten o'clock. At eleven we all went to perform our religious duties. When they were finished, I changed my dress, & the Coach & Post Chaize carried most of us a sort of airing between Church & Dinner, thro' the Park & to different Hills to see the beauties of the Country. We dined as usual with quiet Elegance, & when Coffee was over Mr Archer, the two Mr Houblons & myself went in the Coach to Wickham to pay a visit to Mr Shirley, the Clergyman of the Parish, & to borrow the Church of him on next Tuesday for a particular occasion. We returnd back again, on account of dark nights, before the Ladies had finished what Mr John Shirley calls their *twattling Broth*. We then read the Newspapers, chatted over our Letters, & made *Bouts rimés* verses, till we were called to supper. At Table, Partridge & Rabbits & collared Eels and pickled Pidgeons & Jelly, & many more good things, led us into Temptation; & after a mouthful of excellent Parmesan by way of closing the orifice of the Stomach, the cloth was taken away & we began to be very spirited & lively. But suddenly upon some provocation or other from the gentlemen, (I really know not what), the Ladies in a general whisper agreed one & all amongst themselves, to be totally dumb for the remainder of the Evening.'

It was in consequence spent rather hilariously; card-playing was not considered seemly on Sunday, but the joke of keeping silence led to a scene of much noise and confusion, more like what a party of boys and girls fresh from school would have indulged in, than the proceedings in a country house full of guests, collected together for the purpose of a wedding. Parson Abdy tells us he played the buffoon in hopes of making the ladies relent. He 'turned his wig wrong side outwards. He got on the table; made faces, intreated, begged, scolded, all with no avail.' Attempts were made to pull off the 'ladies hats and caps,' glasses of water were thrown over gentlemen's legs, and snuff distributed liberally, followed by much sneezing. At last a general attempt was made by the gentlemen to prevent the ladies from leaving the dining-parlour; and all this foolish fun was not ended till 'M[r] Houblon, who from his situation was to appear anxious for the sex in general & one in particular,' brought it to a conclusion by assisting them to escape. Mr. Abdy adds somewhat obviously that those 'remaining behind were rather glad to remain quiet and to cool, after this battle of the sexes. We recollected,' he says, 'all the different circumstances of the contention, and the vanquished rather hung their heads upon the occasion.'

The next day was very sultry and hot, but passed much as the preceding ones, varied only for the merry parson in one particular. 'This afternoon,' he writes, 'I buried a Corpse for M[r] Shirley.'

'Tuesday Sep[t] 18th. This was the Day of Days. The morning appeared uncommonly clear and cheerful. I drest myself in my new Habit ready for the celebration of the Ceremony, and everybody except the intended Bride herself seated at Breakfast in the Parlour, in new and elegant undresses by ten o'clock. Soon after

JOHN ARCHER, ESQ.
LADY MARY ARCHER, NÉE FITZWILLIAM.
SUSANNA.   CHARLOTTE.

THE WELFORD WEDDING

eleven o'clock, Mr Archer handed his eldest Daughter down from Lady Mary's dressing Room. Her apparell was a nightgown[1] of silver Muslin, with a silver Blond Hat and Cap admirably adapted to the gown. Mr Houblon in white and Silver, led his future Mother; Mr J. Houblon, the Bride-Maid Miss Charlotte Archer; who looked enchantingly in an undress of white Lustring ornamented with a Silver Blond, with the serpentine Line of Beauty hanging pendent from her neck in the appearance of a Silver Snake. Mrs Abdy, Miss Houblon, and Mr John Shirley closed the Procession.

ARMS OF ARCHER.

'We past through a Lane of Tenants, and a groupe of servants in new rich Liveries, to the Church; and there with the greatest propriety of behaviour in everybody, and the most solemn Decency, Mr Houblon and Miss Archer were legally united in the bands of Wedlock. The Bridegroom then led his Bride out of the Church; the Bride-Maid followed, Mr Archer handed Lady Mary back, the Bells were set a ringing, & we all adjourned to the Drawing Room in order to insert the marriage in the Register. We then (as the morning was exceedingly fine & it was too early for dressing for the great appearance) walked round the garden, & thro' the Wilderness, after which we came again into the Drawing Room, where a profusion of Bride Cake was placed ready for refreshment; & salvers of rich wine, & a gold Cup[2] containing an excellent mixture, were handed round. The Bride and Bridegrooms healths were drank, & pieces of cake were drawn properly thro' the Wedding

[1] Full, or evening dress.
[2] This cup was left as an heirloom.

VOL. II.

130   THE HOUBLON FAMILY

Ring for the *dreaming* Emolument of many spinsters & Batchelors.

'After this, we all parted to dress ourselves before dinner; & by three o'clock there were assembled below stairs, a set of Ladies & gentlemen drest with uncommon Elegance. The Bride looked enchantingly in a very rich white & silver Sack with a Hoop, a suit of very fine Point Lace & all her diamonds.[1] The Bridegroom in a rich suit with silver & shaded of Colours in the Lace; his Hair drest to the Life, & Bag & Solitaire. Lady Mary appeard in a most elegant quiet matronlike Sack of a grey watered Tabby, embroidered with the Leaves, Flowers & small Fruit of Oranges; and Her Ladyship in my poor opinion, never wore a silk that set so becomingly upon her. She too was in all her Jewells. Miss Archer, the engaging Charlotte, the charming Bridemaid, the Soft emblem of Innocency, was in a Robe of a most beautiful blue & white stripe, with flowers of silver & colours. Miss Houblon appeared in a spotted Lustring of Sage green with a very handsome gold Trimming, & a suit of expensive Lace. M^(rs) Abdy was in a new silk of Brown, with Brocaded Flowers. M^(r) Archer's suit of Cloaths were brown, with a rich broad Tamboured embroidery. M^(r) John Houblon in grey with an elegant gold Gauze Lace. M^(r) Shirley in a handsome suit of Cloaths new for the occasion, & an enchanting Wig made by the twister of Crines at Newbury; and, Parson Abdy—after disrobing himself—put on all he had a right to, which was a plain superfine grey Frock & waistcoat, that had never been upon his back before.

'After we had sufficiently admired each others dresses & dazeled our eyes with the uncommon splendour that was before us, we were called to another scene. In the

---

[1] We find by Jacob Houblon's account-book that shortly before his marriage he purchased jewels to the amount of £724 for his bride. Romilly was the jeweller. He also purchased much lace, about £60 worth.

THE WELFORD WEDDING

great eating Parlour, about sixteen servants stood in rich Liveries; the Table was spread in a most elegant & superb manner; the Sideboards loaded with massy Plate; the Bride & Bridegroom sat at the top, the Father & Mother at the bottom; with the worthy Steward John Heath,[1] in a handsome suit of Cloaths, & the Body Coachman behind their Chairs. There were fifteen hard-named dishes in each course, besides Removes. The desert consisted of Temples, gravel walks, Ponds, etc.; and twenty dishes of Fruit, & Champagn, Burgundy, Malmsey, Madeira and Frontiniac, were handed about incessantly. Bumpers it may be imagined were drank to the joy, health, & happiness of M^r & Mrs Houblon; the Bells were ringing the whole dinner time, & in short everything had the appearance of the true hospitality of a fine old Family, joined to the elegance of modern taste. Coffee & Cards as usual led us on to the ten o'clock Supper, which deserves a place on our remembrance equally with the other entertainment. But it is impossible to recollect the different situations, of the Lambkins, the Pegodas & the Colonades, & the Comportes & the Hobgoblin's Heads; nor is it easy to recapitulate the cheerful *Bon mots* or the laughable observations that were introduced, or to describe upon paper that heartfelt joy which appeared upon (almost) every countenance. The joy reached even to the Laundry in the Yard; a Tabor & Pipe were *dub dubbing* there the whole evening, & to that & a Fiddler's harmonious sound, they were footing it for several hours. Nothing, however, the least indecent, riotous, or drunken could be heard; as Othello says:

> "They taught themselves that honourable Stop,
> Not to outsport discretion."'

The chief event of the next day was 'an airing over

[1] A large number of farm and other accounts still exist kept by John Heath.

Lord Craven's fine Park & Plantations. In Mr Archer's Coach & six went Lady Mary and Mrs Abdy, Miss Archer ("that was yesterday Miss Charlotte"), & Mr Shirley.' Honeymoons were not yet; and the bride and bridegroom remained on at Welford till the wedding party broke up. In Mr. Houblon's 'new Coach, with two Postillions in green and silver jackets,' went the newly married pair, together with Miss Houblon and Parson Abdy himself. Mr. Archer and Mr. John Houblon accompanied the party on horseback. The evening of the following day was to the jovial clergyman—who prided himself upon being both the originator and the butt of the fun and frolic of all the young people—supremely happy. After the usual early dinner, where he 'devoured with eager appetite several of Monsr Hash Slash Cook's palatable preparations . . . tiring his arms with handing mottoes & sweetmeats to the Ladies, swallowing two Rounds of Champagne & enjoying half a dozen glasses of good Burgundy . . .' he was sufficiently lively and comfortable to respond with delight when 'a Tabor and a Fiddle invited them to the Hall.' Here 'the Bride and Bridegroom walked a Minuet together; the rest of the company followed their example, & I exhibited my slender shape in that elegant dance to the great diversion of the Company. We then went to Country dances. The three Husbands and their wives together; Mr J. Houblon and the divine Charlotte, (she really looked like a Divinity that night) and Miss Houblon and spruce Mr Cruse, or Mr Shirley—I can't tell which, and afterwards with Mr Archer. We danced with great spirit till half an hour after ten, and then (after refreshing myself with a change of Linen, Cloaths and Wig) we sat down cheerfully to an excellent Supper, at, and after which, we chatted over the figurings in and the crossings over. We then began singing several joyous songs; not such as *Your Water parted from your seas*,

THE WELFORD WEDDING 133

the solemnity of which suited nobody but *Jack Houblon*, but such as Love and Burgundy inspired. Sir John Peyton would have said: *This is Life!* and this Life and spirit continued till past one o'clock.

'Friday Sep^t 21st. About eleven o'clock this morning, we set off in our smart Equipages, with the two gentlemen on Horseback as before, and several Outriders, for the Pelican at Newbury. There, we were regaled with Tea, Coffee, and Hot Rowls. After which we walked to see the Assembly Room, the Town Hall, the Bridge, the Church, the Milliner's Shop, etc. This was a glorious treat for all the inhabitants of the Town; for as the Welford Family are naturally well known and honoured there, and as Mr Houblon was in a white and silver frock & his Lady in the wedding muslin, it was soon whispered from House to House that the Bride & Bridegroom were walking thro' the Town. The Bells were immediately set a ringing, & the doors and windows in every street were crowded with spectators. We returned home to dinner about four o'clock, and in our way to Welford, M^{rs} and Miss Houblon, the Bridegroom & myself, joined in a composition fraught with true wit and Humour upon the subject of our mornings jaunt, to the tune of *Green grow the Rushes oh!* ... At dinner there were two gentlemen from Newbury, both of them agreeable well behaved men. They went away when Coffee was over, and we sat down to Cards. At ten o'clock we supped, and by one o'clock I suppose Mr Shirley was safe & sound *upon his Perch*.

'Saturday Sep^t 22. To the great regret of the whole Party, the lively cheerful & sensible Miss Houblon left us this morning before ten o'clock. Mr Houblon's Chaise carried that Lady and her Abigail as far as Newbury, and we set off, Lady Mary, Mrs Abdy and myself, in the Post Chaize, Mrs Houblon and Miss Archer, Mr Houblon & Mr Shirly on Horseback, in order to see a Malting of an uncommonly curious Construction. It began to rain exceedingly hard just as we got to the Bar upon the Common; but luckily the Chaize returning at that moment from carrying Miss Houblon to Newbury, took up the Ladies & Mr Houblon, before the embroidered Habits and the Hats & Feathers could receive any detriment.[1] We then proceeded with our intention, and at last we arrived at the spacious Malting[2] to the astonishment of its inhabitants, with Equipages and a retinue amounting to fourteen Horses.' —A long description follows of the place and family they had come to see.—'After having looked at everything that was to be seen we got into our Chaizes, and on our way home stopped to see *Doll* play with a mole. During this entertainment Mr Houblon ordered his Chaize to draw up on one side of us, and put into our hands a little piece of Paper on wch something appeared to be written with a Pencil. This we found to be some verses of Miss Houblon's upon her leaving Welford, which instead of sealing, she pinned up, & sent by the servant who returned with her Brother's Chaize. Upon opening the Paper we found the following contents:—

'A quite new song to be sung by Mr Abdy to the Tune of *Water parted from the Sea*, for the amusement of *John Houblon*, Esqr humbly addressed to the Circle at Welford.

'Titia,[3] parted thus from thee,
Tho' she has other Friends to see,
Still must mourn that Fates divide
Her from her lov'd Brother's Bride.
Ne'er sweet Welford can forget,
Land of Plenty, Joy and Wit.
Friendship gratefully does claim
To record each worthy name.

---

[1] They were thus attired on horseback.
[2] Near Half-way, on the Bath road. Some of the buildings still remain.
[3] Laetitia.

THE WELFORD WEDDING

2

' Of her La'ship's goodness boast
Nor forget my gen'rous Host,
Look in my heart and you'll see there,
Sweet Miss Charlotte I declare!
Placid Shirly still must find
A place in every friendly mind;
Now with my fat laughing Friend
And his good wife my Song does end.

'When we were new drest for dinner, the worthy Lady of the House informed us, that Monsr Hash Slash Cook had taken his leave, and that we should feel too sensibly not only the loss of intellectual food by the absence of Miss Houblon, but the want of everything hard named & *out of the wayish* as to eating; and that we must now be reduced to plain mutton and apple dumplin. We, instead of being mortified at this account sincerely rejoiced at hearing it, as our eyes had not been blest with such a sight for above a week. When we came to table we had the pleasure of seeing seven good eatable dishes, and could really tell what they were, and we enjoyed our meal thoroughly. After dinner it was just hinted to me that I had made very little progress in the "Welford Frolic." I had indeed thought a little about it between breakfast and our visit to the malting, and by card time I produced the two following stanzas.' More doggerel follows, the refrain, as in the previous ones, being the same:

' Susan and Charlotte and Letty and all
Jump and skip and caper and bawl;
Frisk in the Drawing Room, romp in the hall,
Susan and Charlotte and Letty and all!'

The 'Welford Frolic' was set to 'the Cotillon Tune of Petit Ballet,' and without its music seems pre-eminently silly, but it served to amuse the light-hearted party at Welford, and was deemed sufficiently interesting by the youthful bride to induce her carefully to copy it out into her commonplace book. 'In the evening we had the usual Cards and Supper, and at parting for the night it was agreed that all should appear the next morning at Breakfast drest for Church in their best Bridal Ornaments.

'Sunday Sept 23rd. I performed the whole Service this morning for Mr Shirley's Brother; and the glistering appearance of the Procession thro' the Isle of the Church from the great House, seemed to set all the Congregation in astonishment. The generality of the audience I am afraid were but little edified by the solemnity of the Prayers, as their eyes seemed to be fixed entirely upon the silver image which Mr Houblon had set up, and their attention to be wholly paid to the Lustre of Lady Mary's Jewels. I preached by the hour to them, and talked earnestly and much of vanity and vexation of Spirit; but they seemed totally wrapped up in the former, and were not at all inclined to be vexed at anything. The appearance was indeed a treat to them; and when all was over, the Bells were set a ringing, and the whole company returned in the same manner they came in to Church, through a crowd of gazing Spectators. A Christening obliged me to stay behind them; when I had finished I came up stairs to change my dress, and found Mrs Abdy reading. Mrs Houblon and Miss Archer soon afterwards were near our door, and by Mrs Abdy's invitation they came in. They chatted with us till near dinner time. At three o'clock the Bell invited us into the Hall, and we busied ourselves with a variety of Eatables till the News and Letters came. I was favoured with a short pithy performance from Mrs Dickens, and a long entertaining account from Mr Altham[1] of Essex Pleasures. The Newspapers raised our apprehensions about an approaching war, told us of

[1] Master of the Essex Foxhounds.

THE WELFORD WEDDING 137

the disposition of Dr Jortin's preferment, and of the death of Dr Potter, Dean of Canterbury. When we had given everything a Perusal and drank our coffee, the evening being tolerably fine we all walked for near an hour. After this we came into Tea; we then with the joint assistance of a German Flute, the Harpsichord, and my enchanting voice, performed four of the religious Hymns out of the Magdalen Collection. From this we proceeded to the inspection of some Magazines, and filled up the time till Supper with trying to unravel the intricacies of some curious puzzles. After Supper we conversed seriously together till about twelve.

'Monday Sepr 24th. The plan for this morning was dragging part of the River Lamborne. The spot was rather tremendous for the Ladies, as the Coaches could get no nearer the place of diversion than a stubble Field next the Meadow. We handed the fair adventurers over the difficult places, but just as we arrived upon the Wooden Bridge, the Rain fell very smartly. We had recourse to the thin covering of some slender Fallows, but the Shelter they afforded was very insignificant indeed. We then bawled for the Coaches; but the Servants wanting I believe a little refreshment (for poor creatures they had drove almost half a mile), were retired out of sight, and put themselves under the protection of some generous Hostess at a Farm House.

'By that time, the brown Lustrings and the smart Hats were tolerably soaked. The Ladies were replaced in their vehicles, Mr Shirley and I attended them home, and left the rest of the Gentlemen to their dripping splash splash entertainment. We all parted upon the stairs, and I retired to my Chamber to read and write.

'When we met at dinner the gentlemen acknowledged they were entirely wet through, but at the same time boasted of their success, as a proof of which they bid us look at and taste a fine Pike upon the Table, which was part of the Capture of the day. Nothing very material occurred from the finishing our wine to the Hour of our going to bed. We had Tea, Cards, and Supper as usual.

'Tuesday Sep^t 25th. This was a wet dismal morning. When we were assembled at Breakfast, news was brought that a Hare was found sitting, and the gentlemen flattered themselves that it would hold up long enough for them to see it coursed. The Ladies gave up the Point. The first part of the morning was employed in getting our Letters ready for the old Post-woman. When they were finished I had a message from Mrs Houblon desiring me to come and read to the Ladies by a comfortable Fire in the Drawing Room. I could not resist the invitation, but immediately obeyed the Summons. It held up just long enough for the gentlemen to course and lose their Hare. Whilst the Ladies were busy at their work, and Mr J. Houblon making a Fishing Net, I was doing as I was bid, reading Baretti's *Travels* (and isn't it Mrs Abdy quite comfortable?) But in the midst of this agreeable employment, curiosity led me to the Hall to see a Miniature Billiard Table. There indeed I staid so long as to incur the displeasure of the Drawing Room; but I don't know how it was, Mr J. Houblon inveigled me to play a game or two, and when the rest of the gentlemen came in, there was no resisting their importunity to join in a Party at Hazards; and this lasted till after two o'clock. When I came down from dressing it was with great difficulty that I could make my peace with the fairest part of our Society; but as they are not made of unforgiving dispositions, I forced some smiles from their sweet Countenances, and we all sat down to dinner in high good humour with each other.

'When we had had dinner it was agreed that as this

THE WELFORD WEDDING

was not the *Anno* but the *Week Versary* of the wedding day, we should call for a Bottle of Champagne to drink the Healths of the Bride and Bridegroom. This we did with great pleasure in a general Bumper. Soon after this we attended the Ladies, and as the day continued wet and lowering we thought it best to shut up the windows, enjoy our Tea and Coffee by a good fire, and have a hearty Battle at Brag. This was really the case till ten o'clock, when we were called to Supper, at and after which we had some very lively conversation.

'Wednesday Sept. 26th. From the appearance of the morning, and the incessant Rain, we soon perceived there would be no stirring out of doors. It was agreed therefore at Breakfast, that I should devote at best three hours to the service of the Ladies in reading to them Baretti's *Travels*. When the first Hour was over, in spite of the refreshing pinches I enjoyed from a frequent application to my snuffbox, I began to be rather tired. Mr Houblon very opportunely came to my relief, and took my place and my book. Mr J. Houblon then left his netting, and we both went to Billiards. This lasted till dressing time. After dinner came our News and Letters; amongst of the latter was a droll composition from Sir J. Peyton. This and the Papers we enjoyed over our Tea and Coffee, and then went to Cards. After supper we recollected and sang fifty old songs, and at twelve retired for the night.

'Thursday Sept 27th. The Weather seemed fine but turbulent. The gentlemen after breakfast prepared themselves for Shooting, and I had determined within myself to walk exactly three measured miles; but before these resolutions could be put into execution, the two Captains Craven and Suckling came to pay their wedding compliments. This brought us all together into the Drawing Room; but I left them after some time, to settle whether there should be a spanish war or not, and pursued my first scheme of walking. During my perambulations round the Ponds, I added three more Stanzas to the Welford Frolic, and finished that curious composition.' We give the last of these :

> 'Health, Love, and Joy to the sweet smiling Bride,
> Bless her, kind Heaven, with each bliss beside ;
> May the Hours all laughing serene round her glide,
> And give Health, Love, and Joy to the sweet smiling Bride.
> Guard dear Charlotte, too, safe from all harms,
> Whilst Time moving gently improves all her Charms ;
>> May Prudence direct her,
>> Till some good Protector,
>> Like Houblon or Hector,
>> Shall fly to her arms !
>
> ' *Chorus*—Susan and Charlotte and Letty and all
>> Jump and skip, etc. etc.

'When the two Captains had finished their visit of congratulation, the Ladies came to me in the garden, and the gentlemen ordered their Greyhounds for a Course. The Ladies bustled and struggled against the Winds, which seemed determined to drive their Caps and Hats into the great Pond, and the gentlemen enjoyed but little Pleasure in their attempts at Coursing, as one of their Servants they were afraid, had put out his Shoulder by a fall against a gate. After dinner came *Darby* and *Joan* ; that is, in the afternoon came Capt Darby to pay a visit with his Lady, who was one of the daughters of S^r Wm St Quinton ; a very agreeable couple, and in point of Happiness in each other, they may possibly outvie the famous couple of old. When they had taken their leaves, we went to Cards. My distress at Brag was exceedingly great, but nobody pitied me. At ten o'clock we sup^d, and at twelve we all parted.

'Friday Sept. 28. I was at my writing table by six o'clock this morning, and wrote Letters to several of my Friends. At Breakfast it was settled that the Coaches

THE WELFORD WEDDING

should be ordered, and that we should go to some Paper Mills about seven miles from Welford. We set out about eleven, and were much entertained with seeing the whole Process of Paper making from the first rag to the snow white sheet. I could not help reflecting that the finest compositions of the greatest genius might be written upon the corner of an old sheet or the tail of a dirty shirt; and possibly the preservation of this most important journal may be entirely owing to the remnants of a rotten table cloth.

'We came home to a four o'clock dinner, after which I received a Letter out of Norfolk to tell me that a quantity of Game was sent for me to Coopersale. I hope somebody has enjoyed it before the *Fumette* became too powerful, for as I am at this instant above fourscore miles from home, I have but little reason to flatter myself with its being sweet tomorrow Sevennight. In the afternoon came a Physician, a Dr Holberd and his two daughters, upon a visit from Newbury. The Dr looked busily important in everything but his Wig. The daughters seemed chatty agreeable women. They stayed till seven, and then we battled it at Brag, and I was carried off amongst the wounded. I hopped about a little tho' before supper in the Hall, and danced the Hay to the Marionette Tunes. We then opened some of Mr Peto's best oysters, sat down afterwards to a splendid Supper, and in good time took our leaves of one another.

'Saturday Sept 29th. This morning was so particularly fine that the whole Party (except Mr Archer and Mr J. Houblon, who were engaged in a fishing scheme at Benham River[1]) agreed to walk after breakfast as far as Boxford, and call upon an old Mrs Tassell, the widow of a Clergyman. We took the greyhounds along with us, and two Servants went before us to try to find a Hare

[1] The River Kennet.

sitting. We found, however, nothing in our going, but the good old Mrs Tassell making a Pidgeon Pye for the refreshment of Mr Watts the next day after the fatigue of duty. For this old Lady still resides in the Parsonage House, and holds in conjunction with her son the glebe Land and the great Tythes, and always takes care to have a clean parlour and a cheerful fire, a comfortable dinner and a warm bed, ready for the travelling Rector.[1]

'Mrs Tassell, upon hearing of our arrival, left the Pidgeons and the Paste and the Giblets in a jumble of confusion, and ran up stairs with an intent I suppose to put on a clean Cap and apron. We were introduced into the Parlour by a smiling pretty Maid, the floor of which was as white as snow; but it did not long remain so, as four greyhounds, three spanials, and a Swedish Pomeranian (who had all the moment before paddled thro' a dirty kennel in the street) followed us in, and besmeared the Boards in such a manner that you could hardly tell what was their original colour.

'We were all exceedingly concerned that so much confusion should be made in poor Mrs Tassell's Parlour, but however the dogs laid themselves at their length, nobody offered to kick 'em out, they had done their worst and we couldn't help it. The proceedings of these dirty dogs, and Portraits in the Room of two Divines of the name of Tassell, of Mr Ben. Tassell in a wig such as no Barber ever made, of " my good Grandmother and Mrs Judith my Aunt," not forgetting Daniel in a den of the oddest Lions that were ever formed, over the Chimney; all served as subjects of Conversation till Mrs Tassell had bedizened herself sufficiently for making her appearance before her Honour My Lady, and the Bride and Bridegroom. At last the Bells began ringing in honour of the new married Squire and his Bride, who had condescended to visit that humble

[1] Rector of Boxford. He was a Pluralist.

THE WELFORD WEDDING 143

Village, and soon afterwards Mrs Tassell made her curtsey at the door. She was exceedingly neat and clean, and in countenance, dress, and size not unlike the late Mrs Nicholas of Albyn's;[1] particularly in the gown she used to wear when Sr John Abdy had the gout, and when she used to toddle out of her own Chamber into his, to give poor Sr John his draught.

She offered us everything her house would afford, and prest us to eat wine and cake; but we were proof against all her solicitations, and after a very little time took our leaves. When Mr Houblon had sent Mr Shirley with something to satisfy the Ringers, and prevent (for the comfort of the Farmers) any more Harvest work going on for at least two days,—we were informed that one of the servants had found a Hare sitting in a most convenient place for the affording a great deal of diversion to the beholders of the Course. We marched on as fast as the rough stones would let us, and were directed to ascend the summit of a steep Hill,[2] and to stand upon the Brow of it on the other side, and then we *should see what we should see*.

When we were all assembled (some panting from the difficulty of getting up the Hill, and others with the eager expectation of seeing a most noble Course), the Hare was *shoo'd up!* She started forwards about four yards, and was immediately frightened back again by some sheep into the mouths of the dogs, and was as dead as a Herring before you could say Jack Robinson three times! We looked a little foolish at one another, and thought we might as well have staid behind at Boxford and enjoyed some of Mrs Tassell's cake. And now we had nothing to do but to make the best of our way homewards. We had two long miles to walk; three more stiles to mount, and the *Devilish Falbrooks*

---

[1] The seat of Sir John Abdy, Bart.
[2] Noar's Hill. The group of trees on the summit still goes by the name of 'Lady Mary's clump.'

Lane full of rough stones, to hobble through.[1] Two of our Ladies were full of infirmities from Head to foot. Mrs Abdy could hardly open her eyes from an immense weight upon their Lids; and Lady Mary from throbbing Corns had hardly a foot to go upon. Mrs Houblon regretted the not ordering the Coach to follow her, and protested she'd give a shilling for a fresh pair of shoes; and Miss Archer, the sweet Charlotte, kept saying continually: *No, but only Mr John Shirley! Well I believe; if you don't carry us the nearest way home, I'll never forgive you! I'm so tired, and I shall never get drest by dinner!*

'At last, however, by Mr Houblon supporting his good Mother in Law, and the young Ladies resting upon me, and Mr Shirley giving his assistance to Mrs Abdy, we reached home, and as there was sufficient time for getting cool and dressing, we all appeared in the Drawing Room when the dinner Bell rang, fresh and lively, and forgot that we had been at all fatigued.

'As this was Michaelmas Day, the generous mistress of the House had taken sufficient care that none of her Party should want *money* during the remainder of the year, if the eating a quantity of Goose would be attended with that happy consequence; for two fine ones appeared in the eating Parlour, to which all proper Compliments were paid; and it was declared, that there were more in the Kitchen for the amusement of the servants. This put me in mind of Soame Jenyns' account of a particular Country, where People lye upon their backs and it rains Pigs ready roasted. Here were geese ready roasted in abundance, but whether the Welford Family[2] all *lay upon their Backs* to eat them is more than I can determine. I am afraid indeed as to the inferior order of Domesticks, so much goose eating served only to put them in mind

---

[1] The present road along the Valley of the Lamborne was then a mere track. The way to Newbury was by the 'Ridgeway.'
[2] The household was called the 'family.'

THE WELFORD WEDDING

of the *want* of money, and to revive some of their *good-natured reflexions* upon the *Loss of Vails*.[1]

'When we had finished our Dinner and Fruit, and drank our usual quantity of wine, Tea and Coffee succeeded. Then Cards were called for.

'Sunday Sep^t 30th. I was once more engaged to do as I had done the two Sundays before, which was perform the whole duty at Welford Church. We all met at breakfast drest for the day, and at eleven o'clock without any form or Parade, we all proceeded as good people should do, to say our Prayers in a private quiet manner. I may here mention that at Welford their manner of singing Psalms is particularly pleasing. The tunes are solemn but exceedingly melodious. Mr Archer's Steward, honest John Heath, leads the set, with as agreeable a voice as I ever heard. The gamekeeper plays upon the Hautboy, and the gardener upon the Bassoon, and these, joined to eight or ten voices, form a Harmony that strikes the attention most amazingly.

'After Church, we all retired to our separate apartments, till we were called to dinner; then came Coffee and the Newspapers and Letters, with the addition of the *Reading Mercury* and the *Lady's Magazine*. In this latter, was an elegant Copper Plate of curious Pattern for an apron; and the young Ladies expressing a desire to have it drawn upon another paper, I offered my services which were accepted, and I immediately went to work. During this employment of mine, the gentlemen read occasionally different articles out of the Papers, and Mr Houblon gave us the proceedings relating to the City Recorder at full length. There was afterwards produced, a *petit pièce* written originally by an ingenious Essex Clergyman, upon Mrs Trefusis

---

[1] A great effort was made at this time to diminish the great tax upon guests in the custom of giving heavy vails (or tips) to servants.

when she was the pretty Mary St. John;[1] in the latter part of which there is a sort of puzzle to exercise the ingenuity of Readers; the first four lines are to be read as they are written.

'The verses are as follows:

> 'If Anne is above
> My vain aspiring Love,
> There's reason manifold
> She's young and I am old:
> She is NOBILITY
> and i
> SHERR i
> 'tis or all
> all
> 'tis or all
> ———————
> all
> in o equal, tho' were both divine.

'This was considered with due attention by all the company, and was at last found out, but not before a thousand guesses, surmises, constructions, and wrong placings of the words, had been made. With these innocent enliveners of that dulness which generally attends a Sunday evening in the Country, and a repetition of the four Magdalen Hymns with the German Flute and Harpsichord, our time was very happily filled up till we were called to supper: and at this, tho' there were nine elegant well drest dishes upon the Table, I had resolution enough to confine myself to one stewed apple and a piece of Bread.

'Monday October 1st. I was this morning upon the walks soon after seven o'clock; Mr Houblon joined me before breakfast, and at our going in, we were met by Mr Archer and the elder *Mr Watts* a Clergyman,[2] who came to pay his personal Compts upon the happy event

---

[1] The Hon. Mary St. John married Hon. Robert Cotton Trefusis, afterwards seventeenth Baron Clinton.
[2] Rector of Boxford.

THE WELFORD WEDDING

in Mr Archer's family. I was pleased at having an opportunity of seeing and conversing with a man generally well esteemed for his uncommon share of Learning, and thorough knowledge of mankind. By the interest of Lord Chancellor Talbot, he succeeded Mr Cranke in the Preachership of Lincoln's Inn, and was much admired there both for the elegance of his Compositions and the gracefulness of his delivery; but after nine years continuance he resigned his office, and retired into the country, where he has lived to the age of sixty-five years, and has at this instant all the life, spirit, and agility of a man of Thirty.

'When we had breakfasted, the other Gentlemen, ever studious of rural amusements, went to their different sports; the Females retired to Lady Mary's dressing Room, and Mr Watts and I enjoyed a walk by ourselves.

'During the course of our conversation, I learnt that there had been a very old friendship between him and the present Bishop of London; that Dr Ferrick was originally assistant Preacher to Mr Watts, and that Mr Watts was the man who recommended him to Sr Joseph Jekyl to be his Chaplain at the Rolls. And now, pray mark the difference of their luck in Life! Whilst *Watts* (who was once in the superior station) is galloping from one Country Church to another, and preaching till his heart akes to a set of Country Louts; and picking up by little and little small Tythes from grudging Farmers; his *Lincoln Inn assistant*, is in fair possession of five thousand pounds p^r Ann. with various opportunities of making ample provision for Sons in Law and Nephews, and his Lady is reclining in a languishing attitude upon a Sofa in St James Square!

'Whilst we were talking over the disposal of some Preferment which had lately fallen, Mr Watts acquainted me with the occasion of the strict friendship that has long subsisted between the Master of Clare Hall, Dr Goddard, and Bp. Ferrick. It seems when they were at College together, the Bishop had a very dangerous Fever, and Goddard sat up with him four nights together. This uncommon instance of affection never was forgotten; and from mere gratitude he gave him a Prebend of Peterborough, and lately another of St. Paul's.

'This morning came a M^r and Mrs Head from Newbury, relations of the Baronet of that name. At dinner appeared the son of Mr Watts, a very agreeable sensible Clergyman, lively and good humoured. Mr Archer gave him a Berkshire Living about a year since, which, added to another not far from Salisbury, enabled him to marry a very deserving woman with a tolerable fortune. We had a great deal of entertaining Conversation at and after dinner; and in the Evening there was a Quadrille Party consisting of Lady Mary and Mr John Houblon, the Father Watts and myself. The rest made a tremendous noise at Brag.

'Tuesday Oct. 2nd. The elder Mr Watts took his leave of us as soon as Breakfast was over. All the gentlemen (except Mr Shirly and myself) went a' Pheasant Shooting. He and I took a quiet walk thro' the Village and upon the Common. We walked by a Row of neat comfortable Cottages which Mr Archer had built for the convenience of his Labourers. Each had a separate Garden belonging to it; every one an Oven, a place for Wood and Turf, and a Hog's Cote; and one Well of fine Water in the centre of all, for the common use of every body. I never saw anything better contrived or more compact.

'Whilst we were admiring the happy situation of these Cottages, with plenty of fine Bacon upon their racks and satisfaction upon their countenances, the Ladies came to us. We sat down in one of the Houses, and chatted with an old widow that kept a little shop.[1] She talked Berkshire pretty broad, and complained much in that dialect of bad times for trusting; so called to her grandchild, "*Tummy, why doesent spike to my Leady, cassent hier?*'

'I was so much struck with these little dwelling houses, that I thought if I should be left by myself and be reduced by any misfortune to forty or fifty pounds per Ann., that I could pass my days with great tranquility in this rural retirement. I fancied myself master of one of these cottages, with a tidy old woman to live in the garret chamber and keep my house clean. I had got in Idea all my books about me, a good quantity of Snuff, some old Hock in my cellar, good Tea & sugar, and Toast and Water for my common draughts, and concluded that, with agreeable dry walks in a pleasant country, I should keep myself in health and exercise; and free from every ambitious pang, should be the happiest Being in the Universe;—when M[rs] Houblon twitched me by the Elbow and insisted upon hearing the subject of my Reverie. I told her the scheme of happiness I had formed, in case of accidents. "Come, come!" says she, "rest yourself contented, and be thankful for your present situation! You'd soon want a little cheerful Society amongst us at the great house; and Mamma never yet had any of the *Cottagers to play at Cards* with her." I thought she was in the right, so we said no more about it, & walked quietly homewards, wishing only by the way for some *little Plum* Cakes from Lamborn Fair, and a Bushel of good Walnuts.

'In the afternoon we set off with a very great Retinue, with the Landau and set of Horses, the Post Coach and two Postillions, and four Outriders, for Capt. Darby's at Newtown beyond Newbury; the Ladies and Gentlemen

---

[1] Both houses and little shop still exist, as also the centre well.

all drest in their wedding finery. When we arrived (which was rather of the latest) the Family had almost done Tea. We found there Sr Joseph and Lady Andrews, two more Ladies and a Capt. Somebody. We made quite a formal circle; but after Tea Mrs Darby broke it by ordering in a Card Table; at which Lady Mary Archer, Lady Andrews, Mr Houblon, and myself played a Pool at Quadrille. Sr Joseph in the meantime was exceedingly conversible. He seemed to be a man of very genteel address, and to have a very good knowledge of the World. We staid till near eight o'clock, and then took our leaves, and when we came home found Mr J. Houblon, Mr G. Watts, and Mr Shirley at Quadrille. When the Ladies had pulled off some of their Finery, we sat down very comfortably to supper. Afterwards we sang several songs, and were very lively and spirited till twelve o'clock.

'Wednesday Oct. 3^d. The family met this morning in the Parlour at half an hour after nine, in elegant morning dresses, in order to breakfast by appointment with Capt. Craven at Benham Place. Just as we were setting out, Capt. Craven made his appearance with the lively looking Widow Taylor, Lord Craven's Sister, and said he was come to fetch us. We immediately got into our different vehicles and soon found what the Capt. called the *Rattletraps* all set in order. The Widow Shuckborough, another sister of Lord Craven's, Mrs Craven, his Mother, and a Sister of Lord Leigh's were ready to receive us. Tea, Coffee, Chocolate, Cakes, hot Rowls, etc., were handed about by a gentleman out of Livery in great profusion; and the Drawing-Room we sat in had some elegant Pictures in it, and was very elegantly fitted up. When we had finished at the breakfast table, we walked all over the House and gardens, and devoured a great quantity of fine grapes in the hot House. Capt. Suckling had his gouty shoe

THE WELFORD WEDDING 151

on, and couldn't stir without difficulty. We staid till past two o'clock, then made our Bows, rattled out of the great Courtyard, and came home to dinner. Between that and Tea time Mrs Abdy and I put, as Mr Crabbe says, *our twos and threes together*, in order for setting out on our Journey homewards the next morning. The family we were with, were so obliging as to express a very considerable regret at the thoughts of parting with us, and frequently declared their wishes that we would lengthen out our stay. This, however, was impossible. Mr Gay says:

'—When a Lady's in the case
You learn all other things give place.'

I was under an Engagement to be in Essex by the tenth of this month at furthest, in order to celebrate the marriage of a Sister. Nothing but this should have moved us from the happy spot we were placed in, till we had paid our personal Compt^s to Mr Archer on his Birthday the Tuesday following, and had attended the Bridal Cavalcade to Newbury Assembly.

'We had Coffee and Cards as usual, and after Supper we took our leave of every body.

'The next morning we were in the Chaize by six o'clock, and arrived safely in Town between three and four. We staid there till Saturday three o'clock, and by half an hour after six that evening, I once more took possession of my comfortable Study at Coopersale.'

In curious contrast to the account of the wedding-party we have here inscribed, is the following little note, a relic of a past of stately ceremony and formality already fast disappearing. The widowed mother of the bridegroom thus greeted him and his bride on their marriage:—

'Mrs Houblon presents her compliments to M^r & M^rs

Houblon; received the favour of a letter from Mr Houblon which inform'd her of their marriage. They merit every good wish, and Mrs Houblon begs they will accept her sincerest wishes that all happiness may attend them. She depends on their goodness to excuse her that she is not able to congratulate them in a manner more suitable to so joyful occasion.—Oct. 9, 1770.'

CHAPTER VI

'GENTLEMEN OF THE MILITIA'

'We talk of nothing but encampments. The hurrying life I lead makes me envy Solomon's subjects who dwelt safely each under his own vine and under his own fig-tree.'—*Correspondence of the Countesses Hertford and Pomfret*, 1741.

JACOB HOUBLON and his young wife spent a considerable part of the next two years in town, though the former was frequently at Hallingbury watching the progress of the rebuilding of the house. A letter to him from Mr. Lipyeatt written late in 1771 describes the 'pulling to pieces of your house' as viewed from 'the rectorial window across the park, in order to render it stronger and fairer.' From this we infer that, as was the case with many old houses at that time, considerable alterations had become necessary owing to decay. Unfortunately these alterations were frequently so extensive as to destroy the character of the old buildings, and even to transform them entirely. Nevertheless it must be admitted that the red brick houses of the eighteenth century are both handsome and dignified in their way, and are eminently characteristic of Georgian development in comfort and convenience. In the present instance much thought and ingenuity were displayed by Jacob₄ Houblon and his architect in producing a Georgian mansion without entirely destroying the old one; though we cannot but regret the picturesque old half-timber house with its long gallery and latticed casements, as also the clearing away of the beautiful 'linen-

1771

fold' oak wainscot with which its walls were lined. Of this one small door alone now remains, which, doing as well as another, was utilised for an attic under the eave of the roof of the present servants' hall. The rest was probably broken up and consumed as firewood. This hall had been a later addition built of brick, about the time of William and Mary. The old half-timber house was now recased with solid brickwork, the outer walls on the north side now being of unusual thickness; a whole network of great oak beams were thus embedded within an outer case of red brick. Considering this architectural patchwork, the whole is of great solidity, and the work was evidently carried out with skill and honesty, the roofs and upper story alone exhibiting the great age of the original structure. Meanwhile the gallery—always on the first floor in Tudor houses—was divided up into rooms, and the original mullioned windows and casements replaced by large light Georgian windows. The flanking towers, or four-story turrets at the corners of the house, were also recased, and surmounted by lead conical roofs with gilt vanes;[1] and while so much alteration went on below them, the old roofs were retained, and it is through this fact that it is possible to trace in great part the plan of the old house. Of the chapel—of which we hear in a seventeenth-century inventory—no trace remains, nor yet of the 'chapel-hall,' which must have been large and chilly from the great quantity of logs consumed on the hearth, a note by the squire's steward, of the amount burnt in one fortnight in the year 1735, having escaped destruction. It is possible that the interior of the chapel was of stone, fragments of early English ecclesiastical work having been found. After the completion of the reconstruction of the house, Jacob

---

[1] The towers at Osterley were recased in the same way about the same date as Hallingbury. Though larger, Osterley is very like Hallingbury.

'GENTLEMEN OF THE MILITIA'

Houblon appears to have personally superintended the carrying out to its completion every detail of ornament and fittings. The whole of the specifications and many drawings are preserved amongst his papers, and together form an interesting study as illustrative of contemporary prices and materials.[1]

Jacob₄ Houblon's eldest child was born on the 5th of July 1771, and was named Maria. The following year another daughter received the name of Laetitia, and nearly two years later a boy was born and called John, whose arrival was greeted by his father's many friends and kinsfolk with warm congratulations. Amongst their letters one from Mr. Bamber Gascoyne of Bifrons in Essex, M.P., is characteristic.[2] Though older than the squire and his brother, this eighteenth-century man of the world and high Tory loved them both. 'Monday morning, six o'clock by moonlight,' he writes: 'God send this new comer health, and may he escape Arthurs', Booths', Almacks', and Newmarket! and may he live to root out Presbytery from yᵉ land!' A charming letter to his father-in-law of this date shows perfect harmony to have subsisted between the squire and his wife's family. Mr. Archer served as High Sheriff for Essex in 1773, and demanded counsel of Jacob₄ as to his Under Sheriff. After supplying the information desired, the latter concludes: 'We and the charming Children are better than could be imagined. Please accept our most affectionate Duty and our best Love to the Dear Charlotte.'

By June 1773 the work at Hallingbury Place was sufficiently advanced to enable the family to occupy part of the house; young Mrs. Houblon records this fact in her commonplace book, and also remarks that

[1] These papers have been arranged and noted by C. R. Ashbee, Esq., architect.
[2] Later Receiver-General of Customs and a Lord of the Admiralty. *Dictionary of National Biography*, vol. xxi.

they at first occupied the 'north front' only. At this time the house was still in the hands of the plasterers, painters, glaziers, and plumbers, all of whom were busily engaged on the south side, most of which was new. Capability Brown did some work about the grounds at this time, and probably planned a large sheet of water in the park, which was made not long afterwards.

On the commencement of the alterations at Hallingbury Jacob's mother and sister had removed from the old home, and letters written by Laetitia to her brother are dated from Stoke House near Plymouth,[1] from which place his mother took pleasure in sending him fish periodically. The advent of little John$_6$ had caused equal delight to both his aunts, Laetitia Houblon and Charlotte Archer. 'I'm just mad to come to town,' wrote the latter from Welford, 'to see my sister and the boy!' while large untidy handwriting is excused to her brother-in-law, by the hope he would forgive 'hurrys and flusters!' Her high spirits are somewhat pathetic in view of her subsequent sad history.

So long as Lady Mary Archer lived, communication between the two families was frequent, especially while the Archers were residing at their Essex home—Coopersale, near Epping. Mr. Archer was affectionate and cordial to his elder daughter and her husband, but a curious letter from him to the latter, written about this time, reveals plans in respect of the younger one which partly explains his unkind conduct to her at a later date. Writing to the squire of Hallingbury he announced a visit for the purpose of drawing some of his son-in-law's coverts the following day, provided the weather remained open. He proposed bringing with him—besides his daughter—his hounds, horses, and hunt servants, for all of whom he expected as a matter of course that room

[1] Stoke House belonged to the Hynde Cotton family, and was rented by Mrs. Houblon from her brother.

SUSANNA HOUBLON (NÉE ARCHER) AND HER DAUGHTER MARIA.

'GENTLEMEN OF THE MILITIA' 157

and hospitality would be afforded. But at the same time he requested Jacob to refrain from inviting to his house during the period of his visit a certain young squire, a neighbour, and the owner of a fine property.[1] The said squire had so much to recommend him as a guest that Jacob Houblon, while professing himself as delighted to receive his father-in-law and his numerous retinue, insisted on being told the reason of this strange prohibition. The explanation was then vouchsafed, that the gentleman had made a proposal for Charlotte's hand, and that he—Mr. Archer—had declined it; the young lady had evidently not been consulted in the matter, but a meeting under the circumstances was undesirable. Subsequent letters reveal a similar refusal in the case of another aspirant for the hand of Miss Archer.

Lady Mary Archer seems to have fallen into bad health about this time, and Mr. Lipyeatt, writing to Sir John Hynde Cotton, mentions Mr. and Mrs. Houblon as having only just returned home after a long absence, and that 'Lady Mary's complaint having taken a favourable turn has restored our good Esquire and his family to us.'

1775

Lady Mary was a woman of warm impulsive nature, adored by her family, and of sufficient character and ability to render happy and contented her somewhat volatile spouse; though it would appear she was unable to control a magnificent expenditure which was greater than his estate could bear. After her death in September 1776, Mr. Archer's character appears to have rapidly degenerated, mainly through the influence of a lady, whom Mr. Bamber Gascoyne describes in a letter to Jacob Houblon as 'insinuating and deep designing.' But he was at first overwhelmed with grief at the death of his wife, while many letters from relations testify not only to the sorrow they felt at her loss, but to their high

1776

---

[1] Mr. Maitland of Stansted Hall, Essex.

estimate of her worth. Lady Mary was the youngest of the three daughters of John, second Earl Fitzwilliam. There are frequent references to her sisters in letters to and from the Houblon family, especially to the eldest Lady Godolphin, who, dying childless at a later date, bequeathed her beautiful diamonds to her niece Susanna Houblon. They are said to have been bought by Lord Godolphin[1] at a sale of the jewels of the unfortunate Caroline, Princess of Wales, wife of George IV., and are still in the Houblon family. Lady Mary's other sister was Lady Betty Fitzwilliam, a somewhat fastidious and aristocratic old maid whom her nieces appear to have held in some awe, though amused by her airs. She lived in Princes Street, and our friend Parson Abdy enjoyed her friendship and patronage.

At the time of Lady Mary Archer's death it is probable that Mr. Archer's business affairs were already somewhat embarrassed. It may be seen by Parson Abdy's journal that his style of living was suitable to a man of large fortune, and he was credited with the possession of £10,000 a year; but though the owner of several large estates, we know by some letters addressed to him by his mother in 1751, the year of his marriage, that they were burdened with mortgages. This lady was a most remarkable person; many of her business papers and letters are in existence, and show her to have been a woman of strong will and great capacity. She was the second wife of Mr. William Archer (formerly Eyre) of Welford, and was the daughter of Sir John Newton of Barres Court, Gloucestershire, and of Culverthorpe, co. Lincoln, Bart. Her husband dying while his children were young, she managed not only his properties, but her own, which were very extensive in consequence of her having succeeded to the family estates of Newton on the death of

---

[1] Francis, Lord Godolphin, nephew of the statesman. Born 1706; married secondly Lady Ann Fitzwilliam 1748; died 25 May 1785.

'GENTLEMEN OF THE MILITIA' 159

her brother, Sir Michael Newton, without children, in 1743. While her elder son John succeeded to his father's Archer property, the second, Michael, assumed his mother's name of Newton, and in time succeeded to her estates.

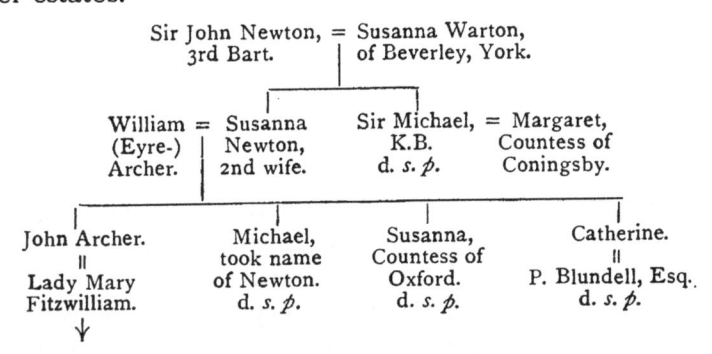

```
           Sir John Newton,  =  Susanna Warton,
              3rd Bart.         of Beverley, York.
        ┌─────────────────┬──────────────┬─────────────┐
   William = Susanna   Sir Michael, = Margaret,
   (Eyre-)   Newton,       K.B.       Countess of
   Archer.   2nd wife.    d. s. p.    Coningsby.
   ┌──────────┬──────────────┬─────────────┐
John Archer.   Michael,     Susanna,     Catherine.
    ‖         took name    Countess of      ‖
 Lady Mary   of Newton.     Oxford.    P. Blundell, Esq.
Fitzwilliam.   d. s. p.     d. s. p.      d. s. p.
    ↓
```

In spite of his mother's warnings, John Archer's expenditure was not restricted. Open handed, not to say lavish, his fortune was not equal to the demands made upon it by wide hospitality and frequent journeys to and fro to his different country houses. A curious account, cut from some newspaper, has been preserved of one of these progresses; in the present instance from Welford in Berks to his Gloucestershire estate of Hylow. Besides the coach and six and other carriages in which he and his family and household travelled, his pack of hounds, horses, and hunt servants in 'scarlet and gold lace' accompanied him, while a special guard of armed men was deemed necessary as escort to the cavalcade on account of the value of the family plate! A large quantity of this plate still exists and bears witness to the good taste of its owner, whose arms are engraved upon it impaled with those of Fitzwilliam.

We have seen Mr. John Archer bringing his hounds from Coopersale in order to draw the coverts of the squire of Hallingbury, and it would appear that this erratic little gentleman was wont to 'carry them' with him wherever he went; a strange proceeding in view of rights and privileges exerted over each several 'Country' by packs in these days. It is evident that a century and a half ago these rights were less arbitrary and defined than they are now!

There are a large number of bills and other papers relative to the few years during which Jacob$_4$ lived with his family at the newly rebuilt Place. The squire bought Thremhall Priory the year of his father's death, and Mr. Wogan and his family now became his tenants. The house was furnished partly from Hallingbury, for young Mrs. Houblon added to what was already there, while much of what was then thought old fashioned was sent to the Priory. Some of the new things purchased for Hallingbury—the bills of which still exist—can be traced, though it has been fetched out of lumber-rooms and attics and even the stables. Lovers of old furniture in these days have rectified the mistakes of the early Victorian period which banished the Chippendale and Sheraton furniture to the oblivion of the attics.[1] A few of the pretty elbow chairs, painted white and silver, of young Mrs. Houblon's drawing-room still exist, and we learn these were then covered with blue and silver silk damask, the curtains of the room being of the same. Four-post beds, single and double, were exclusively in use, and till long after this time were surrounded with curtains on all sides, our ancestors holding the belief that they could sleep with neither comfort nor safety without being completely enclosed in stuffy draperies. It was further considered suitable to the dignity of every great house that it should have its state bed, and such a one existed at Hallingbury early in the eighteenth century, when we hear of 'the velvet Bed.' These beds were

---

[1] A pair of cabinets by Chippendale, made for Mr. Archer at Coopersale, have lately been valued at £500.

The Children of William and Susanna Archer, 1747.

usually 'upholstered in Genoese velvet, and were beautiful in material and workmanship, the canopies being covered with the velvet and frequently surmounted at the four corners by upright plumes of feathers. Though the old Hallingbury bed is no more, the state bed of Madingley last century found its way there, together with the family cradle, or rather crib, a beautiful piece of Sheraton workmanship.

In an old house where great destruction has not been wrought amongst the crockery, we can frequently find traces of the taste and fashion of generations in what survives of each period. A stately dame, by name Mrs. Roberts, was housekeeper at Hallingbury during the two generations of Jacobs. As she still reigned there when the second of the name died, and the family left their home for some years, she must have been in authority for nearly half a century. Under such rule, crockery was not wont to be broken unduly, and therefore remnants of services of china exist, reaching back to an early period.[1]

Early in the eighteenth century, families with armorial bearings frequently took pleasure in sending sketches of them to India, where, under the auspices of the East India Company, they were reproduced on sets of Indian china, and sent home as dinner and other services. Such a dinner service was manufactured for the elder squire of Hallingbury, and decorated with his arms impaled with those of Cotton of Madingley. As gaps occurred through inevitable breakages, it was the custom in the country houses of Great Britain for careful housewives to replace them by other pieces; but being unable to do so from India, they had them copied in England, hence we have old Worcester or Lowestoft

[1] In a book of accounts of Mrs. Houblon senior, in the early part of the century, are some rules laid down. By one of them she received Mrs. Roberts in her chamber at eight o'clock A.M. in order to give her her orders for the day.

VOL. II.

china filling the gaps in the India sets, and painted like them with the arms of their owners. Some of this old Worcester is still at Hallingbury, as well as part of the original service of Indian ware. Relics of other oriental sets also survive, in a considerable number of the gigantic plates for which we can imagine no domestic use; but they are very fine, and are now valuable.

By the evidence of several long bills of Josiah Wedgwood, a large amount of his beautiful and then very popular ware was bought by the squire and his young wife when they settled at Hallingbury after its rebuilding; but owing to its fragility as compared with the robuster oriental of the previous generation, but little remains to this day. Later, Crown Derby held its sway, much still remaining. Of this a small lemon-yellow tea service, belonging to Susanna Houblon, is said to have been removed by her after she became a widow. More than a hundred years subsequently, it once more found its way to Hallingbury by the will of her grand-daughter. The same fate befell Jacob$_4$ Houblon's watch—a beautiful chased one of the 'turnip' type—which, parted then from its bunch of seals and fob, left behind at Hallingbury, was again united to them by the same testamentary means.

Blacksmith's bills show the squire's stables to have usually contained about twenty horses—hunters and coach, while occasional entries refer to a fine stud horse of the name of Ajax. Very soon after he succeeded his father at Hallingbury, we hear of his 'hounds.' They were not the foxhounds of which Mr. Altham had been Master, but harriers.[1] In Daniel's *Rural Sports* the author, writing in 1801, speaks of 'the Beagle crossed from the dwarf foxhound, of which the late Mr. Houblon of Hallingbury (and another gentleman) had each

[1] In 1759 Sir Richard Chase kept a pack of harriers.

'GENTLEMEN OF THE MILITIA' 163

a pack, the most complete specimens as to size and figure ever seen, and the fittest for a Champaign country.'[1] Jacob₄'s friends banter him occasionally in their letters on his love for his 'little hounds,' which he declared gave better sport than could be got with the foxhounds. One letter from his cousin John Hynde Cotton, when on a visit at Clumber, tells a tale of sport there, which he hopes will convince Jacob as to the superiority of fox-hunting: 'though it seems you prefer your own *tours, grands et petits* and hare hunting to it.' That he was not always content, even with his beagles, is shown by a letter from his sister from Stoke, in which she asks: 'What's the matter with your Hounds? I fancy the bad weather put you out of sorts, and made you expect impossibilities! Don't quarrel with them, they are your best Physicians.' Possibly the poor sport with the Essex foxhounds at this time was due to the huntsman, as John Cotton, in another letter to Jacob₄, describes a fine run spoilt by his mismanagement. 'Hounds met at Hormead park,' he wrote, 'and Conyers and I lost a good day's sport through the obstinacy of King, who would go off with two couple of hounds when the Pack followed a fox almost in view. We found at Shales park—I think the place is called—and ran almost to Newport, where the hounds for want of a huntsman would not go on after the first check. A charming country, which made it the more provoking.'

Charles, Sir John Cotton's second son, was now in the Royal Navy. His letters exhibit the warmest affection and gratitude to his aunt Mrs. Houblon, not only in respect of interest exercised with regard to his advancement in the service—in those days generally essential,—but in the matter of presents sent him of various kinds, and especially of the *shirts* which at that

[1] Daniel, *Rural Sports*, p. 329. Bunny and Gold, 1801.

period formed so costly an item in a gentleman's wardrobe.[1] With the care of her youngest nephew Edward, who was almost an infant at the time of his mother Lady Cotton's death, Mrs. Houblon appears to have charged herself entirely, and in her will she left a sum of money in the hands of trustees for the purpose of completing his education. Nor during her lifetime did she forget her other nephews. Sir John Cotton was always dilatory in business matters, and needed *reminding*, by Mr. Lipyeatt, 'of Mrs. Houblon, his sister's wish that he would not delay using his influence with the First Lord of the Admiralty' on behalf of one of his twin sons, George and Alexander. This should be the more easy to the indolent Sir John as Lord Sandwich, then the First Lord, was his intimate friend.[2] Their father's seeming neglect did not cause his children to love him the less. One and all were devoted to him, as were also his nephews and nieces, and he warmly returned their affection. He was in fact a characteristic Cotton, like his Jacobite forebears, generous and warm-hearted to a fault. But while upholding the weak and oppressed, and spending time and money upon those unworthy his care, he was often unwittingly unmindful of the ones who had most claim on him. To please his daughters he built them a 'magnificent ball-room'; to please his parish he rebuilt the church; and to please his own love of beauty he decorated it with stained glass and ornaments which his neighbours thought popish.[3] His house was crowded with works of art, pictures, furniture, china, bronzes, books; but his son's careers were left to the guidance of his sister Mrs. Houblon, while an ominous silence respecting his disordered affairs filled them all with uneasiness and anxiety.

[1] More than once a set of shirts cost the squire £35.
[2] *Navy Chronicle*, No. 162.
[3] See Cole's MS.

'GENTLEMEN OF THE MILITIA' 165

In a letter dated from Copped Hall, and written by Mrs. Conyers, we have come across a reference to a family gathering in the year 1776. Speaking of Sir John's eldest son, lately staying there, she says : 'Mr. Cotton is gone to see his whole kith and kin assembled together at Hollingbury.'[1] But in a short time this happy circle was broken up and scattered. Lady Mary Archer's death this same year was the first of many griefs which entailed far-reaching changes in the family, while not long after, John Hynde Cotton himself lost his life by the accidental discharge of his gun while shooting in Madingley Park. Mr. Archer greatly missed the influence of his wife; so much so that he made a foolish marriage scarcely two years after her loss. He had already embarrassed his estates, and they were still further encumbered by the demands now made upon him by the 'expenses of a young wife and extravagant brother-in-law.'[2] His proceedings alienated his daughters' affection; Susanna was proud, and greatly mortified by her father's behaviour, while Charlotte soon left him and joined her sister at Hallingbury. Under these circumstances we hear first of his anger against them, then of his grief, and 'even tears when speaking of their neglect.'[3]

That Mr. Archer's life from this time forward was controlled by some sinister influence seems certain. It was not that of the young wife, who seems also to have suffered from it, and who after a short unhappy married life abandoned her husband altogether. No divorce followed, though a long lawsuit resulted from her brother's claim to the whole contents of the house at Bath they had occupied, and which he declared had been given to his sister by her husband. A curious outcome of this lawsuit, ultimately given in Mr. Archer's favour,

1776

[1] It is pronounced thus.
[2] Letter from Mr. Bamber Gascoyne.   [3] *Ibid.*

was that the contents of this house, in which was much plate, the family jewels, and Mr. Archer's wardrobe, was delivered up to the lawyers, packed in boxes and deposited by them in Coopersale House, which mansion had been shut up by its owner since Lady Mary Archer's death. With the exception of her diamonds, which Mr. Archer gave to his daughters, everything remained there packed up, for thirty years. Without such a strange chapter of accidents, an eighteenth-century gentleman's wardrobe complete in every respect would hardly have been handed down in the perfect condition in which it was found by his great-grandson, and in which it exists to this day. Some idea may be gained of its luxury by the lists of Jacob Houblon's clothes in a former chapter, though the gorgeousness of Mr. Archer's small person—as displayed in the famous Pump Room at Bath—must even have surpassed that of his son-in-law in his early youth. Such beautiful stuffs are not to be seen nowadays except in museums or in cherished morsels—relics of past splendours of our great-grandmothers' Court plumage! Nothing is wanting, from dress suits to scarlet hunting frocks and embroidered dressing jacket; not forgetting the huge silver-mounted spectacles from the depths of a pocket, and the favourite gold-topped malacca cane engraved with the owner's initials.

1775   Some letters written by Charles Cotton (then a lieutenant in the Navy) to his cousin, Laetitia Houblon, during the war in America are at Hallingbury, and, until the intervention of the French in the quarrel, are very illustrative of the lack of energy with which it was carried on. He talks of 'Rebells,' it is true, but during the intervals of fighting an excellent understanding subsisted between the belligerents; the former 'behaving exceeding polite and not disturbing us
1776 the least, while we passed as pleasant a time as our situation would admit of.' Under 'their heaven-born

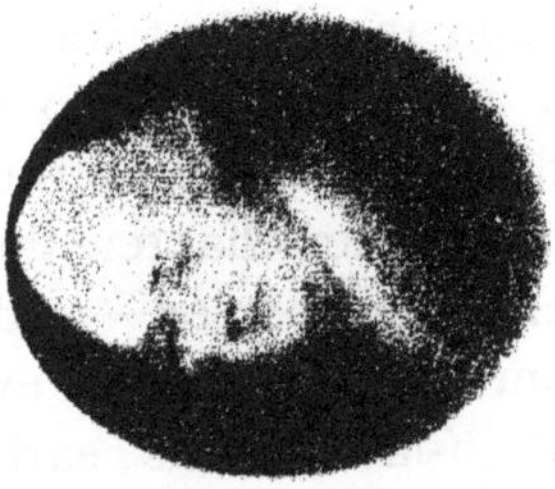

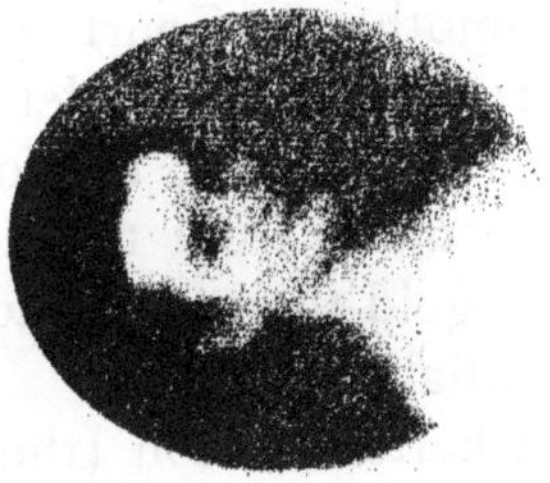

was that the contents of this house, in which was much plate, the family jewels, and Mr. Archer's wardrobe, was delivered up to the lawyers, packed in boxes and deposited by them in Coopersale House, which mansion had been shut up by its owner since Lady Mary Archer's death. With the exception of her diamonds, which Mr. Archer gave to his daughters, everything remained there packed up, for thirty years. Without such a strange chapter of accidents, an eighteenth-century gentleman's wardrobe complete in every respect would hardly have been handed down in the perfect condition in which it was found by his great-grandson, and in which it exists to this day. Some idea may be gained of its luxury by the lists of Jacob Houblon's clothes in a former chapter, though the gorgeousness of Mr. Archer's small person—as displayed in the famous Pump Room at Bath—must even have surpassed that of his son-in-law in his early youth. Such beautiful stuffs are not to be seen nowadays except in museums or in cherished morsels—relics of past splendours of our great-grandmothers' Court plumage! Nothing is wanting, from dress suits to scarlet hunting frocks and embroidered dressing jacket; not forgetting the huge silver-mounted spectacles from the depths of a pocket, and the favourite gold-topped malacca cane engraved with the owner's initials.

1775 Some letters written by Charles Cotton (then a lieutenant in the Navy) to his cousin, Laetitia Houblon, during the war in America are at Hallingbury, and, until the intervention of the French in the quarrel, are very illustrative of the lack of energy with which it was carried on. He talks of 'Rebells,' it is true, but during the intervals of fighting an excellent understanding subsisted between the belligerents; the former 'behaving exceeding polite and not disturbing us
1776 the least, while we passed as pleasant a time as our situation would admit of.' Under 'their heaven-born

Susanna and Jacob Houblon. 2

'GENTLEMEN OF THE MILITIA' 167

general,' as Cotton calls Washington, the Americans were determined and united, but they appear to have cherished no animus against the mother-country, looking on the war from the first as the 'King's war.' On the arrival on the scene of the French squadron under Count d'Estaing, however, all was changed. 'He has blocked this Port up for ten days and disgraced the British Flag vainly imagined Mistress of the Ocean,' bewailed Captain Cotton;[1] 'and as to the Americans, you may easily suppose how they are exulting, on the appearance of their trade being open'd by so formidable a Fleet, and their receiving an Embassy from the grand Monarque!'

1777

Captain Cotton's subsequent hopes of 'giving some account' of the French fleet were disappointed, for D'Estaing's orders were such as to debar the British from the chance of a pitched battle;[2] but in the moral support he gave the States of America he had already accomplished the object for which he came, without risk of loss in ships and men. The disastrous effect of the American policy of King George's Government was now apparent, and Great Britain awoke to a full sense of the crisis, for her forces were at the seat of the war, and, as has always been the case in face of a quarrel with France, the question of invasion once more assumed a threatening aspect in men's minds. But in France there was jubilation! D'Estaing was the hero of the hour, and that weathercock of French sentiment, the *toilette des dames*, reflected the pride of Parisiennes at having worsted *la perfide Albion* on her native element. Queen Marie Antoinette crowned her stately head a yard high with emblems of victory; frigates in full sail nestled in the powdered pates of great ladies, and everything *Américaine* or *à l'Estaing* that could be put on and worn was the supreme mode.[3] At home confidence soon

[1] He was posted to the *Boyne* in 1777.—*Dictionary of National Biography*.
[2] Captain Mahan, *Influence of Sea Power*.
[3] Racinet, *Le costume historique*.

returned; the Militia was called out and assembled in the several counties in March.[1]

Various letters addressed to Jacob₄ Houblon and his brother after they had joined their regiment—the Herts Militia—are strong evidence not only of the tenseness of the public anxiety, but also of the deep relief which filled all hearts at the prompt response of the counties to the call to arms, and this for the second time in the space of twenty years. The squire and his family were in London when the regiments were called out, and Jacob's sudden departure with his brother left his wife very low and miserable. That her sister had for some time made her home with the Houblons, probably greatly relieved the squire's mind, for not only was Susanna expecting another child, but she had been fretting greatly over the estrangement from her father, and the strange alteration in his character and habits. Indeed the excitement and alarm everywhere exhibited, together with grief and annoyance, were too much for poor Susanna, and very soon after the squire's departure, Charlotte wrote to him announcing a 'mishap' which had occurred. Her entreaties that he would at once come to her sister were not likely to have been complied with; for other letters show the bustle and business at the camp at Cocksheath to have been very great. Susanna's anxiety that her husband should not attribute what had occurred to any neglect on her part leads one to

CHARLOTTE ARCHER.

[1] *Annual Register*, 1778, p. 173.

think that her naturally quick temper and wilful disposition had not met the change in their circumstances with overmuch philosophy! Indeed the good-tempered Charlotte, while confusedly urging the squire's return, assuring him her sister was 'pure well' and generally making excuses all round, attributes all misfortunes to 'the vast depression of spirits' Susanna had laboured under, and 'which you yourself have been a frequent witness of.'

Mrs. Houblon appears to have soon recovered her health and spirits, and the following month we hear of her and Charlotte visiting the camp at Cocksheath, which seems to have attracted a large number of visitors and spectators to view it, and to witness the exercises and field-days with the troops, of which some 15,000 were encamped there. An almost childish pleasure in the military exhibition furnished by the numerous camps planted about the country, had succeeded the general alarm, and as the royal family made progresses for the purpose of inspecting them, and possessed then the same love of military pageants and uniforms as it does to this day, it followed that martial ardour filled every bosom.[1]

Situated near Maidstone, many officers took houses in the neighbourhood of Cocksheath for their families. Amongst these was the Conyers family of Copped Hall, Essex, and an amusing journal kept by the youthful Juliana gives a naïve account of her visits to the camp. The honours of the militia regiments were done by the wives of their officers; and we hear of Lady Cranborne's 'receptions' in the tent of the Colonel of the Herts—Lord Cranborne, and how the ladies of the county 'drank tea' there. On a certain occasion when Mrs. Houblon and Charlotte

[1] We have found formidable bills for regimentals and accoutrements of this date.

Archer 'drank tea' in the camp, little Juliana Conyers (who was there with her mother, Lady Henrietta) describes with much delight a review or field-day which they witnessed; whereat 'the sun shone and made a fine appearance upon the *Armor*. It was the prettiest sight she ever saw! They had a mock fight amongst the bushes, bush fighting. They fired cannon and guns, and played music most delightfully.' A few days later the camp was visited by the King and Queen, and a little unofficial note from General Keppel still remains among Major Houblon's papers, begging him to deliver two letters to the Colonel and Lady Cranborne announcing their coming. The latter being expected to wait on the Queen, a separate tent was made ready for her Majesty and the Princesses.

Henceforth, all business matters of the Houblon brothers were set aside for the one absorbing occupation of military duty, and to the purpose of working up the regiment to the highest point of efficiency.[1] How earnestly both laboured to this end is amply shown in letters and papers remaining of this period, and this in spite of an unusual amount of other business pressing upon the squire of various kinds; but lawyers and attorneys, estate-agents and bailiffs, had to travel to the camps to report business, and receive instructions from England's country gentlemen in the early days of the embodiment!

Smallpox was raging at this time, and people were now very generally having themselves and their children inoculated. Severe as the results of this operation were, it was regarded as an 'inestimable boon to mankind,' so dreaded was the disease. Through a letter from Lord Oxford to their father, we find that Jacob Houblon's little children underwent this ordeal in 1778.

[1] The old Herts Militia is now the First Battalion of the Bedfordshire Regiment.

'GENTLEMEN OF THE MILITIA'

In the same letter, in which Lord Oxford congratulates the squire and his niece on the 'recovery of their little family from the small pox,' he goes on to express what we have already noticed, viz. the gratitude of all classes to the militia. 'We often thought of you and Mrs. Houblon at Eywood,[1] as well as Miss Archer, during the summer, and are sorry for so long an absence as you have had from so fine a place as Hallingbury. The Nation, I am certain, is indebted to you and to the rest of the Gentlemen of the Militia, for standing out so nobly in its defence. It is an honor to you as well as a real service at this time to the Kingdom. His Majesty (Lord Oxford was Lord of the Bed-chamber to George III.) is sensible of it. I hope the people are so also.'[2]

JOHN₆.

Not only the Houblons, but the Cotton family experienced a great loss the following year by the death of the elder Mrs. Houblon at the age of sixty-three. On Mr. Wogan's death, which took place in 1778, and the removal of his widow and Mrs. Sancroft to Tunbridge Wells, Mrs. Houblon and Laetitia had left Stoke House, and taken possession of Thremhall Priory. Writing to Sir John Cotton in April this year from the seat of the war, Charles Cotton speaks with pleasure of this change, which he well knew would be agreeable

LAETITIA₂.

[1] His seat.
[2] Lord Oxford when Lord Harley, 11 July 1751, married Susanna, daughter of William Archer, Esq., of Welford. He succeeded as fourth earl, April 1755, and died 8 October 1790. Lady Oxford ob. 10 November 1804.

172   THE HOUBLON FAMILY

to his aunt and cousin, and in the same letter refers to both her sons—the Mr. Houblons—being with their regiment. Her new abode was not to be long enjoyed, for Mrs. Houblon died on the 19th of May 1779. A curious little incident shows her political sympathies to have been unchanged from those of her early youth. The draft for her will, drawn up in 1776, bears a seal, on which the head of poor Prince Charlie is engraved.

A quaint relic of family history is now in the possession of the descendant of a relation of both Cottons and Houblons. Originally the property of Mrs. Mary Houblon, it was subsequently given by a member of the family—probably by Laetitia—to the granddaughter of Lady St. John, who had been so dear a friend to all the cousinhood. It is a small gold box or bonbonnière, encircled with rows of alternate rubies, diamonds, and emeralds, between which its owner had caused to be engraved the names, and dates of the decease, of those most dear to her. The first name in order of date is that of 'Sir John Hynde Cotton, Bart., Ob. 4 Feb: 1752,' her father. Next, that of the 'R^t Honble. Lady St. John, Ob. 17 Nov: 1769,' her cousin. Next, that of her husband, 'Jacob Houblon, Esqr, Obit 15 Feb. 1770, aged 60,' also the names of two cousins, Philippa and Ann Walton. The next name was probably added by Laetitia Houblon, for it was her own: 'Mary Houblon, Obit 19 May 1779, aged 63.' Two more names follow only too soon. They were those of her two sons, Jacob$_4$ and John$_5$ Houblon, who died within a few months of each other in 1783. On the lid of this jewelled box is a 'landscape worked in hair.'

The squire's regiment was chiefly stationed at Hertford during 1779 and the following two years, and communication between him and his family was thereby greatly facilitated. Writing from Hallingbury to her father, little Maria Houblon, now about eight years old,

'GENTLEMEN OF THE MILITIA' 173

speaks of his expected arrival there, where Lord Cranborne was awaiting him. For some reason or other he did not arrive. 'Dear Papa, Mama would have met you herself, but did not know what time. We could not send the post chaise because Lord Cranborne had broke the springs.' In view of the durability of eighteenth-century vehicles, we surmise Lord Cranborne to have been no slight weight!

Meanwhile Susanna and her sister Charlotte, together with other ladies whose husbands and brothers were tied to the camps and depôts by their martial duties, attended military balls and assemblies in the winter, as well as field-days and tea-drinkings in the summer. As it is typical of many another function of the same nature, we give young Mrs. Houblon's very feminine account of a regimental ball at Hertford (the present headquarters of her husband's regiment), which took place on the 21st of January 1780. Accompanied by Miss Archer, she drove over from Hallingbury in her coach, having previously engaged a lodging for the night in the town.

MARIA.

> 'Account of a Ball given by the (then) Lord Cranborne[1] at the Town Hall at Hartford.
>
> *January* 21, 1780.
>
> 'Arrived about 20 minutes past one at a very comfortable Lodging at Hartford. Found Mr. Lacey ready to dress our hair. Miss Savage and Mr J. Lipyeatt jun^r arrived ab^t 3 q^{rs} after us.
>
> 'We dress'd and dined very comfortably—(Mr H. etc. at the Mess room). Soon after 6 by desire of Lady

1780

---

[1] As colonel of the Herts Regiment.

Cranborne we went to the Town Hall, where we found her Lady[sp] and Lady Anne Cecil, and two or three more Ladies; and some gentlemen of our Corps, with M[r] Lambard of the West Kent, soon joined us. About eight the room began to fill, and before ten made a very gay appearance. The whole county were invited. All the Ladies appear'd to have exerted themselves to the utmost, and the powers of fancy and labours of the toilet were evidently display'd; tho' it must be own'd in different ways. Variety is always charming, and here it was seen in perfection.

'Some few were dress'd with that neat elegant simplicity that surpasses every distinguishing ornament, and must at least pass uncensured, as it is unstudied. Some were gayly apparelled, but with taste and elegance. But more had called every flower, ribbon, and feather to their aid! And yet it is most probable that among all this motley crew none had the least idea that they were not well dress'd! As to the gentlemen, they were, I believe, all very properly dress'd. The 18 of our Regiment who were there could not be otherwise; and all others who had a right to regimentals wore them, not excepting Lady Cranborne herself, who had on a gown of scarlet sattin with buff ornaments. On her head she wore a Devonshire Hatt, turned up before with a cockade and diamond button and loop, with several scarlet and Buff feathers. Her dress and her affability became her so much, that everybody admired her. The supper was exceedingly elegant and well conducted, and Lord and Lady Cranborne were most remarkably civil and obliging to everybody.

'The minuets were began at one end of the room by Lord C. and Lady Shelburne, and at the other by Major Houblon and Lady Cranborne. *Mem^d*: My Dress was a new polonese of dove colour'd sattin trim'd with ermine; apron, etc. etc. of Brussels Lace, pink

'GENTLEMEN OF THE MILITIA' 175

ribbon bows and diamonds . . . Lady C. went up next day to the Opera, and we return'd to a late dinner at H. Place. I danc'd the two first country dances with Mr Lambard. The two second with Lord Cranborne, and one after supper with Mr Altham. There were two sets; chang'd partners every two dances.'

Scarcely five months later the scene was changed to Hyde Park, and the Herts Militia was engaged in helping to restore order for the much-perturbed Londoners, frightened to death by the famous Lord George Gordon Riots. There had been signs of discontent in many quarters with regard to the act recently passed for relieving the Roman Catholics from the many disabilities with which they were encumbered. Though they had long been law-abiding and patient under these heavy disadvantages, so deep was the mistrust that still obtained towards the Roman Church, that any measures for their relief brought to the surface slumbering animosity and fear. Possibly these may not have taken shape in violent action, but that the more turbulent among the party found a leader in Lord George Gordon, a fanatic well fitted to lead such men as they. The George Gordon Riots were long remembered as among the worst that ever disgraced London, for so great was the paralysis of fear everywhere exhibited, that for some days the mob had its own way to such an extent, that Roman Catholic houses and chapels were burnt and sacked almost unchecked. Meanwhile amongst the regiments hastily ordered to town was the Herts Militia, and by the 5th of June the Houblon brothers were encamped in Hyde Park, having marched that day from Whitechapel. It had been an unprecedentedly wet spring, and the summer was as wet. A long bill of the upholsterer, William Gates, gives a dismal picture of wet tents, bedding, and other paraphernalia, spread out to dry before the tents were pitched, and all 'the things' brought up to the camp. Two days later, so wet was it still, that the tents were struck and a floor laid down in the major's marquee before it was pitched again. It is notable that all this tent-pitching, and carriage from one camp to another, was done by workmen of an ordinary London upholsterer, and paid for by the officers. Meanwhile there was plenty of time for the Herts Militia to expend its efforts towards making itself comfortable in Hyde Park. The rain which flooded the camp was also some deterrent to the ardour of the mob, which was perhaps fortunate; for the authorities, mindful of the anger displayed when they had summarily dealt with the Wilkes rioters, were fearful of using the troops, and they remained in camp. 'Black Wednesday' thus came and went. Newgate was burnt and the criminals there released, and the Bank of England was actually in danger before the soldiers were allowed to charge and disperse the mob. The troops remained in Hyde Park till near the end of July, when all fear of disturbances was at an end.[1]

1781-2 Between January 1781 and June the following year the main part of the Herts Regiment was stationed at Hertford; companies being also at Hatfield, Welwyn, Ware, and Hoddesden. Amongst Major Houblon's papers is a long letter from one of the captains—Lord Fairford—proposing a plan by which those officers stationed at Hertford should lodge at the Castle, which was his property. This plan was carried out accordingly, and we find by his account-book that the senior captain, John Houblon, managed the accounts of their mess; and from various private letters addressed to both brothers, it would appear to have been a most harmonious party. Some of these letters exhibit the warmest affection and confidence towards both Houblons.

[1] See interesting account of the Gordon Riots, Lecky's *History*, vol. iii.

JOHN₅ HOUBLON.

'GENTLEMEN OF THE MILITIA'

Colonel Lord Cranborne had now succeeded his father as Earl of Salisbury.

We give the names of this little group of officers, viz. :—

Lord Salisbury, Colonel.   Sir Richard Chase, Major.
Jacob Houblon, Major.   John Houblon, Captain.
Lord Fairford, Captain.   Westrope, Captain.
Garrard and Johnson ditto.
Watson, Ellis, Wilcock, Gibb, Willis, and Williams, subalterns.

The militia was disembodied in November 1782, and to the intense relief of all who had been so long away from hearth and home, the long four years of service came to an end. For some time John$_5$ Houblon had been in failing health. We hear of his suffering greatly from his feet; he went more than once to Bath in hopes of alleviation, and at one time got much better; but unfortunately he appears to have been a somewhat heavy drinker. A very general favourite in his regiment, he was lively and amusing, very kind-hearted, besides being a well-read man with many interests out of the common run. That his study of astrology, at this time very popular, militated against his happiness and that of those dearest to him is likely, for so strong was the belief in planetary influence, that men's lives and destinies were often fatally clouded and controlled by the drawing of their horoscopes even by some smatterer in the art. By the linking of the fates of two persons born under the conjunction of certain planets, for instance, the adverse fate of the one might—it was believed—entail a similar misfortune to the other. It is a fact that misfortunes frequently followed the very fears which gave birth to them. Such is the credulity of man and such the weight of the chain with which he binds himself even to this day.

John and his brother were scarcely ever parted throughout their lives. After their father's death his younger son still made his home at Hallingbury, and many are the messages and questions about 'Johnny' in letters addressed to the family home. Among his papers we found two bills paid but very shortly before his death. They are both characteristic of his idiosyncrasies: the one is a long list of books, purchased or bound, from the bookseller Bathurst; the other the account of an apothecary at Bath, where the poor fellow had had a severe illness. Whether his death was occasioned by the disease from which he suffered or by the drastic remedies applied, according to the custom of the day, may be a matter of doubt; for, during the short space of eight days, forty-seven 'draughts' at one shilling and sixpence apiece, were absorbed by the unlucky invalid. Jacob Houblon travelled to Bath in June and brought his brother home; but he died on the 13th of July and was buried at Hallingbury. A neighbour and brother-officer—Sir Richard Chase, in writing to the squire, speaks of him thus: 'In the meantime accept my condolence for the loss of a worthy man *without guile*. At this moment, frugal as I am of Tears, a tribute of one drops to his memory. The concern I have felt for the repeated loss of my friends round this neighbourhood, having almost dried up the fountain.'

Laetitia Houblon's happiness at finding herself once more settled close to her old home, and at the return there of the squire and his family after the war, was quickly marred by the death of John, followed but a few months later by that of the squire himself. John$_5$ died at the age of forty-three; but while he had been an occasional 'martyr to the gout,' Jacob$_4$ was a strong and healthy man, and had never been ill or suffering in his life till death overtook him at forty-seven; and for the second time in the history of the Houblon family, it was reduced

'GENTLEMEN OF THE MILITIA' 179

in the male line to one small boy of under ten years old.[1]

Singularly lonely and desolate was now the poor young widow Susanna Houblon, her married life having lasted but thirteen years. Estranged from her father, she had nobody to turn to for help and advice, when, unacquainted with business, she found herself all at once face to face with the whole mass of her husband's affairs, and of a very serious and depressed condition which had affected the whole community. The late war and what it entailed in the way of expense had also for the time burdened the family fortunes very considerably. Not only had the militia officers given their time, but their expenditure had been very heavy, for on them fell a large amount of the burden attendant on the embodiment, and the squire had found it necessary to borrow money to meet the initial expenses in 1778. Fortunately the close of the war brought about the return home of one who was henceforth to be a true friend and unselfish adviser to the Houblon family, till little John$_6$ grew up and was able to take his affairs into his own hands. Failing any testamentary disposition by the squire (who died before making the change in his will necessitated by his brother's death), Captain Charles Cotton, R.N., was appointed 'Receiver' for his estates by the Court of Chancery and guardian to his little heir. Cotton had been appointed to H.M.S. *Alarm* in April 1781, which, ordered to the West Indies, was one of the repeating frigates in the memorable victory of Rodney in July that year over the French fleet, and De Grasse. At the peace the *Alarm* returned to England, where she was paid off. Till the year 1793, when he was appointed to the *Majestic* for service in the Channel Fleet, Captain Cotton saw no service; he was thus at liberty to devote himself to the work which

[1] Jacob's only son, John$_6$, was born 1 December 1773.

devolved on him by appointment of the Court of Chancery.

Under the entry of the squire's name in the burial register of Great Hallingbury Church, its rector wrote with a heavy heart:

'Quis desiderio sit pudor aut modus
Tam chari capites?[1] . . .

---

[1] Another rector has thus translated it:
'What limit shall any sense of self-control
Impose upon our grief, at the loss of one so dear?'

CHAPTER VII

LAETITIA

'Philip, whom have we here?' 'A good maid, sir; neither old nor young.'—ANONYMOUS.

THEIR residence of several years at Stoke House, near Plymouth, had kept Laetitia Houblon and her mother in constant touch with Charles Cotton and his naval contemporaries. They had many mutual acquaintances, and frequent references in letters and journals of after years, show that the vivacity and good temper which had made Miss Laetitia so great a favourite, were not forgotten in the service.

After Mrs. Houblon's death her daughter continued to live quietly at Thremhall Priory for some years. The many sorrows and losses she had sustained, for the time subdued her naturally joyous disposition, but her warm heart, ever seeking for objects upon which to lavish devotion and service, more and more fixed itself upon the nephew and nieces, who with their mother were now all that were left of the Houblon family. Susanna's cold nature melted before the onslaught of affection lavished on her brother's widow and children by the hungry heart of the lonely Laetitia, for though possessed of endless friends, her brothers had been the central thought of her life.

No longer young, Laetitia retained many elements of youth, while enthusiasm and a strong imagination led her to see nought in those she loved but the qualities she most desired should distinguish them. As Mrs. Houblon's disposition led her in a somewhat opposite direction, the friendship was advantageous to both. Soon after Captain Cotton was appointed Receiver to the estates of the late squire, the little heir, John Houblon, was sent to the Charterhouse, where we may still see his name deep cut on the keystone of the ancient arch, which was carried with it by the great old foundation when it migrated to the country some years since. Meanwhile Hallingbury was let to Lord Mountstuart[1] for three years on a lease which was subsequently renewed, and in 1786 the rents in the Essex and Herts estates were raised.

1784

1787 In the year 1787 Miss Laetitia Houblon came to the momentous decision to go abroad. She consequently let Thremhall Priory to Captain Vachel, placed all her affairs in the hands of the kindly sailor cousin—whose good sense and clear head had already been brought to bear with advantage upon the business concerns of the family—and packing up her belongings she departed. This decision might never have been arrived at but for the kindness of heart which always characterised Laetitia. Miss E. Watson, whose family was connected with her own,[2] was in delicate health. English people were already in the habit of flying southward for sunshine and health, and Miss Houblon offered to take the young lady abroad. Spinsters of her years in those days occasionally assumed the title of Mrs., and she gave directions that her letters should be addressed as Madame L. Houblon, *Dame Angloise*. Beginning with a cousinly feeling in respect of each other, the sentiment between the travelling companions gradually ripened during their sojourn abroad into the 'tenderest attachment.' As the elder lady possessed the happy faculty of quickly adding

[1] Born 1744. Eldest son of the third Earl of Bute (the statesman).
[2] Watson of West Wratting Park, Cambs.

to her already large circle of acquaintance, and was also an excellent linguist, it followed that the pair enjoyed themselves greatly. Needless to say that from the day of her departure, accompanied by Miss Betsy and attended by Ovington and Nobe Northey, her man and maid, as well as a courier, Miss Houblon kept a diary. They travelled in her own coach, fitted as was customary with every convenience, and built with an eye to durability and resistance to an ordeal of wear and tear such as no modern vehicle could bear. Miss Houblon's diary included her current cash expenditure, and it, together with her letters to her sister-in-law, make an exceedingly entertaining narrative, longer extracts from which we would fain have transcribed. 'My first writing from France is justly your due,' she wrote to Mrs. Houblon after landing at Boulogne from a stormy sea,— 'My heart indeed asserts the truth of Solomon's saying, "*many waters* cannot drown love!" and I add, neither can sea-sickness put you and your dear children out of my mind!'

Joseph Dombrey, the courier who had met them at Dover, was engaged at £60 wages per annum, and apparently proved himself very satisfactory to his mistress, as she kept him for two years in her service. That he was a good courier as couriers went then, is probable, for no less a person than the 'Traveller and Historiographer,' Sir Nathaniel Wraxall, approved him as 'parfaitement au fait de son métier.' This gentleman, as he records in his *Posthumous Memoirs*, 'passed part of this Autumn in Paris,' and was the fellow-traveller of our two ladies on the first part of their journey. They crossed the Channel together, and were apparently mutually pleased with each other's agreeable society. 'Our sorrow at parting with M[r] Wraxall quite astonished myself,' wrote Miss Laetitia, 'tho' no more than due for the kindness and civility He showed us. When he left us in the Coach, we seemed turned quite desolate into a strange country unprotected! Most fortunately we have wanted him in nothing but His agreeable and instructive conversation. His extensive knowledge and willingness to communicate, makes Him the best of travelling companions.' Doubtless the gentleman himself enjoyed holding forth to so keen and intelligent a listener. Letters were afterwards exchanged, and one from Paris gave Miss Houblon full directions as to what she was to see and admire at the various places they were about to visit on their way to Nice, their destination for the winter. Meanwhile materials for his *Memoirs* were being gleaned in Paris, where, in his own pompous words, ' the utmost effervescence, not unmixed with gloomy apprehensions of futurity, began already to diffuse their influence over society.'[1]

Miss Laetitia appears to have been a good exponent of advanced eighteenth-century female education. In a day when a vast number of fashionable women were at once coarse in mind and ignorant, the elder squire, her father, had been fully alive to a much neglected duty; for while sparing no pains in the education of his sons, his daughter came in for her full share of culture and advantage. Had she been possessed of more pretension she would probably have belonged to the Bluestocking Club,[2] for many were her interests and accomplishments. While possessing both the wit and 'sensibility' to steer clear between the coarseness and freedom of the earlier years of the century, and the sillier if more refined characteristics of the typical female of the latter portion of it, she was yet no prude. Her strong sense of right and the religious bias inherited from her forefathers were never lost sight of; and though wit and power of repartee were undoubtedly great, had she ever indulged in

[1] See Sir N. W. Wraxall, Bart., M.P., *Posthumous Memoirs of My Own Time*, v. 38. Ed. Wheatley, 1884.
[2] See Lecky, *History*, vi. 166.

them ill-naturedly she would not have been as popular as she undoubtedly was with both sexes. Beauty, in whatever form she found it, whether scenery, art, music, or people, captivated this cultured woman, whose chief charm would appear to have lain in the simple and unaffected enthusiasm and *verve* with which she went through life. Her sister-in-law writes apologetically of her *style* in her somewhat laboured epistles;—Laetitia begs her to be easy on that score; as to herself she had *no* style—had never pretended to any. The consequence is, that for the eighteenth century her letters are models of ease and charm. With so much intelligence and so keen a power of enjoyment, the journey just begun promised much, and the more so that sorrow and loneliness had for the time overshadowed a life that was made to be happy and full.

It took the ladies twelve days to reach Lyons. They had no adventures on the road. Highwaymen—still common in England—they apparently did not fear. The patrolling of the roads in France by the *Maréchaussée* rendered them much safer than at home, and they were probably reassured by Mr. Wraxall on this point, though they were anxious on another against which they had been warned, viz. possible wounding of their feelings of delicacy and even safety—in respect of impertinent fellow-travellers of the opposite sex at the inns and elsewhere. In one way alone, however, were the feelings of our ladies outraged during their wanderings in France and Italy; the most superb Greek or Roman statuary failed to excite any sentiments but disgust, nor did they attempt to overcome their sense of indelicacy in any representation of the undraped 'human form divine.' With respect to the dread of the ladies as to possible insult to their modesty while on their travels, it was at least very excusable. Even during the later years of the eighteenth century both at home and abroad, women had occasionally good reason to be afraid. The incidents related in contemporary novels are not representative of the impossible nor of a time gone by, but founded on actual occurrences in the life of the period. Miss Betsy's fears are often referred to in the letters and journals of her companion. Romantic and timid and with the smiles and easy tears of the *female* of late eighteenth-century date, she presents us with a type of which the novels of the Misses Ferrier and Edgeworth give us examples. As an 'elegant female' she was 'well-bred,' pretty, and perfectly amiable, while timidity was so much expected in a young lady of her rank and disposition, whether in the case of precipices or accident, insult or ill health, as to be regarded as a normal condition of mind. Needless to say, we see no expression of feebleness or fear on the part of Miss Laetitia. Belonging both in education and habit to an earlier date than her companion, she was made of a stuff wholly different, though sufficiently rare in her day for us to find few delineations of a similar character in contemporary writings.

Dombrey, the courier, as was customary, travelled on horseback and in advance of the coach, in order to ensure horses for the next stage being ready on its arrival, or to engage rooms at the inn if it was intended to remain the night. Upon the efforts of this functionary the comfort and convenience of the party depended especially when other travellers were also upon the road. For their immediate protection in case of emergency the ladies had Ovington, Miss Houblon's man, whose delight and wonder at his novel surroundings she describes as causing him to wear a 'perpetual grin.' The coach, drawn by four or six horses according to the condition of the roads, was roomy, and in it the ladies—as well as their maid—were apparently able to lie down; for prone in the vehicle (which was strapped to the deck of the packet) and grievously sick, they had crossed the Channel. Neither did they always leave it in order to dine in the middle of the day, an arrangement advised by some old travellers, which they found both saving of expense and time.

Could we afford the space, the account of the journey through France would be worth inserting here, but suffice it to say that their first stopping-place for more than one night was Lyons. Here, scarcely had the hastily summoned hairdresser 'drest their heads,' than introductory letters to Mr. Eynard (the English *Chargé d'Affaires*) and his wife, brought kindly people about them. Sights were seen, a silk manufactory explored, caps, silks, lawn and velvet purchased, followed by a visit to the opera and a ball. Lady Rivers, an old friend of Miss Houblon's, was there, also on her way to Nice, of which she was an *habituée*. After a somewhat adventurous journey from Lyons they travelled as far as Avignon by *bâteau de poste* on the Rhone, and in spite of broken bridges, floods, and bad roads, finally arrived at their destination—Nice, then part of the kingdom of Sardinia. Here, in the 'neatest tiny house you ever saw outside the town, combining the attractions of a lovely prospect, and a delightful garden, separated only by its wall from the Mediterranean, and in the enjoyment of agreeable society,' the ladies spent the next six months.

'Your welcome letter and every proof of your affection, is most dear to my heart,' wrote Miss Laetitia to her sister-in-law early in November. 'This indeed is a most pleasant place, it is astonishing how well I am, and the diversity of objects assists my endeavours to banish thought. The climate is heavenly, you would suppose it a fine May; strawberries, peas, etc., in bloom; a profusion of fruit on our table, and every kind of vegetable in perfection and excellent fish; we dined yesterday at

1787

188   THE HOUBLON FAMILY

Mrs. Penton's on a *Empereur* (Smollett will tell you of it). Veal we have none, but all other butcher's meat is very good, besides excellent game and poultry; so we need not starve. . . . An English frigate has just passed so near that with my glass I could see the men shifting her sails.'

Lady Rivers, who had preceded the ladies from Lyons, had announced their coming, and now made it her business to introduce them to all the 'best people,' both of the little côterie of English and the large and varied society comprising the resident 'Nissards' and many other visitors, both of French and Italian nationality. Rumours of Betsy Watson's pretty face had already been sounded from Lyons, where her fresh English complexion had gained her the title of '*la belle Angloise*.' At the house of a charming and hospitable old lady, Madame la Baronne Tondut, they first found a welcome. This lady was wont to have weekly assemblies, 'where all the first people and where we received a thousand civilities. I shan't be ruined by gaming, for I find they doubled the stake out of compliment to me at my table, and yet we played shilling whist. Most took Miss Betsy for my daughter. She flirted with Signor Grimaldi, the first grandee of this place. Lady Rivers introduces us.'

In a very short time the pair were in a whirl of gaiety and engagements. Their great popularity is evident. 'We dine out five days a week. English and Irish are very sociable, and the Nissards shew us a thousand attentions. The assemblies are very pleasant. *My bon ami* (for there's no living here without one) has taught me Reversis $\frac{1}{2}$ *sols* a fish; and I am already enriched very near threepence halfpenny English! But it is proper to introduce you to the man who attends me everywhere, takes my cloak, calls my carriage, and never suffers me to stir without His Hand; visits me every afternoon, unless he is on guard, and is, in short, the most obsequious of slaves. His name I can neither say nor spell, but he is a Saxon Baron; (of course he says related to me, tho' we must trace the parentage some Hundred years back). In the Sardinian Regiment; vastly agreeable, speaks most languages, English very tolerably; has read most of our best Authors; an Enthusiastick admirer of Milton and Pope; will talk for an hour of Tillotson, Blaire, and Sterne's sermons! Detests Paint and Papists (so, of course, I don't Rouge or go to Mass, tho' I hope soon to see a Nun professed).[1] As to your question about the French language, it is out of my power to answer it till we have been in Paris, for I suppose I have not heard a word of *good* French. I know I understand and make myself understood, and Here they speak no [other] language.' French was in fact then, as it remained till Bismarck broke its claims, the universal medium of communication between all nations, and Miss Laetitia spoke and wrote it with ease and idiom, while she was even among the earlier translators of French plays into English. But Miss Betsy was weak in French, and consequently conscientiously studied it with a master during her stay at Nice. This example of diligence was followed by the elder lady, but in respect of Italian, a favourite study with the more highly educated English women of the century, indeed Laetitia was already sufficiently acquainted with the language as to be able to enjoy the literature, to translate, and, as we now find, to understand *sermons!* The Italian friars were great preachers, and all, including English Protestants, flocked to hear them.

We have been told the supposed necessity for the

---

[1] As to the title of *bon ami*, here used in so different a sense to that in which it is now presented, it must be remembered that we are writing of some hundred and twenty years ago, and that both manners and modes of expression have greatly altered since then. For the rest—*Honi soit qui mal y pense.*

attendance of a *cavaliere servante* or *bon ami*, as the French called him; the gentleman who filled this position in the service of Miss Houblon was Baron von Feilitzsch. So accustomed were the ladies to his presence and to that of Miss Watson's attendant in the same capacity, that Laetitia's journals record their coming and going as 'B & C.' 'B' was the Baron, 'C' the English Consul, Mr. Green. The fair invalid had meanwhile much sympathy bestowed upon her. 'She could have had almost as many Nurses as there are gentlemen and Ladies in Nice,' writes her partial companion. 'They are all so captivated by Her Person and Manners. If it goes on I shall be sent home alone, unless my Baron can get leave of absence! But, joking apart, the English Consul's assiduities—if he has not adopted the mean-nothing manners of Italy—look more than those of a *bon ami*.[1] He seems very worthy.'

'I thank God for your spirits mending,' she wrote on Twelfth day to her sister in London. 'I banish retrospect as much as possible. Assisted by variety of objects and this heavenly climate, I have obtained an exemption from bodily ills; can scarcely believe that "I be I." My dear fellow-traveller is certainly much better; folk say she grows fat. This is a very busy time. We were obliged to visit and be visited by every one we knew on New Year's day. Nobody lets in; but you must go, so it is fine exercise for the servants (you would not know Ovington, he wears long Ruffles and learns French)—as many live up 4 pairs of stairs, and all the Rooms lofty. We dined at Sir W. Gordon's, and afterwards Baronne Tondut took us to the Commandant's who shams sick, so we had not the plague of seeing his ugly person. The Intendant is one of Betsy's *inamoratos* and the liveliest good old fellow possible, so we had half hour's laugh with Him, then paid our respects to

[1] The attentions of the latter were regarded as purely formal.

the Bishop, who is charming. I wish you could have seen the little man, with a broad red sash and cuffs of the same color to His black dress: fine lace and a magnificent cross round his neck. We are just come from the Cathedral where He celebrated high Mass, and afterwards preached an excellent sermon in Italian. Betsy says she is sure I shall be perverted, for I was attentive & pleased, altho' it lasted 32 minutes. But indeed there was not a word that the Bishop of London might not have said at St. Pauls; and He said he hoped to meet us all in Heaven! The dressing and undressing at the Altar is a droll part of the Mass. They put Him on nine fine things one after the other, then took them all off again. The last looked like a shirt that I expected to be obliged to hide my eyes, and that He would get cold.'

'So C. C. has fixed his affections!' she wrote soon after. 'It is where I always expected. God send him happy.[1] Fear money may be wanting. How generous the Empress behaves. Pray describe Miss Rowley.' Charles Cotton had just become engaged to Philadelphia, the lovely young daughter of Sir Joshua Rowley, Bart., and Sir John's income did not admit of his doing much towards the settlement of his eldest son. The 'Empress' alluded to as generous was the now venerable Mrs. Wogan his aunt, whose old-world etiquette and ceremony kept all younger than herself at a proper distance. It will be remembered that the family formerly lived at Thremhall Priory near Hallingbury. A keen Jacobite and aristocrat to the last, the 'Empress' dwelt on a pinnacle of her own building, looking at life and its changing scenes with amusement tinged with scorn. The daughter of a Sancroft and a Cotton, and married to a Wogan, she could have regarded it, as it now was, in no other way. Living at Tunbridge Wells

[1] Charles Cotton, R.N.

she watched the *beau monde* there during the season of water-drinking, and took the measure of those who went seeking for health, and those who only followed the fashion, while all alike sought excitement and amusement. The habit of keeping late hours was increasing, and 'the Quality,' of whom she related 'there were more than ever this year,' did not consider going to bed early as part of their cure. 'Among them,' she wrote, 'there are many flirtations, but no serious attachments. The plays have been greatly supported by y^e *Noblesse*, who bespeak them every night, & People think themselves oblig'd to attend them which spoils the Rooms; after which there are great suppers either at ye Tavern or at their Own Houses; where they stay till 3 or 4 in ye Morning. The Party consists of near 30, with ye Dutchess of Ancaster at their Head. She stays here a Month longer.' It is pathetic to find the leader of this gay band, less than two years after this time, consumptive and wasted at Nice! There, hours were still early, and life and its amusements simpler.

'Miss Fuller (who arrived at Nice in her own chaise some time since) is now greatly better,' wrote Miss Houblon. 'She is talked of for a French Chevalier, but here as everywhere else, you must marry all you speak with! Balls are begun, and very pretty they are. Betsy has danced at two without suffering from her side. I wish for my Nieces skipping on the brick floors! tho' I do not think this would be a proper place for young women to make their first début into the world. The men are too assiduous, and the women are too unprincipled. But there are some very estimable, and all have a good-humoured friendliness that is enchanting. We are certain we shall not like any other Italian society so well, therefore propose returning next winter. I have a box at the Opera, which is good. Lord Pembroke's Melocini is first dancer—wondrous heavy—but men say very handsome,—near. I must tell you a thing you would never suppose. My dress is the most admired in Nice! and I excel the Duchesse de Brissac and Prince Camill de Rohan's Madame (I forget her name) by an embroidery and grebbe[1] trimming on my black velvet. It is really handsome and sets off my best lace; for the Ruffles are so deep here, that they required very little turning in. A clever Milliner for 2 livres has made smart, neck fallals, and we are in love with the old Hair Dresser. He surpasses any I ever saw; makes us vast smart both, in half an hour. Feathers, Flowers, Ribbon, and gauze alternately ornament Betsy, and what delights me (tho' I look high frize) He has never curled but once, and I can comb it all thro' as if nothing was done! Desire Mrs Revel (Mrs. Houblon's abigail) to explain that, for we can't.

COIFFURE DE GRANDE PARURE (1786-1788).[2]

Paris did not at that time everywhere control the fashions, and when 'the daughters of the late Lord Mayor brought hats from Paris, they were the astonishment—not admiration, of all Nice.' Though the craze for modes à l'Américaine had passed by, the headgear of Marie Antoinette's Court had now reached the climax of absurdity, and was ripe for the change which

[1] Grebe, the water-bird. [2] See Racinet, *Costume Historique*, vol. vi.

she herself is said to have brought about in a single night. Women were wearing flower-gardens and farmyards on their heads, when Marie Antoinette appeared at the opera with the modest *coiffure* with which we are familiar in De la Roche's picture of the beautiful Queen in her sad day of humiliation. Frequent questions occur in Laetitia's letters with respect to London's prevailing fashions, especially with regard to hairdressing, which was still so elaborate as to be unattainable to the skill of the ordinary lady's maid. The local hairdresser therefore dressed the heads of our ladies when they went into society 'high frize.' Two years after this time a great alteration took place in women's dress very typical of the general change in thought brought about by the Great Revolution, and it was so much simpler in respect of coiffure, that we hear of Miss Houblon's maid habitually dressing her mistress's hair. 'I think I have craññed this sheet well,' she says at the close of a long letter, 'but I cannot stop when talking to you, tho' this is the worst place to write I ever knew, and proves that those who have nothing to do, are always the most employed.'

Meanwhile the assiduities of the Saxon Baron whose name she could neither speak nor spell—and no wonder, for it ended in five consonants—had continued unabated till, like those of Mr. Green the English Consul, they appeared to the busy-bodies of society as more than warranted by the duties of a *bon ami* or *cavaliere servente*. He was not young, and therefore had probably been regarded as suited to the service of the lady who had been so kindly welcomed at Nice by all the 'best people,' now watching for a possible *dénouement* with an amusement shared by the lady herself. Miss Houblon, though of the same frame of mind, had already unconsciously allowed 'my Baron' to occupy her thoughts and time more than she was aware of. It was perhaps not wonderful, for many records of this gentleman's amiability have come down to us, but being a woman of the world and wise enough to know its ways, she preserved both her dignity and the respect of the gay *monde* of Nice. Her sister-in-law at home joined in the banter. 'Write what you like to Baron de Feilitzsch,' she answered—'I defy you, for yesterday I was assured I received an unfailing proof of the sincerity of his attachment. It was not of the *most* pleasant kind. As it is a mode of tryal of which you perhaps, like me, had never heard,—shall disclose. On my asking him to draw a Card for me at Faro, one of our Grandees whispered Betsy: "Now we shall see if He loves her, for if he does she will lose." True enough I paid seven louis for the favor. Rather a dear bargain and a great reduction of my winnings.' In answer to a question as to Lord Landaff, who was also a constant attendant on Laetitia, and was then at Nice with his wife, she continues: 'Lord Landaff and I are very fond! Of course I don't like his lady, but I doubt he does, which is not gallant.' Lady Landaff had lately given a ball, 'where all the best company, sixteen couple of dancers, three rooms for cards, refreshments continually handed round but no supper.' One day Countess Cesole 'brought her three lovely girls who danced and sung and entertained us mightily.' A friendship was established with these children, and we shortly hear of her taking 'the little Cesoles' to the opera.

So permeated was the whole society with French thought and idiom, that it is impossible always to know if the people mentioned are Italian or French; for Nice was so near the French frontier that there were nearly as many French as Italian families in its neighbourhood. The difficulty is the greater, that the terminations of Italian names are frequently changed to French, or even translated. We hear, for instance, of a Marquis de Châteauneuf, but it is as likely that his real name and title was the Marchese Castelnovo. Oddly enough, the first time Miss Houblon met this gentleman, she wrote his name as Châteauvieux! He was evidently a local magnate or grandee, as she would have said; and we are later told of our ladies going to see his daughter's 'wedding cloaths; not the ones her father had provided, but those her fiancé the Comte de Villeneuve gives.' The Marchese took part at the New Year in a *quête* for the benefit of the local hospital, a custom which has continued to the present time in catholic countries, though the attendance of a gentleman on the begging party is now generally dispensed with. Not so the choice by the clergy or conventual authorities of the most beautiful or fashionable ladies at their disposal, as their envoys in soliciting alms. Possibly the peccadilloes of these ladies, rendered the work of love very remunerative to themselves, in the way of remission of coming years of purgatory. It is certain that fashion, beauty and high birth, continue to extract money even where it is grudged. 'The Marquis Châteauneuf,' writes Miss Laetitia, 'this day attended the beautiful Beggars Mesdames de Ramini and Verani, to collect for the Hospital; a sure method of receiving. Nobody gives less than a crown, so the sum must be great indeed, as they apply to every one. They made a short stay.'

1788   'On January 22 : Father Thomas came with the Baron and Consul to walk with us to Lady River's Hermitage. The Baron had split an artery(!) running to be ready to hand us out at the Baronne Tondut's the night before, yet lame as he was, he would assist me up a steep precipice which we were obliged to ascend, to a very neat Cottage, which commanded a most beautiful view of the Town, Harbor, Sea, Country Houses, Rocks, Mountains and gardens, all adorned with olive, orange, and almond trees in full bloom, and every ornament of the most luxuriant spring. Such the southern aspect now displays.' After a long climb they rested on the steps of a little chapel and ate oranges from a tree near by, then pursued their way by a sheep walk to the top of the hill. The descent was by a rugged path; truly a laborious afternoon for a man who had but the day before 'split an artery' handing a lady out of her carriage. Intelligent as she was, Miss Houblon's studies had not taken her into the domains of physiology, nor had the impertinence of quack advertisements enlightened her. Happy century! when ignorance was bliss, and saved many an excursion into as yet unknown and unsuspected ills of the flesh. Consumption and gout were sufficient woes for the time, outside the faculty.

'To Marquise Ferraro's ball. All the best Company in Most elegant apartments, detained us till near two in the morning.' This was a most unusual dissipation, for hours were early in Nice. 'I lost sixty-six fish at Reversis, and won four Crowns at Faro. Lord Maynard, who arrived the night before, appeared in a wondrous gold Coat. His Lady danced with the youngest till four in the morning.' Miss Betsy took a bad cold at this time; but unwilling to forgo the pleasures of society, she continued to attend balls, assemblies, and the opera, and receive friends at home, disregarding 'her painful state.' This went on till it was necessary for her 'to be blooded,' which operation apparently relieved her immediately, and the following day she and Miss Laetitia attended an assembly at the Countess Torrino's, where the latter 'lost seventy fish at Reversis but won twenty-nine Louis and three Crowns at Faro.' 1788

Playing day after day whether at whist, reversis or faro, Miss Houblon's gains and losses as recorded in her diary, appear to have for long pretty well balanced themselves; but she was proverbially lucky in most things, and in the end her winnings were considerable. The stakes at faro seem to have risen gradually during this winter at Nice. Players of whist and other games of skill were content with almost nominal stakes; not so at faro, for the delights of which the light-hearted, shrill-voiced company forsook the quiet tables. That it was not entirely a game of chance in the estimation of Miss Laetitia, we find by a lamentation after a faro party at the Countess Cesole's, where 'the ceaseless chatter of the Duchesse de Brissac had spoilt her play' and resulted in the loss of many louis d'or. The passion for faro in England had been immense; men and women alike frequently losing or winning hundreds in a night. 'Faro's Daughters'—three ladies of fashion —led the craze, which George the Third in vain tried to control; at Court it was not played, but elsewhere it had its way, for society was permeated with the spirit of gambling, a taste which the state had itself unwittingly fostered and encouraged by the public lotteries. Indeed, the cash account-books of the time record at regular intervals the purchase of lottery tickets, and Miss Laetitia's journals note several winnings; though usually these were few and far between; but, as we have already observed, she had a lucky hand, and when she left Nice in April, she relates with much satisfaction that her total gains amounted to seventy-two louis thirteen livres. It is amusing to find what 'Great George' failed to accomplish till fashion changed, the King of Sardinia succeeded in doing. So concerned was he at the growth of gambling at Nice, that he endeavoured to check it by an order which, though it was evaded at first, was obeyed in the end. Mrs. Houblon having caught the fever, wrote from England desiring her sister to venture a sum of money in play on her behalf, but Miss Laetitia replies jokingly : 'His Sardish Majesty,—who is much offended that you do not consider the poverty of His subjects but encourage them to gamble, orders me to inform you of an edict the very date of your letter, that if you presume to play at Faro or any game of chance : for the 1st offence you pay 100 Crowns : for the 2nd 300, and if you persist, a Convent receives you for life!'

'B & C and Father Thomas came to the Marquis de Châteauneuf's Champagne,'[1] she wrote in April, 'a terrible long way on foot. Count and Countess St. Tropice and Countess de Laval came thither on horseback.' For a delicate girl, abroad for her health, Miss Betsy's pedestrian performances were considerable. The two ladies, accompanied by their *bons amis* and frequently by the Baron's friend Father Thomas—an Irishman—took long walks in the neighbourhood of Nice. Baron von Feilitzsch shared Miss Houblon's enthusiastic love of nature, while he and the Consul were already well acquainted with the country around, then free from the encroachments of endless villas. Miss Laetitia's journal records many of these rambles, together with her delight at the beauty of the scenery and of the plants and flowers she met with. Things horticultural and botanical had long been a source of happiness to her, and she had a considerable knowledge of both. 'Vastly entertained,' she exclaims one day after the examination of 'an Horti-siccus at the Consul's, the work of a Botanist who had been 40 years collecting it on the Mountains between Nice and Turin.' Sometimes the Baron 'brought an Ass' to the little villa, on which Laetitia and Miss Betsy rode alternately ; but some of the French ladies at Nice habitually rode on horseback. 'Lounging rides' were considered in England as a self-indulgent pastime introduced from France,[2] and Burke thought men should make more use of their limbs than to 'saunter on horses.' Be that as it may, the Houblons had always been fond of riding,

1788

---

[1] Campagna—Country seat.
[2] See Lecky, *History of England*, vi. 153.

both as a means of locomotion and for pleasure only. Not only did Laetitia in her youth frequently follow the hounds, but her mother was accustomed to ride almost to the end of her life. A letter of her daughter recalls this fact, and that when 'she felt herself grow weak,' unwilling to give up the pleasure—'she took to a poney.' Ladies who were timid, 'rode double,' that is on a pillion. We should imagine that the agreeableness of this mode of exercise would have depended somewhat upon the other occupant of the horse's back, to whose waist the lady was forced to cling! Miss Charlotte Archer, in her solitude at Welford at this very time, was solacing her lonely hours in this manner. We believe she considered it conducive to the health of her liver; it led, however, to serious results to herself and others.

Much as Miss Laetitia loved flowers, she was subject to a weakness with regard to the scent of jonquils, which certainly was not affectation in one so robust in mind and body. Her journal records more than once her fear of these flowers; but on a certain occasion some jonquils at Mrs. Penton's 'affected' her. 'I immediately left the room,' she writes, 'but could not get downstairs. So was supported to Mr Green's (the Consul lodged in an apartment above) where I fainted repeatedly on the sopha. When a little better had the Chaise and came home. Miss E. W. as ill as I by the fright. B & C were so good as to come attempt Whist with us in the evening.' Next day: 'Lady Rivers hearing I was ill, came and sat an hour, which revived us a little. Took an airing, and met Mr Faraudi (the Apothecary) who was bringing me medicine by the Baron's desire. Some Julep revived me.' 'I paid my Apothecary's bill just now,' she wrote later to her sister-in-law, 'the enormous sum of 3 livres, and that I owe to Mrs Penton's jonquils. I suppose they are more powerful in this warm climate, for I never was ill a week with them before. I was mightily nursed and sent home in a few hours. I am quite stout again now, tho' I have not dared to go to an assembly since, but we shall to the Play this evening, where Betsy's Love the Intendant Général's box will contain us.'

This prejudice is rare among English people, but Italians to this day dread the supposed poisonous effects of flowers, said to be exuded at night. The author has known the time when the only flowers sold in Florence consisted of large flat nosegays of neatly wired camelias, in alternate rows of crimson and white, occasionally embellished with a pattern in the middle of purple pansies. These, fringed with cut paper, were sent (with billets-doux) to ladies on their fête-days,—they were scentless and wholesome! for the same reason the china rose was a favourite, indeed there were no other roses. Italy owes her glory of flowers (other than wild) to northern taste, not her own; and probably still cultivates them mainly for the same reason. Meanwhile Miss Laetitia's experience and Italian prejudice suggest the query. Did the jonquils affect her through her nose or through her mind? Perhaps, 'As a man thinketh in his heart; so is he.'

Mrs. Houblon and her daughters were now in London; the latter were considered as grown up, and were to be taken into society for the first time by their mother. A letter from Miss Archer comments upon the clothes they wore on the occasion of their presentation at Court, where all were received with flattering kindness by their Majesties. 'What joy,' wrote their other Aunt from Venice, 'to see the two dear *young Women* reflecting credit on their dear Mother!' Maria and Laetitia[2] Houblon, whose début was watched with so much interest by their two fond aunts, were in course of time to develop very opposite characteristics; but for the present both were equally dear, equally charming. No one remarked upon Maria's good looks, it is true; but Laetitia was decidedly pretty, and comments on her appearance were received with delight by her elder namesake abroad.

1788   April saw the departure of Miss Laetitia and Betsy from Nice after many P.P.C. adieus to their friends. Before leaving, Miss Houblon agreed with a gentleman for the hire of his villa for the following winter. Meanwhile they proposed travelling in Italy and spending the summer at the Lakes, a good friar having assured Miss Laetitia: 'Como in June was *nearly* heaven!' 'This trip,' writes Laetitia in joke to her faithful correspondent, 'will prove if I can do without my *bon ami*. If not I shall bring him with me, and expect Sir P. P.'—a home devotee of many years' standing—'not to give himself airs!'

Miss Houblon's letters home during her travels in Italy are both amusing and interesting. To her every difficulty and adventure came as an enjoyable experience, though bad roads and precipices still filled her companion with dismay, and Italian food with suspicion. They went by sea to Genoa, and then in their coach to Venice, where a delightful fortnight was spent. They witnessed the famous ceremony of the wedding of the Adriatic by the Doge in all its magnificence, and together with Lord and Lady Grey[1] (who had preceded them from Nice) went into Venetian society and received much kindness. From Venice Miss Laetitia wrote, telling of the 'melancholy parting' at Nice between her young companion and the Consul: 'There is a serious *secret* attachment. If it *can* be I shall be pleased, if not it is a pity.' From Venice they proceeded to Milan, and we hear much of all they saw there and of the agreeable people they met. In the present instance

[1] Baron Grey de Wilton, cr. 1784, extinct 1814 (Egerton).

LAETITIA 203

Miss Houblon had an introduction to a wholly different society from the usual circle visited by the *Corps diplomatique*. This was through the auspices of a kind ' learned man ' at Nice, who gave her letters to certain of his own *confrères* in the domains of literature, science, and art. Among these gentlemen was the Abbé Amoretti, a distinguished Italian geographer and naturalist,[1] who was also Keeper of the Ambrosian Library, where he had 'an handsome apartment.'[2] Extremely occupied, the worthy Abbé at first found it impossible to attend to the ladies; so they went on an expedition to Pavia, leaving the servants and the dog ' Ran ' behind, and taking with them other letters from the Abbé to several 'learned men' there, chief among whom was the famous Volta, professor of physics at the University of Pavia. The next day while the professor was 'delivering his Lectures,' Padre Menegliotti and Professor Scanagatta did the honours of Botanical Gardens ' etc.—of which we have full accounts from the nature-loving Miss Houblon — after which they were conducted to the Museum by its Keeper, where ' Mr. Volta joined us, and showed us the new Theatre and all his Apparatus Philosophical. He also most obligingly shewed us some experiments on English Machines.' It would be interesting to know what the experiments were which Professor Volta exhibited on this occasion; for he had been for many years labouring in the experimental study of electricity.[3] But a few months after Miss Houblon's visit to the University of Pavia, another Italian worker in the same field of inquiry, Galvani, was led by his accidental observation of the movements of some frogs under certain conditions of contact with two metals, to

[1] Rose, *Biographical Dictionary*, i. 405.
[2] J. Thomas, A.M., M.D., *Universal Dictionary of Biography*, p. 115. Under the Abbé Amoretti's auspices a library of ' 14,000 choice volumes had been lately purchased, for which the government paid £1000 sterling.' See letter.
[3] *Imperial Dictionary of Universal Biography*, iii. 873.

believe the solution of these phenomena to lie in *animal electricity*. But Alessandro Volta was already on the right track. The kicks of the frogs may have opened the door for the greater discovery, but he shortly afterwards found the true law of the form of electric action observed by Galvani, in the arrangement of two metals and the solvent fluid which is necessary for its production. Thus was discovered the Voltaic pile or battery, sometimes called by the name of Galvani, or the Galvanic battery.[1]

After the fatigues of much sight-seeing, the drive back to Milan in the lovely spring evening, the way lightened by the sweet *Lucioli* (fire-flies), loved of those who love Italy, may have been, we trust, not a little soothing to Miss Laetitia's troubled companion, as well as delightful to herself. For Betsy was even now revolving in her mind if she should accept her Consul or reject him! The first she was longing to do, the second was taken out of her hands by Miss Laetitia. She had written promptly on receiving Mr. Green's proposals to Betsy's parents, who accepted them on behalf of their daughter. This information they received on their return to Milan, so pretty Betsy during these days became engaged to Mr. Green.

1788   On Miss Houblon's reappearance at Milan the Abbé Amoretti fulfilled all her expectations as a *cicerone*, and delightful hours were spent at the Brera and other places of interest.[2] But though for the time her love for 'the

[1] The moment of his discovery was not propitious; for the French Revolution had but lately begun; so Professor Volta came to England for appreciation and sympathy, and in 1792 read a paper to the Royal Society of London which, after five years' consideration, awarded him the Copley medal. In five more years the French Institute gave him another, and at last he found himself a great man and senator, by the patronage of the Emperor Napoleon. Several discoveries and inventions are connected with Volta's name, amongst them the 'electric condenser.' See also *Nouvelle Biographie Générale*, xlvi. columns 356-363, and Thomas, *Universal Dictionary of Biography*, ii. p. 2212, etc.

[2] The Abbé Amoretti, who was born in 1740, was author and translator of various works on art. He was a contributor to the *Transactions de la*

MISS LÆTITIA HOUBLON.

best society' was swallowed up in the absorbing interests of science and art, yet, as was her wont, she made new friends, and next day found herself on a damask-draped balcony introduced by the kindly Amoretti and shared by two Venetian ladies—witnessing a gorgeous procession in honour of the festival of the Corpus Christi.

Miss Laetitia's lively conversation, together with the fascinations of Betsy's 'person and manners,' appear to have attracted all at Milan with whom they came in contact; and during the last few days spent there, they appear to have been attended wherever they went by an admiring circle, whether of professors, clericals, or gentlemen friends of Mr. Ritchie, the English minister at Venice. These included a friend of the Baron von Feilitzsch, and a Milanese gentleman, whose love for England as the 'Country of Angels' pleaded his excuse for an introduction! This took place at the opera, where 'a friend of the Abbé's, Cavaliere Carcano, lent us his box, and where the Abbé also visited us, so that we had Men in plenty; one on each side of each, to hand us to our Coach.'

It was already becoming too hot to linger longer in the Lombardy plains and cities, so Miss Houblon now carried out her plan of going to the Italian lakes where she proposed spending the summer. Meanwhile Mrs. Houblon had left London, and was with her daughters at 'Baylies' near Windsor passing the summer with her aunt, Lady Godolphin. John[6]'s mother, always diffident as to her powers of making her son happy, arranged for him to spend his summer holidays away from herself and his sisters; so we hear of him 'at Madingley again.' To him his aunt wrote from Como a kind

Société Italienne, the *Magasin Encyclopédique*, etc., and wrote a valuable Biography of Leonardo da Vinci. He was member of the Italian Institute, secretary to the Patriotic Society, etc. See J. Thomas, *Universal Dictionary of Biography*, and Rose, *Biographical Dictionary*, etc.

letter full of good advice. The behaviour of some of the young Englishmen whom she had met at Nice and elsewhere, and who had 'spent time and money to disgrace themselves and our nation,' furnished her topic and served to point the moral and adorn the tale, while she entreats him to avoid 'that most despicable of all vices, the love of Liquor.' 'Avoid it, my dear, as you would perdition. Lord Belgrave (one of these youths on the Riviera) paid dear for his want of sobriety, having broke an arm and some ribs, insisting on being drove over a mountain in the dark.'

Miss Betsy's engagement to Mr. Green was now announced. Though she had been very unwilling to leave her friend before her return to Nice, the marriage was to take place at Turin by the English minister's chaplain; 'For one can't be lawfully married easily abroad!' Lord Mountstuart, who had been British Envoy there from 1779 till 1783, had given Miss Houblon letters to several of his friends at Turin. 'We are told this King's second son will there wed the Archduchess of Milan; if so, we shall have great gaiety. Meanwhile, my dearest Sister, you are very kind to my Baron! I believe he consoles himself with a Comtesse at Nice, and I don't believe he will meet us at Turin. But he must return to his duty when I appear!'

In a 'spacious house at Como, in a delightful situation, the hosts most obliging,' and to which they had been recommended by M. Bonnet, the banker at Milan, the ladies remained for three months, their only difficulty being that of understanding the patois spoken by the good people of the house. 'We are recommended to several agreeable people here,' Miss Laetitia wrote to nephew John, 'and pass our time much to my taste after our long journeyings, and hurries in great Cities. Too much cannot be said of the charming borders of the Lake of Como. We were last week at the House which was inhabited by both the Plinys, and we are much obliged to the descendant of another Latin writer, Count Giovio. He is a very pleasant man, and learned people tell us the Literary Laurels of the Family will not fade in His hands.' They fared well, as they had hitherto everywhere done, as to kindness and hospitality from those to whom they carried letters of introduction, and in a short time the best society of Como and its neighbourhood was open to them. Except for a couple of Englishmen, who hearing at Milan that two English women were gone to spend the 'heats' on Como and determined to follow their example—they were the only foreigners there. Count Giovio, the young poet, was the nephew of the Cavaliere Carcano, their acquaintance of Milan, who had recommended our ladies to his and his wife's special care and protection during their sojourn on the Lake. Another lady to whom he also recommended them was his sister, Donna Vincenza Paravicini.

Donna Vincenza lost no time in fulfilling the wishes of her brother, for no sooner had she received the letter of introduction which Miss Houblon sent her, than she 'flew to visit' them at the 'Prudenziale' where the ladies had taken up their abode. She brought with her the Abbé Volta, brother of the professor with whom they were already acquainted at Milan, and who also enjoyed the honour of being Madame's *cavaliere servente.* 'She took us to the Corso in her Coach and is vastly civil, and promises to be as agreable as her brother the Chevalier.' The next day 'came Count Giovio to call, and sat with us two hours.' This was the usual length of a visit. 'We gave him tea which he did not like, but He did like to show us great attention; ambitious, as he said, to obey his uncle's commands and make the *séjour* of Como tolerable to us. I believe he is the first man here.' The next day the young Count came again, this time bringing the Countess with him to call on his uncle's friends. They came in their coach, 'with all the parade of running footmen, etc.,' and presently took the ladies with them to show them some of the sights of Como. They went first 'to the Chanoine Gaetoni's Museum, where were fossil birds, etc., and much learned writing hanging about to explain.' Then 'to the Borgo di Vico (the borders of the lake opposite our House), where many Milanese are building Palaces; a truly delightful situation.' Here the young 'Lord of the Lake,' for such apparently he was, was also building a house for the summer. They afterwards saw much of the Giovio pair, who were at once pronounced interesting and charming, especially the Count, whose family had reigned over the lake since his Roman ancestor composed Latin odes on its bosom. 'They are a pleasant and for Italians a very extraordinary Couple,' wrote Miss Laetitia, 'for they seem to love each other! She is rather shy; has been married eight years, and is only 24!'

The weather, which 'was only fit for Macbeth's witches,' prevented them from returning these visits next day, but meanwhile 'a French officer, Captain Paravicini and Don Giuseppe Salas, visited them with proffers of preventing ennuy!' and the next day they 'Drest and got the queerest little Chariot which carried us to call on Donna Vincenza Paravicini.' On seeing their funny little vehicle she with much courtesy, 'after giving us *rinfrescos*, insisted on our dismissing it, and begged she might have the happiness of conveying us wherever we chose to go. We only desired to visit her daughter (the Countess Giovio), so away we went. We found them at home, with a little crooked Relation, a jolly Dominican, and three fine children; the eldest six—a very intelligent Child; the second quite a beauty in spite of coloured frocks—blue linen bib and apron (quite shocking and so unlike children of fashion). But yet the Babe was quite engaging and gave us flowers! Last appeared the young Heir, the fattest fair thing ten months old, wrapped in a long mantle like an old blue curtain! They showed us the house and garden, both fine, and then took us a drive *al Corso*'; the usual *finale* to a day's outing, except when they sat in their coaches in the piazza and ate ices.

With occasional airings in Donna Vincenza's coach, scrambles up the mountains, and the visits of their friends, the ladies passed a pleasant time. One rainy day they accompanied Count and Countess Giovio to a concert, 'to hear a woman play on the flute. All the company stared at the English travellers, and every man who could jabber French and was of rank, was introduced, and some Contessas. The music was not much, but seeing so many of the Noblesse paid for being out in such a horrid night, to us at least! what the Running Footman thought I can't tell.' On June 16: 'All storm and no Company. We took a walk in the evening. Met the Marquis Cigallini riding, with his running Footmen before him. Odd equipage to English Eyes.' The next day: 'After dinner that Marquis made us a visit. Then Captain Paravicini brought a Brother Officer who seemed to enjoy our tea. A nice chatty man. The Donna called us for a drive, but we refused. Got four letters between 10 and 11, so went to bed content.

'Captain Paravicini & Don G Salas came for us at eleven. We walked with them to a school instituted by the Emperor.[1] 63 Girls are taught all sorts of work and weaving silk. A certain number are maintained and educated, and for the rest their parents pay 20 livres[2] a year. They seem well instructed. The Emperor has several of these Institutions. From thence to a convent, but it was noon and all were sleeping.' Soon after

[1] Joseph II.
[2] Equal to a pound.

this they were conducted to see another convent of Capuchin nuns of the order of San Carlo Boromeo. The abbess was a noble Genoese lady, *dei Marchesi* Ferraro. Very old, she excused herself, an ancient nun doing the honours. To the nuns and their abbess the care and education of twenty young ladies of family were entrusted. All these little maidens seemed to the visitors sleek and well fed, but the order was severe, though less so than before a peremptory command from the Emperor to relax their discipline. This was in consequence of several of the nuns having died from the hardships. So the old nun related, and lamented the change.

Back at Milan late in August, the ladies were once more welcomed by those who had been kind to them on their previous visit, and first among these was the Abbé Amoretti.[1] Count Giovio's uncle, Cavaliere Carcano, now presented them to his wife, and a new acquaintance, the Marchesa Menafoglia, lent them her box at the opera for a grand concert and masked ball, where a friend of Baron von Feilitzsch's, Colonel Lerchenfeldt, attended them, besides Don F. Visconti and their two Abbé friends. Marchesi, the famous singer, had chosen to spend the morning partridge shooting 'mid leg in water' to Miss Laetitia's indignation, 'so he was quite hoarse. But it is nevertheless the fashion to applaud and be delighted!'

'Now for an answer to your ever kind Letter,' Miss

[1] It was not till six years later that the Abbé Amoretti published a work which contributed greatly to his reputation, describing the geography and natural history of the three great lakes of Italy, and entitled *Viaggio da Milano ai tre Laghi*. The manuscript (though in the form of letters) was already completed at this time, for the Abbé entrusted it to Miss Houblon, who carried it with her when she left Milan with the intention of translating it into English. This she accomplished during the following winter at Nice, with the assistance of Baron von Feilitzsch, who was himself an accomplished Italian scholar and even poet. We are unaware if the translation was ever published; but it certainly was meant for publication, and to meet a great want, for 'no English guide to the Italian Lakes existed' at that time.

LAETITIA

Laetitia wrote to her sister-in-law before leaving Milan. 'Betsy is all gratitude for your good wishes. Her spirits are more composed, but we frequently weep! She has a thousand fears. Matrimony she has always thought ill of. And how a Man of 50 without advantage of Person or fortune could enchant her I can't tell! He is certainly sensible, agreeable, & I believe truly worthy and good tempered. I teaze her for Her assertion which in England used to be very frequent, that She never could be in Love. I always replied time would come! . . . Direct Poste Restante, Turin, *Dame Angloise.* I will enquire for and hope to find a letter, as soon as we arrive.'

'A delightful drive' from Milan took them up mountains and down valleys to Varese, from which place fourteen miles of the worst roads she had ever experienced, made the owner of the good English coach think it 'was built even to swim or fly if necessary.' On the 'Noble Lake' (Maggiore) they embarked coach and all, and many are Laetitia's raptures over what she saw. On the Isola Bella—'bellissima it should be'—the fair Boromean palace was then still in its choice freshness of architectural beauty, the interior filled with pictures, statues, and gorgeous furniture—'fit residence for some benign Fairy!'

They arrived, August the 30th, at Turin—capital of the kingdom of Sardinia, whose 'Charming broad clean streets as full of neat people as London,' delighted the ladies. Lord Mountstuart,[1] who was at Spa with his wife, had recommended them to the care of his friend, Mr. Trevor, while the English Chargé d'Affaires, Mr. Jackson, was also well known to Consul Green, and during their stay at Turin proved most kind and assiduous in his attentions to the travellers. In a friend of Baron von Feilitzsch, Captain Albani, 'whom we are

[1] Lord and Lady Mountstuart were now tenants of Hallingbury Place. Some interesting letters of the latter are among the family papers.

in love with, which he returns'—they found a guide who undertook to show them everything. The town was full of people, though 'all the *beau monde* (contrary to Miss Houblon's expectation) was away in the country': but not so 'Mr Fox Lane who is still chained to Turin by the Marquise Lance, both Soul and Body.' After some difficulty, Mr. Jackson procured the ladies a private lodging at the house of Count Nuvolone, who was away in the country, for like all Italian inns in those days, theirs was unfit for a long residence.¹ As soon as the 'fallals' were unpacked, the English Chargé d'Affaires conducted them to the palace of the ancient society queen of Turin—the Comtesse de St. Gilles—and presented them to her. Thirty years had passed by since in 1758 Jacob₄ Houblon had been a student at the Academia Reale of Turin; and a familiar figure in society then, she was still a prominent one. But 'Madame de St. Gilles'—she was probably the Contessa di San Gallo—was now old and feeble. She had long survived in Jacob's memory as all that was gracious and charming in woman, and as such Miss Laetitia looked to find her now. Propped up by pillows, the old lady still held her little court; the ancient *habitués* of her salon continued to assemble at her house, but they were now faded and grey and *passés*, like herself. So after two or three visits, the brilliant Laetitia voted the circle *ennuyeux*. The Countess, however, received her most graciously, and arranged for her presentation, and that of Miss Watson, at Court, deputing her niece, Countess Brizzio, to be her representative in this matter.

Besides Captain Albani, who spoke English very well, and was 'most charming,' a Chevalier Polon (Polone?) was frequently in attendance on the ladies during the month they spent at Turin. One or other of these gentlemen always went shopping with them, and aided in the

¹ They were generally infested with bugs.

purchase of finery for the approaching presentation at the Court, which was now at the castle of Moncaliere.[1] The banker, Signor Negri, who had an English wife, was also most attentive. The Negris lived in a villa beyond Moncaliere, and the account of a visit there is interesting. The lady was said to be a 'Wit and poetess, but of a sad Muse.' She turned out to be a charming, simple, English woman, who wept when she parted from her English guests. A contrast to her in temperament was another lady, the Countess Bogaretti, who, as a friend of Lady Mountstuart, arrived at their lodging in a hurricane of animated talk, and 'loading us with professions and embraces.' Of these Miss Laetitia seemed a little doubtful, till the impulsive dame proved her sincerity by many kindnesses, one of which was energetically bargaining for a cap for Betsy and some gold buckles, which she got many livres below the stated price. 'She preserves the remains of the most beautiful woman in Turin.'

'Mr Jackson came in his Coach and four at ½ past six. Took us first to Contessa Brizzio's, who accompanied us to Moncalier. Here she first introduced us to the Dame d'Honneur of the Princess of Piedmont (there was then no Queen of Sardinia). The royalties passed through the Ante-chamber where all waited—to a long gallery, and after a short pause the English ladies were called for.' Since Charlemagne, it is to be supposed, presentations to royalty have been conducted much on the same lines. Outside its special circle, the crossing of the barrier within which it hedges itself, is generally attended with awkwardness unless it is purely automatic. When Miss Houblon, followed by her cousin, was ushered into the Sardinian presence, 'Three Princesses stood forward' ranged in front; a little distance behind stood the King with five sons and a brother, in a row. Beyond that

[1] To this day a favourite country residence of the royal family of Italy.

again, the Court. The audience lasted twenty minutes. The King's daughter-in-law, the Princess of Piedmont, received them kindly, but had nothing to say. 'Madame Félicité, however, His Majesty's sister, a delightful old maid free and engaging,' when she found she had to deal with a pleasant English woman neither frightened nor abashed into idiocy, brought her nephews and introduced them. The shy constraint with the foreigner then broke down, and the King and his eldest son 'came and said a deal to us.' The Duke of Aosta, who was to marry an Archduchess of Milan, was brought up to talk of his intended, whom Miss Laetitia had seen there, and all was general conversation till much courtesyings and *bon-voyages* finished the ceremony, and they retired. Meanwhile other ladies had been introduced, but neither the King nor princes said a word to them.[1] Etiquette took them after this 'to Madame de St. Gilles, where we complimented half an hour.'

Soon after, they were invited to a 'Stag hunting with the Court' at Stupinigi. Accompanied by Mr. Jackson and some other men, the ladies were driven there in a '*Berousch*,' where they found fresh horses. 'I thought myself on Hatfield Forest, the woods and soil so like,' wrote Miss Houblon. 'The Forest is as dirty as ours, but I enjoyed the splashings, they were like home. . . . Not so the appearance of the Sardinian Court, the Huntsman and Piqueurs in scarlet and gold, and the gorgeous equipages of the royal family and Court; the only Lady on horseback was Princess Carigniano.[2] . . .' 'We followed Princess Félicité in her Chariot. The stag died near the Palace, which is very elegant.'[3] What was most remarkable in this stag hunting was 'the great

---

[1] Three of the King's sons were afterwards successively Kings of Sardinia.

[2] Of the younger branch of Savoy Carigniano. She was the sister of the Princesse de Lamballe, who was guillotined during the reign of terror. See genealogical table *Encyclopædia Britannica*, Savoy.

[3] The Stupinigi palace and hunting lodge, about eight miles from Turin.

number of fine horses.' But Turin had long been remarkable for these, and was still the school of horsemanship and the manège, for Europe.

The gaieties of the ladies came to an end now, and it is doubtful if poor Betsy, whose approaching marriage filled her with all the nervous apprehensions detailed in the fashionable novels of the day, could have much enjoyed them. The bridegroom's arrival is thus described: 'At six came Mr Green all rapture. She all confusion; could not look up or utter a sillable for a long time. But we got composed.'

On the 2nd of October 1788 'Mr Green showed the happiest face I ever beheld, when he received the most trembling of all Brides from the English Chargé d'Affaires in Mr Trevor's house.' The ceremony was performed by his chaplain—a Swiss—in French. The fine muslin, the silk, the *Blone*[1] and Valenciennes, and the crape hats—all of which were the work of the Queen of Naples' mantuamaker—are duly described, besides the blue and silver-laced garments of the bridegroom. Dinner was early, and after it the trio retired to a villa in the neighbourhood of Turin, called Gierbido, belonging to Count Villani, from whom Mr. Green had rented it for the honeymoon. Here they remained for the next ten days, the third party being apparently not in the least in the way. This ended, they all proceeded on the journey back to Nice, where Miss Houblon proposed passing the winter once again. We hear much in her journal of the dangers of the way, especially of the transit of the 'terrible Col de Tende.' It is curious to find that Italian engineers were even then discussing the possibilities of 'piercing an hollow way' through the mountain, the starting point being about half way up, in a cave of great extent—nigh on 300 yards.'

One post from their destination, 'at the door of the

[1] *i.e.* blond.

little dirty Inn at Schiavenna, kept by a dirty old French woman who *boasts* herself the daughter of the Cardinal Bernis,' a familiar figure was standing by his horse. 'My Baron' and the Vice-Consul had ridden out to meet them. Arrived at Nice, except that the ladies were divided by the length of Miss Laetitia's garden, the old life was resumed pretty much as before, though Mrs. Green, as the wife of the English Consul, had much visiting and entertaining to do. But almost every day, the one 'ran' to the other, and when not out of an evening, the rubbers of whist were resumed. For Baron von Feilitzsch returned to his duty towards his *bonne amie* as a matter of course. 'As I told you he would be,' she wrote to her sister, 'He is more my slave than ever.'

CHAPTER VIII

'MY BARON'

'My people shall be thy people. . . .'—RUTH

MEANWHILE all at home was peace, and the country prospering under the firm and wise government of England's 'great Commoner.' Since 1784 Pitt had been Prime Minister, and his first five years of rule had been fruitful ones to England. But in the words of a modern statesman—'the new element was soon to cloud the whole firmament,' and Pitt, though for long obstinately determined on maintaining neutrality in the coming storm, could not but perceive 'the heavens blackened and the sound of the rushing mighty wind that was soon to fill all Europe.'[1] And so it came to pass that all progressive legislation—though most unwillingly—was perforce laid aside. This reaction was due to the fear lest the 'mischief making' of the revolutionary emissaries from France, and there were many, should kindle a similar conflagration in this country.

'Letters have been dreadfully delayed,' wrote Miss Houblon from Nice. 'Indeed it made us all almost mad when the state of England was so critical, for we thought there must be something important done, and now we find you are all so good you need no government! Mr. Poyntz grieves much he is not at home, for He says He longs to do just as he pleases for once in His life.' The agitation here referred to was probably that caused by

[1] *Pitt*, by Lord Rosebery, p. 280.

the King's mental illness, and the impending Regency Bill which was happily rendered unnecessary by his recovery.

Miss Laetitia passed the winter of 1788-9 at Nice, and the same visits, walks, and card parties are recorded in her diary, though we hear of no faro; if played, it was in secret. The attentions of the Baron von Feilitzsch also continued as before. The 1st of December 1788 was John$_6$ Houblon's birthday, and his aunt Laetitia commemorated it at Nice by a dinner party, consisting of some of her best friends, of course including the Consul and his wife and Baron von Feilitzsch, as also the Barons Stein and de Alderstein, Cavaliere Ardessone and Mesdames Artaud and de Broutin. In anticipation of the necessities of the occasion, a cask of English ale had arrived shortly before, and it was tapped with all solemnity for the drinking of the health of the young head of Miss Houblon's family. Soon after, she gave an evening party.

'NICE, *February* 15, 1789.'

' Mme L. Houblon prie Mme Houblon et les demoiselles ses Filles, de lui faire l'honneur de passer la soirée chez elle, Jeudi le 19 du courant.—R.S.V.P.'

'As I have invited all I visit,' she wrote, 'I did not chuse to omit you. Trust you will bring with you your *Cavalieri serventi!* I found it was expected, as I had a large house that I should open it so. Heaven knows how we shall accomplish the business. Ovington and Nobe are in a grand fuss. The Baron says I shall faint before the evening's over, but I don't feel so, though 108 are on my list!

' Lady Maynard has taken an House here for 9 years. I wonder at Her, for she is very little noticed. But her attraction for young Men is wonderful. Mr Bell a Relation of the Edens (under age) is now absolutely fascinated by Her, and Lord Gore an astmatick Boy of 19 is for ever quarrelling with his mother about Her. Are the Greys de Wilton in Town and how do they, and is Miss Egerton marrying? Do you see Lady Coventry?[1] I know nought of Her and have but just answered a letter of 7 months date to Lady St. John. I fear to enquire for your nearest of kin, for I am sure was there anything good you would have mentioned it. But I hope your good Aunts are well. Oh! I had like to have forgot to inform you that I have risked a part of your "Clotty,"[2] and you are to gain the 6th part of 24,000£. I hope you don't object. I never could find a better way of spending it to advantage, and I believe if you don't send an express to forbid me I shall spend the whole in Lotteries. My Baron got 50£ for 5 last month. You will please to observe that £ here means shillingsworth. . . . I must dress to dine at the Consuls' (they dined at four) 'for we spend our Sundays alternately. We shall have a nice walk after dinner till Sunset. Can you do so in February?'

She was reading *Hayley* aloud to the Baron at this time.[3] When Miss Houblon returned to Nice, it is certain that she did not regard this fine soldier's attentions as serious; so accustomed were women abroad to what she herself called the 'mean nothing ways of Italy,' that the devotion of the *cavaliere servente* was accepted as a matter of course, and probably as often resulted in boredom as it did in pleasure. But that true and solid friendships were occasionally built up between two people whom custom hedged round with an *Honi soit qui mal y pense* which protected them from scandal, when none existed, is undoubted. Possibly English society in these days would be none the less pure, if honest friendship between the sexes was not so often made an unpardonable offence by Mrs. Grundy, who still knows no

[1] *née* the Hon. Barbara St. John.
[2] Clotty = Lottery?
[3] ? William Hayley, poet and painter. Friend of Romney.

other name for the male friend of a woman than 'tame Cat!' Wisdom and prudence were certainly sufficient armour in respect of Miss Laetitia, but a warm and close friendship had sprung up between these two, which community of tastes and mutual appreciation of many fine qualities on either side, tended daily to increase. A crisis, however, was hastened by a sudden order for the regiment in which the Baron served, to prepare to march for Alessandria. The prospect of a separation unsealed the lips of the Baron, who perhaps only now fully realised that life without his *bonne amie* would not only be uninteresting, but unhappy. What she thought herself we shall see.

1789 'March the 6th—We spent the last evening. At ¼ past 11 we took a tearful parting. He was to march next morning at 5, but the Batallion were not ready till ¼ past 7.[1] Mrs Green saw them pass. I did not rise. She came to me at 9, and I went to Her house to see the (other) Piedmont Regiment come in.' No one was allowed to guess that the soldier Baron had won the ever-green heart of Miss Laetitia, who had so often parried the jests of her friends on his devotion. But so it was, and a promise was made which sent him away consoled. The same afternoon the stream of visitors was not denied, and we hear of some one bringing to see her 'two fine young Men, Princes of Montmorency, travelling for three years, the eldest being just married to an Heiress aged eleven!' Then, 'Lady Anne Hatton drank tea; and Lord and Lady Landaff brought the Comtesse Piccolomini,' and Lord Bristol also 'drank tea.' Soon after this she was bled. Bleeding was considered calming to the mind as well as salutary to the body.

The King of Sardinia[2] was a quiet kindly man, united

[1] A second battalion marched three days later, when 'Baron de Beck took leave.'
[2] Victor Amadeus III.

and domestic in his family relations, but politically ambitious and intriguing. As Duke of Savoy and Prince of Piedmont he had successfully assumed the foremost rôle among the princes of Italy. Seeing many signs of approaching trouble he had long been anxiously endeavouring to strengthen and consolidate his position and that of his country; to this end he spent many years in training and exercising his army. Experienced officers from abroad helped him in this work, and amongst them our acquaintance 'the Saxon Baron' took service some years previously in the Sardinian regiment now stationed at Nice on the French frontier.

The Von Feilitzsch family belonged to Upper Saxony. They were possessed of 'many Fiefs,' though it is to be doubted if they were much overburdened with money. They were, however, an ancient race 'eight hundred years noble,' and as proud and exclusive as people of blue blood in Germany were then, and as they are still. Baron Friedrich, however, united with these characteristics, experience and knowledge of the world gained from much travelling and study; these had made him a thorough cosmopolitan. His father died in 1770, and among the cherished papers found after his son's death—which include some graceful poetry, both French and Italian—is a long printed poem in which he expressed his filial feelings on the former melancholy occasion. An engraving of a drooping nymph weeping over the urn of the departed, graces the top of the faded yellow, black-letter page. Wilhelm, his only brother, served in the Saxon army, and was later a major-general on the staff of the Elector of Saxony. It was probably after his father's decease that Friedrich left home, finally taking military service in Italy. That he was devoted to the profession of arms, and the ancient traditions of his house we may deduce from Miss Laetitia's remark just before his departure, on the eve of new and momentous developments in European politics. 'So at Geneva,' she writes, 'they have resumed their ancient Constitution. It has cost some lives; but Baron F. says that is no matter, for no death is so desirable as from a Musket; and he seems to envy all who fall so! The whole World appears in agitation,' adds the poor lady, 'so what will come of it, God only knows!'

The people were all 'dancing round the May Poles' when Miss Laetitia was ready for her departure from Nice on her return to England in the spring of 1789. The Consul and his wife were established in a new and charming villa which she had helped them to arrange, and now nothing remained but to make her farewells. This was not accomplished without regret, for she had made many friends, and, in the case of the Greens and the kind old Baronne Tondut, not without many tears. The friendly coach was put on board a felucca and, 'if the wind was right,' she was to sail the morning of the 6th of May for Toulon. It is curious to find that Miss Laetitia's plans were upset by Algerine pirates! Just before the felucca was to sail which she had hired to take her the voyage to Toulon, the Consul arrived in haste to say five Algerine vessels were on the coast of France, and he was closely followed by the owner of the felucca, declaring 'it was folly to pass Point Garouse, indeed he *would* not sail, for the Turks would show no favour to Genoese.' But as the coach was already on board his vessel, he agreed to take the lady to Antibes and from thence she could proceed by land. So Miss Houblon 'breakfasted by Mrs Green's bedside' and departed. Jolting roads and solitude (except for Nobe who complained bitterly 'her bones would soon be thro' her skin') made the road through France by which she had come less fascinating than on the first occasion. The mountains appeared less high, and, in spite of 'Nightingales singing and Rhododendrons blooming,' the early part of the journey was tedious, and anxious thoughts were less pleasant companions than pretty Betsy in the day when both were heart-whole, with Europe and its newness lying before them.

Three days brought them to Tarascon, where they crossed the Rhone partly on the bridge of boats, partly on a ferry,—the ice of last winter having destroyed the centre causeway,—and from thence to Nismes, where at the inn Miss Houblon overtook Lady Rivers, who was on her way to Lyons, where she usually spent the summer. With Lady Rivers were Madame Artaud and Mr. Pitt and Mr. Lee. 'They desired we might not separate, an happy proposition for me who had had no society for three days!' Mr. O'Byrne was added to the company at dinner, and 'gave us excellent *Vin de Grave*, and to those that liked it, old Port. We had a very social meal. Then O'Byrne would make Coffee, for He carries every luxury with him. Some Florence silks—for which Nismes is famous—were brought. Lady Rivers bought two pieces and I hope to smuggle home three, for which I paid five Louis. Mr Pitt selected them so they must be high Ton. This great business over, we proceeded to survey the Roman works, Lady Rivers in a Sedan and the rest on foot . . . Of the Baths nothing remains but the unfathomable source and the steps which go down into it. All the rest is gone or perverted into a gallic Promenade, where we viewed and were viewed by all the Beaux and Belles of Nismes. One very fine young Lady took the opportunity of suckling Her Child, to the great amusement of our three men. We entered the Temple of Diana which is unroofed, but enough remains to show the superiority of ancient architecture. The people of Nismes take great care now of all the antiquities, and are purchasing the Houses which disgrace the inside of the Amphitheatre, in order to clear it; and then, though smaller, it will be preferable to that at Verona, as the outside is more perfect. We looked into it, took a chat, and at nine retired to comfortable Beds.

'Madame Artaud called me at ½ past 5, and before six I drank of Lady River's Chocolate and they took leave. Set off soon after them, having made an assignation with Mess[rs] Pitt and Lee the night before to meet at the Pont du Gard. They, travelling on horseback, were off early. Changed horses at St. Gervaze. Sad to see almost all the olive trees dead in Provence; a proof how much softer the climate of Nice is, none being hurt there, only the Fruit destroyed last winter.[1] At Remoulins at 8.20; and about a mile from thence came up with the gentlemen at the Pont du Gard; an amazing structure, the proportion of the im̃ence arches strikingly beautiful. A pretty addition to the scene was part of a Troop of Dragoons, which had halted at the end of the bridge; tho' the gallick smartness accords not much with the idea of the founders of the Aqueduct.' This wonderful monument of Roman greatness having been explored with the gentlemen, Miss Laetitia took leave of Messrs. Pitt and Lee[2] and proceeded on her way. What was Mr. Pitt doing now, travelling in France with a friend? Early in May, was not Parliament sitting? In truth this could not have been the statesman, for though the House adjourned for a week on the last day of April, Pitt was reported as again speaking in his place on the 12th of May, but a few days after the gentlemen were riding across the Pont du Gard on their way northwards.[3]

Only a few weeks before this time, the heretofore all-

---

[1] The winter of 1788-9 had been an exceptionally severe one. It was that of the 'Great Frost' in England.
[2] Probably John Lee, lawyer, politician, and King's Counsel, b. 1733, d. 1793. See *Dictionary of National Biography*, xxxiii. p. 361.
[3] *Morning Star*, 1 May 1789, No. 68; and *Ibid.*, 13, May, No. 78.

powerful Pitt had been unostentatiously preparing to retire into private life, and was even contemplating resuming his practice at the Bar. At the zenith of his Minister's power the King's reason showed signs of failure, and as business was at a standstill, the question of a Regency became the vital problem of the hour. Pitt's power depended upon the support of the King, not on that of the people, though they were at one with him in aim and policy. But the Prince of Wales hated Pitt, and all knew that in the event of his becoming Regent he would at once dismiss him and that Fox would take his place. While the Regency Bill was actually passing, the King recovered, and Prince and opposition were alike disappointed of the power they thought within their grasp. Well for England, that at the opening of the greatest crisis of the century, the great Revolution, the hand of Pitt was not removed from the helm of the State. But for these discrepancies of date, it is conceivable that, during one of the frequent adjournments of the House during the troublous spring of 1789, the strain of anticipated retirement from office followed by the succeeding triumph of finding himself more firmly seated than before in power, was relieved by a change of scene, and that in this riding tour Pitt not only found relaxation, but opportunity for seeing and judging for himself at first hand, the trend of public and private opinion in France.

1789

But though to any one behind the scenes, the volcano might have seemed near eruption, Paris, when Miss Laetitia reached it, appeared outwardly gay and bright as ever, and her thinking she saw beneath the surface that 'all was ripe for revolt' was probably not due to what she beheld, but was rather the echo of what she was told there, and of the talk at the inn at Nismes, when her friends discoursed on France and her future over

Mr. O'Bryne's *vin de grave*. This was in May, and the Bastille fell on the 14th of July.[1]

Miss Houblon had not yet seen Paris, and had made many plans for the short time she was to stay there on her return home. 'I wish you were here,' she wrote to her sister-in-law, 'though you must be quite stout, for I really am more tired every night than with a day's posting. M^r[2] and M^{rs} O'Dunne and M^r and Mrs Lutwyche shew me the greatest kindness. M^{rs} O'D. says she is so happy to see a Relation that she is ever calling me niece, for such I am it seems *à la mode de Bretagne*. For the Lutwyches acquaintance I am indebted to Mr Poyntz. They are a most agreeable couple settled here about ½ a year. He was at Harrow with my Brothers, and his Father was a great intimate of my Uncle's (Sir John Hynde Cotton). A lawsuit which *They gained* and cost them 25,000£ sends them on the saving schemes. Between one and the other I am to be shewn everything. Whitsunday is a great day at Versailles when I shall see all the Court, etc. I hope to get away the Tuesday after. I believe my head will be turned; I am sure my purse will be emptied; everything is horrid dear, and the Head dresses so ugly, a mile high, there's no sitting in a carriage. I hope that fashion is not renewed in England. I have been to two Theatres and am to go to five more.'

On May the 21st the journal, which is very laconic, records: 'Drove in the Boulevards. Saw a deal of fine World, horse and foot. Guards everywhere. All ripe for riot. Presented to Lady Lambert, a fine old Dame above 80. . . . At the Beaujolois (Theatre). The words all by people *behind the scenes.* . . . Dined at the Count O'Dunnes. . . . Went to see the Gobelins Tapestry made. Some charming pieces

---
[1] Pitt is said to have been abroad but once in his life; in the recess of 1783. See *Pitt*, by Lord Rosebery, p. 42.
[2] He was a French Count.

done and doing. Saw three laughable pieces at the Variétées Amusantes.' Next day 'At the Comédie Française. . . . handsome Theatre. . . . The actor, said to make Himself the exact representation of the Great Frederic. . . . Went to Neuilly to the House of the Comte St. Foy. Very fine. Went to the Opera. Violent squalling, and no good dancing. French don't sound well in recitative.'

On Whitsunday Miss Laetitia's visit to Versailles took place. 'Hair drest at ½ past 5. Went at 7 to take up M^r and Mrs Lutwyche in a coach and four to Versailles. . . . At the Castle, a Swiss placed us in a superb gallery where we stood till twelve before the Procession past. A noble sight. The Cordon Bleu all in their fine robes; more than forty. The little Duc de Berri and another who were to be invested, were all in silver as they went to the Chapel, returned with amazing long trains. The King looks heavy and bloated, and waddles. Monsieur the same. Comte d'Artois a fine figure. His sons fine Boys. The Queen's, a majestick figure. Madame Royal ugly, and looks sulky. Madame Elizabeth a pleasing Woman. The Savoyards not so. . . . Whilst they were at Chapel we saw the King and Queen's apartments. The summer furniture only, but charming embroidery. In winter Mr Lutwyche says, the richness is astonishing. Some fine pictures and china.' The party waited to see the return of the procession from the chapel where the investiture had taken place, but not to 'see the King dine, which he and the Queen did in public.' After this they 'went in Chairs to see the Little Trianon for which Mr Hubert had got us a ticket. The House is small indeed, and nothing in my opinion admirable, except the furniture of the famous Boudoir, into which we were admitted, as our Ticket was for particular attention. . . . The garden is delightful; the expence to form it enormous. Mountains,

1789

Rivers, all *à l'Angloise*. A mock village—delightful. The dairy all Sèvres china, as we saw thro' the windows, for we were not let in. Some of the Cottages are nicely furnished for eating rooms, Work, etc. In another part, grottos and Temples, etc.'

Authority was fast slipping from the grasp of Louis XVI. at this time, and in little more than two months, in the fall of the Bastille, the doom of the French monarchy was sounded, and with it fell the system by which it was upheld. Among the private letters of Horace Walpole to Hannah More is one congratulating her on this event, which in common with all generous-minded English people—ignorant of what was to follow—she had hailed with joy, as presaging a day of liberty and enlightenment for France. 'I always hated to drive by it,' writes Walpole, 'knowing the miseries it contained. . . . Every crowned head in Europe must ache at present.'[1]

On the second of June Miss Laetitia left Paris; but before her departure she wrote an important epistle to her sister-in-law, who had just left town for Margate, that young Laetitia's health might be benefited by sea-bathing. 'I think you very right to go to Margate. But for my own sake I cannot wish you to stay long there, for—well 'tis a very silly affair! But my Heart can keep no secrets from you, and I beg you will not mention this to anyone, as M^r and Mrs Green alone are acquainted with it. I cannot hope you will approve. It is certainly twenty years too late, but the Fates would have it; for what less forcible motive could induce the Baron de Feilitzsch to imagine the remainder of his Life must be unhappy unless He had me to plague Him; or make me quit my Country and dear Friends! How it happened neither of us I believe can tell; but we

[1] *Private Correspondence of Hon. Horace Walpole*, iv. 481. London, 1820. It is nevertheless said, that when broken into, no more than seven political prisoners were found in the Bastille.

certainly did not part without a promise to meet again for Life, very early in Autumn at furthest. So I doubt I must not make three months stay in England, as He cannot come there, but will next year.[1] Keep my secret, my dearest Sister, and blame me as little as you can. When you know Him I think you will find me very excusable; but till then my evidence I can expect to have but very little weight. But I may say everybody respects Him; His Family 800 years Noble, in Upper Saxony, and Fiefs, numerous. I often think something will prevent; but I know my mind was never in such a situation. I must give up the Priory; and settling all my affairs is an horrid task to me who hate business and money matters above all.'

So much did Miss Laetitia dread the meeting with all her relations and friends and the coming explanations, that she even thought of giving as the excuse for her proposed marriage, that she was 'fearful of the Winters in England.' Meanwhile 'I hope I shall find many of my Friends in London: Lady Coventry, Lady St. John, Mrs Feake, Pennants, etc. etc., and that you will come to the Priory as soon as you have done washing.'[2]

How detached from Europe this country still was by the turbulent channel, Miss Laetitia's account of her return voyage amply shows. A post from Boulogne, a packet captain spied the approach of the lumbering coach, and hastened to offer his services. 'I told him I would *see* at Boulogne, where we arrived at 11.30.' She then agreed with the man to charter his vessel, and the carriage was embarked ready to start the following morning. The transit was to prove not only expensive and costly of time, but at the outset perilous. 'Went on board; no wind, obliged to row out of the harbor. The Pilots drunk and quarrelling amongst

---

[1] He proposed to resign his commission.
[2] Sea-bathing.

themselves, and would not row. A very great Sea, and so much time lost that we struck the ground many times. As we were turning to come in again a Rope broke, and the Packet ran on the outward Wall and stuck. The shock threw us all down, frightened Nobe and a French man terribly. I was bruised, and the sea came into the ship every time she Rolled, that our situation was very disagreeable till a Boat came and took us off.' Out of the boat they had to be carried to shore, as the 'tide was gone.' Some stalwart fishwives performed this service for them, and Miss Houblon and the terrified servants went back to the inn, several English gentlemen congratulating them on their escape. Later in the day 'walked to see the Packet where she lay dry, a vast piece of the keel broke but no other damage, and she was brought back evening tide and repaired at daybreak.' Meanwhile 'our wretched Pilots went mackrel fishing, and still inebriated overset their Boat with 1200 fish, and out of nine Men, three were drowned.'

The next morning 'Mr Wolseley (probably the Consul) sent to beg I would permit a gentleman to go, who was in great haste to get to England. I agreed, and He introduced Him as Mr Meadows, agent in the Kingstone Cause. But we were all disappointed, for the Wind was so violent there was no sailing.' Two more days they awaited the calming of the winds and a 'monstrous Sea,' when the voyage took them eight hours till they anchored outside Dover, and awaited a boat which took them off. But it was not yet over; for though it was 'a nice four-oared boat, and the sea smoothe as glass that we should have had a most pleasant Row, the tide Ran so strong that we were obliged to go 4 miles and then turn 3 more, to get to Dover, and so landed after another 2½ hours at ½ past 9. Walked to the Ship Inn, where got some Soop, and to Bed with the pleasing thought that nine Ells of Lawn was seized out of the Coach

Seat, which we had brought with us for our night things. No bribe could get it back from the Custom House. They opened every paper and unpacked all. Paid the Captain for the Packet and for the Sailors £7. . . .' Truly a hundred and odd years have worked much change in nautical locomotion! Possibly ere long a service of aerial machines may do the business.

Miss Laetitia met with warm sympathy at home. Her sister-in-law had probably long expected the *dénouement*, and received her with true kindness and consolation. Some might think the marriage had come 'too late,' but it concerned no one but herself, as she was practically alone in the world. So Thremhall Priory was given up, and many tearful adieus made. The following letter from Sir John Hynde Cotton—the much-loved uncle of the Houblon family—gives a pleasant impression both of him and his niece.

'MADINGLEY, *September* 15, 1789.

'MY DEAR NEICE,—It has been a great mortification to me that I could not follow my full intention of waiting upon you, either at the Priory before you left it, or now in London. But my weak and scorbutick Legs, which are scarce able to support me, have joined to other Infirmities which dayly so much Increase upon me, that I am become of late quite unable to attempt it; and I find I must content myself to make this letter my deputy to express my sincere wishes for your future Happiness, which I pray God to pour down upon you in the fullest abundance of his most gracious Providence. But yet, dear Neice, your Friends & Relations at home do and must lament the Loss of you, and I know well from the Love you have always shewn us, some little Corner of your Heart will be reserved to us, though you are going to give the other great share of it elsewhere. I hope and Trust it will there be received and kept close to his own ever after for a Token of your great generosity to him.

'I cannot flatter myself through my age & Infirmities I can ever see you again; but it will ever be the greatest satisfaction to hear, as long as my Life continues, of the uninterrupted Wellfare of yours.

'I am sensible your Time & Thoughts must now be so much employed, that I beg not the least Intervals may be taken up in answering this letter to your affectionate Uncle, who now concludes with repeating Two little words generally coupled together, which may you always enjoy in the true meaning of them.

'Farewell! Farewell!   J. HYNDE COTTON.'

Laetitia's marriage to the Baron von Feilitzsch was to take place at Turin, where the Consul of Nice and Mrs Green proposed to meet her, and whence the Baron was to come from Alessandria on leave from his regiment. The journey to Piedmont was difficult and full of delays. In a letter to Captain Cotton Miss Houblon remarks, had he seen her for some days past he would never 'accuse me of the family complaint (quick temper); I am vastly vain of my patience, for sure it is some tryal to wait four hours at a time for Horses on the road, and in 12 hours not get 30 miles! The roads good, Horses stout; but when one has waited, the vile Postilions won't put them in a trot. They complain that the French are perpetually on the Road, and tire them to death! From Brussels we went to Liége and were there stopt at the gates till we were furnished with Patriot Cockades; for, till we had them on, the Burghers would not let us pass! But the next morning at the first stage Dombrey was put into the Imperial Guard House for having one in His Hat! On pleading compulsion, however, he was released and sent back to us that we might doff ours.' During many days we have the same complaint in the journal of 'belated or tired horses, & of my poor new Chaise getting terribly scratched' with hard usage. 'From Carlsrue—a mighty pretty town and superb Palace of the Prince of Baden—we travelled almost the whole day between an avenue of poplars. For three days before, apple-trees lined the roads, so loaded with fruit they had to be propped up.' A long wait at Krotzingen, which was caused by an ambassador from Turin to Berlin having taken all the horses, brought them to Basle at three o'clock on Sunday. Here they were kept waiting for another reason, ' The good folks allow no carriage to enter their City during Service, and that would last $\frac{1}{2}$ an hour yet.'

Arrived at Geneva after about a month's travelling, a pause was made, for the Baron was to meet her here. But neither knew where the other was to lodge, so a day was spent in tremulous expectation. At last Dombrey found the expectant bridegroom, and 'he was at my feet by eleven. Joy was nearly oversetting both.' At Turin 'M^r and Mrs Green and the Babe' were awaiting them, and on the 24th of November 1789 the marriage took place. The following is the letter of the Count de Lautrum (the Piedmontese Commandant) on the occasion of the Baron's wedding.

'A Monsieur, Monsieur le Baron de Feilitzsch, Capitaine-Lieutenant du Régiment de Lautrum, à Turin.

'Monsieur,—Comme le mariage que Vous allez contracter, Monsieur, me paraît tout à fait a Votre avantage, Je m'emploie volontiers à en demander l'agrément de S.M. Et comme je ne doute pas que le Roi daignera l'accorder, je Vous en fais d'avance mon Compliment sincère, aiant l'honneur d'être, avec ma consideration distinguée, Monsieur, Votre très humble, très obeissant Serviteur, LAUTRUM.

'ALEXANDRIE, Le 1er *Novembre* 1789.'

The Baron and Baroness proposed paying their respects at the Sardinian Court before repairing to Alessandria, but this took longer than they had expected. 'All this fuss we had no idea of,' wrote Laetitia from Gerbe, 'or I believe we should not have waited. But now 'tis begun it must be gone through with. But the Baron —though he was presented 17 years since and frequently at Court since, and I was received last year—on this occasion must prove an unstained Nobility of many generations, and I must get our Minister to assert that my Rank entitled me to appear at St. James'! . . . I am told too I must receive everybody in form. How delightful to be stared at and commented upon by a whole City! Let me have the comfort of a letter.' At the same time the Baron wrote to the young head of his wife's house in pretty formal English, protesting his joy will be perfect if he would in future place him high on the list of his affectionate friends, and thus add to the happiness which his dear aunt had so recently lavished upon him. Entreating his respectful compliments to Mrs. and Miss Houblons, he is, 'with the most inviolable attachment, Dear Sir, your affectionate Uncle and obedient Servant, Frederick Lewis, Baron of Feilitzsch.'

Rumours of war kept the garrison at Alessandria constantly on the alert, and the Baroness wrote, 'How cruel it is that my friends cannot this year witness my felicity! and what is worse, a Camp seems now certain, and an active one not as impossible as was supposed; but if I write on that subject you may not be suffered to read, and the post is provoking enough without any excuse. My Lord orders me to say He is very thankful for all the kind things you say. Indeed nobody can have the least regard for me without loving Him, whose every thought appears to be for my happiness.' Meanwhile there was no lack of gaiety at Alessandria. 'Balls

JOHN ARCHER HOUBLON, ESQ.

are numerous—My neices would shine in this land of dance! The most capital Performer is my Lord's bosom Friend. He excells even Slingsby in the Allemand, I think. My "old Gentleman" has left off dancing these twelve years; but I am told he surpassed them all. I wanted Him to renew, but that is the only contradiction I have undergone. Now all is over, till the grand Fair in May . . . God knows where then we shall be. But the same Providence is everywhere. Is the King's health re-established, and are you to have any royal Weddings? Is London very gay, and any new fashions? Clements (her maid) wants to know if there's any material alteration in Hair dressing? She is a capital performer in all that relates to smartifying. My dress had been the admiration and talk of Alexandria. A young Marquis described me from head to feet to Mrs Gay! Is not that a pretty way for a man to employ His thoughts?'

Royal gossip was a favourite topic in those days as now. Writing to Charles Cotton on the 5th of May 1790, 'I hear,' she says, 'the King of Bohemia[1] is much grieved that an English Princess will not give Her Religion for His eldest son, as he is very desirous of a strict alliance with England. All his daughters are disgustingly ugly, so much so, that as they passed by, the Milanese were so struck they forgot to bow, and the first impulse was to turn away their heads. Not very flattering to young ladies!' To those who know the beauty-loving Italian, this story is very credible. 'Oh, pray tell me,' the Baroness continues, 'Lady Craven's age, and what Children she has. She is playing the D . . . at the Margrave of Anspach's Court. She reigns despotick, and has made him discard many of His oldest servants,

1790

---

[1] Leopold (Grand Duke of Tuscany) succeeded his brother, Joseph II., in February 1790. Elected Emperor, September 1790.—*An. Register*, vol. xxxiii., 1791. The Hapsburgs were hereditary Kings of Hungary and Bohemia, and Archdukes of Austria.

and is generally detested.' The following year a letter from Miss Archer, at Welford, to her sister, Mrs. Houblon, speaks of Lord Craven's recent death, and affectionately of his daughter. Benham, where the family then resided, is near Welford, and Miss Charlotte reports the anxiety of the neighbourhood lest his strange and erratic widow should take up her residence there, 'It being her jointure house.' She adds, however, that Lady Craven having other plans, 'wrote to Lord Craven when she heard of his illness to beg he would leave her his house in London! They say she is certainly to marry the Margrave of Anspach.'[1]

1791   In the summer of 1791 the Baron and Baroness made their first visit to Dresden since their marriage. It was many years since the former had been at home. They went first to Weisdorff, near Münchberg, in the Margravate of Bayreuth—a property belonging to the Baron, where they remained for about two months. Although this place was in Bavaria, the Von Feilitzsch family belonged to Upper Saxony. Writing in July from Dresden Baroness Laetitia says: 'We have been so visited, revisited, and feasted that it was impossible these 9 days to steal an hour from company and frizing to express my gratitude for the happiness your letter half gave me. I wrote to dear John as soon as we got to Weisdorff. It rejoices me much that he leaves school (John$_6$ was leaving Charterhouse for Cambridge). Maria wrote me your reasons for preferring Emanuel College. My Father and many of our Relations was at that College, though my Brothers were at St. John's on account of the Lipyeatts. But there is no good to be got from that name now. *I* doubt if ever there was. We are with my Baron's darling Brother here. They had not seen each other since the year '80' and their meeting was truly affecting. He is universally esteemed, and

---
[1] See Horace Walpole's letters to this strange lady.

has a Wife worthy of Him. (How happy am I in Sisters-in-law!) and two fine Boys. She is one of the first Families, that we move in the grandest circle. To-night we sup with the Prime Minister, Count Shoenberg, Her Uncle. Yesterday we past at Her Father's Fief, an hour's drive. All are anxious to shew respect to my good Man. Our letters of recommendation procured us an excellent dinner & vast civilities from Mr. Eden[1] & Lady Elizabeth. C.C. we are much obliged to for one we found here from Mr. Frazer. Lord Mountstuart had made us expected 6 weeks since, & we brought one from Lord Coventry. Here are very many English; Lord Albemarle is just gone & much regretted. Lord Dalkeith is an amiable youth; has been here near a year, but goes to-morrow. M[r] Garthshore is His fellow traveller. The former is a fine young man, & will leave great part of his heart with an officer's Lady here; but, I suppose, like the Polypus hearts of that age, 'twill bear much cutting & grow again.

'My de Feilitzsch returned mightily delighted from the Coffee House the day after our arrival. He had overheard a long conversation in English concerning us; & my Family mentioned very highly. When the speaker left the room He inquired & found His name was Archer. He set Him down for a near Relation of yours, & consequently that I should be rejoiced to see Him. It puzzled me vastly, not recollecting any Male but your Father, & He it could not be, as He had a son with Him. Mr. Eden solved my difficulty by explaining this gentleman to have been a Banker, & Partner with Baron Dimsdale. I was not acquainted with him, but am much obliged to Him. 'Tis charming to have one's Family extolled in the ears of those we best love.

'The Electress has gone to look for a son in some

---

[1] Subsequently Sir F. Morton Eden, Ambassador at Vienna, at this time Chargé d'Affaires at Dresden.

Baths a day's journey from hence. It is not supposed she will succeed, as she has exerted Her utmost endeavors near 20 years, & produced but one girl who is now 9. We got here the Friday, & as she was to depart last Monday, Lady Elizabeth (Eden) said I must be presented on Sunday. So all was hurry, the dress bought & made the Saturday.[1] Clements made up my finest Lace, & when all was prepared it was announced *No Apartments* as it is called, as she was to set out early, & to save taking leave. Mr Eden was so good to present my best half in the morning. The Elector asked why He had recourse to the English Envoy? My beloved answered, that having married an Englishwoman & rec^d great civilities from Mr E. He could not do otherwise. Truth was He did not chuse to kiss Hands, which He must have done had He been introduced by any of His Saxon Kin. The Electoral family is so polite that I believe we must wait Her return if she does not prolong Her stay till too late to get to Nice before the cold sets in here. . . . You will be so good as to continue directing to Weisdorff as they will forward without loss of time wherever we are, and we shall be there again on our way to Nice. All looks like England here; so many talk the language that I feel quite at home. Did you meet a Count & Countess Schall last winter? They are very agreeable, talk incessantly of London. Have more than 10,000 sterling a year. We are to eat some of it Tuesday.

The Electress of Saxony's 'efforts' towards presenting her lord with a son were destined never to be fulfilled. At this very time the need was deemed so urgent as at once to flurry and mortify the poor lady. The crown of Poland—though he was even now to be forbidden by the imperious Catherine of Russia to accept it—had been offered to the Elector, and the fact that he

---

[1] Huge hoops were still worn by ladies in full dress.

had no male heir complicated the matter of succession, and let loose greedy thoughts and designs upon the child of nine who was his heiress. There were plenty of aspirants for the hand of the Princess of Saxony in spite of her youth,[1] and her fate entered into the Conference which was shortly to take place, as a pawn in the game being played by the great powers of Europe. The Elector was hereditary Marshal of the Empire; that is, the great Roman Empire, of which the Emperor Leopold II. was now the head. In view of coming events at Dresden—many great personages were expected, and the Conference of Pillnitz was to be held in a few days —was it to be wondered at that 'No Apartments' was still the order of the day when the Electress returned? Through coming years of sorrow and anxiety she was to be the honoured mistress and friend of the Baroness Laetitia, but for the moment the latter's presentation at the Court of her husband's sovereign had to be postponed.

Horace Walpole's prophecy as to the crowned heads of Europe had already come true. They were all 'aching' badly; while one of them was not only aching, but in danger of being 'lost,' more through the indiscreet efforts and selfishness of his own friends than through either his own fault or that of his people. Nothing contributes more to one's understanding of the rottenness of the *Ancien Régime* of France, than the history of the selfishness, cowardice, and haughty pretensions of the Bourbon princes, and the crowd of 'noble' emigrés who had fled from France to save their skins and wealth, leaving the unfortunate King to the mercy of his enemies. Miss Houblon after her visit to Versailles— a few short weeks before the fall of the Bastille—spoke of Louis XVI.'s person as 'heavy and bloated,' and of Monsieur as 'the same.' But in the hour of adversity the former was sustained by a spirit of Christian

[1] Von Sybel, *History of the French Revolution.*

patience and courage, very far from the sentiments of his ignoble brothers. The princes and emigrés had been besieging the Courts of Europe with clamours, almost threats, for armed help; help to reinstate them and the King in their heretofore power and prestige,[1] unmindful that they were inviting other nations to introduce foreign troops to French soil, and to 'inexorable war' with their own country. The kingly instinct in Louis felt the anomaly, and he persistently deprecated armed interference between himself and his people; as a matter of fact, so soon as French territory was invaded by the allies, the King's doom was sealed. Meanwhile, though the Princes of the German Empire felt the general danger—and the agents of the French Revolution were assiduously sowing the seeds of their doctrines in every state—the representations of the Comte d'Artois at this very time only served to disgust, while enlightening them on the preposterous selfishness of his proposals. No one could have been more anxious to ensure the safety of the French royal family than the brother of Marie Antoinette; and Leopold of Austria was more likely to listen to herself and Louis than to either Artois or Monsieur. Moreover, neither he nor the King of Prussia had any desire for war, grave as was the situation. The person chiefly interested in that contingency was Catherine of Russia, who desired to see them both with their hands full in a French war, that she might be free to fasten her grip on Poland, which was in due time to become the prey of the Russian vulture. That the German eagles insisted in the end on sharing the spoil, was neither her fault nor desire.

The Elector of Saxony, having been encouraged by his late powerful guests to accept the crown of Poland, was, as we know, forbidden to do so by Catherine, who

[1] Von Sybel, *History of the French Revolution*, i. 362.

wanted it for herself. The poor man's condition of mind, when once more left to face the situation, can be imagined. Soon after this, Baroness Laetitia's presentation took place, and she and her husband departed for Nice; but meanwhile she wrote home to Charles Cotton a short account—sent by a private hand—of the recent great events. We may read between the lines that the result was known; for the present there was to be no war. As at this time it was generally believed that Naples and the King of Sardinia were ready to go to war with France, while Gustavus of Sweden, in alliance with and subsidised by Catherine, had engaged to do the same—the relief as to the outcome would have been great in respect of the Baron Friedrich's situation as a Sardinian officer. Bouillé, who was to lead the Swedish expedition, found himself at Dresden during the Conference, and remained behind after the monarchs were gone, in close intrigue with the French Princes.[1] But Sardinia, and his duty as a soldier, alone concerned our Baron. He desired to be free of foreign service in this critical time, so as to be ready to draw his sword, if needed, in that of his own country. Though the Italian states were still furious with the French, they were nevertheless thankful to be still at peace,[2] while Russia's game of aggression was perforce postponed by the result of the Conference. All now appeared as if promising a lengthy peace,[3] and this being the case, the honour of the soldier was satisfied, and shortly after the Baron resigned his commission in the Sardinian army with a clear conscience.

The first half of the letter above mentioned as written to Charles Cotton from Dresden was begun on the 21st

[1] The famous coalition of the powers of Europe against the French Revolution had its birth in the Pillnitz Conference, though for the present active measures were to be resorted to 'in case of necessity' only. This was in sum the answer given to the Comte d'Artois after the Conference of 27 August 1791. See Von Sybel, *History of the French Revolution*, i. 364.
[2] *Ibid.*, i. 368.
[3] *Ibid.*

of August, and after an interval of a week Baroness Laetitia continues : 'We were feasting on account of a family birthday, when Thursday arrived the Emperor[1] and Arch Duke Francis, the King of Prussia and Prince Royal. This has made the Crowns to fly swiftly out of the Elector's Trunks, a thing He is not said to be very fond of!' Though at that time very rich, the Elector was mean and apparently not much loved.

As she had not yet been presented at Court, the Baroness Laetitia 'could not be invited to the state dinners and suppers' in honour of the august guests of the Elector—with her new relations; but she accompanied them to a function at Pillnitz where she met 'this Assemblage of Royalty, including the Comte d'Artois and various other celebrities.' The entertainment included 'a superb illumination and wondrous Fireworks on the Elbe.' She also attended a great masque ball in the Opera House at Dresden, where 'the Grands took two or three turns round, and then seated themselves in a Box for an hour, whilst some of the Princes danced. The King and his son are extreem fine figures; the Arch Duke (afterwards the Emperor Francis) a very pretty man. But his Father has nothing Imperial about Him! Count Artois is still here; the rest went yesterday, Sunday; one to be crowned, the other to marry two daughters, extraordinary princely Weddings—& as it is, Love reciprocates ! It is said here, the King not only gives His daughters an iffience portion, but pays the Duke of York's debts to the amount of 5 Million of Thalers! How can He owe so much! We also say that all is settled to reinstate the King of France, and that the first blow is to be struck in 14 days. I think if that was so, Bouillé would not still be here nor yet the Prince' (Artois). In response to questions from Eng-

[1] Leopold II. See p. 235.

land respecting Poland: 'Tell Miss Cotton I see many Poles, but know nothing of Revolution, only that everybody is disatisfied, and the Monarch said to be in danger. We shall soon leave this agreable mansion (her brother-in-law Baron Wilhelm's palace in Dresden) and begin our long journey; but meanwhile my Lord has been casting covetous eyes on the flocks of Pheasants, Partridges, and Hares, which abound in the country round about, and which indeed meet us at every turn, but the shooting of which is prohibited at all seasons. So they go to a Family Fief. I wish you good luck next Thursday in your sport.' After this, the Baron's leave being at an end, he and the Baroness rejoined his regiment at Nice, at which place they remained till May 1792.

War was not yet declared, but the disturbed condition of France made the exchange of letters with England very irregular, though during the past winter a larger number of English people than ever before flocked to sunny Nice in search of health. It was long before the Riviera was again the resort of either English or any other strangers, but meanwhile 'they keep coming, whenever the weather will permit.'

'Relations of yours,' she wrote to her sister-in-law, 'a most pleasant Couple, made me conclude my last letter in a vast hurry, Mr Eyre & Lady Mary, I fancy you don't know them much,[1] but I am in love with both, tho' I often threaten to pull her Cap, as she persists in declaring a passion for my Baron! Mr Eyre is astonishingly better, and intends a second winter here, as does also Lady Glyn. I sent John a list of our Country folk here. Miss Pocock is vastly better, and I hope will recover. They are vastly agreable and *prudent*, which is not the case of all Wives and Misses this year. 'Tis still doubtful if the Duchess of Devon, etc., will add to

1792

---

[1] Mrs. Houblon's grandfather, William Eyre, Esq. of Holme, co. Derby, took the name of Archer on his wife succeeding to Welford, Berks.

our party. Lady Duncannon has borne the journey to Lyons better than was expected, some think they will stop at Hyères. The Duchess of Ancaster is in a deplorable state; no hopes I fear. Mrs Graham, Lord Cathcart's sister, Mrs Dumbleton and Miss Russell are our last invalids, except Mr Foster, the Irish speaker's son, who arrived four days since and by all accounts will hardly exist as many more. I never heard a more amiable character than His. Coxe the writer's [1] Brother is with Him, and appears a Worthy Clergyman. Indeed we abound this year in decent Priests; no less than three Christmas Day. Dean Coote assisted Mr Middleton in administering the Sacrament. Do you know Mrs Coote? she was niece to Lord Bathurst; a funny little old Woman, who my Lord says would like a healthy young Husband better than Her infirm old Dean. He is ungrateful and saucy, as she takes vast notice of Him! To-morrow we are asked to *broach a goose Pye* at your Cousin Eyre's, who is just recovering from 2 months Gout. Mr Green has again suffered grievously, but can again get out. How do your good Aunts? Tell Mrs Feake it was childish to get sick at Bristol.[2] I beg she will put on Her best looks for our arrival, and I will allow Her to flirt as much as she pleases with my Baron.'

In April we hear more of the poor searchers after health at Nice, in a letter from the Baroness to Miss Cotton at Madingley. She begins by describing the latest addition to the Green family in a ' Babe that is the admiration of all; draws up its head with the stately air for which its grandmother Watson was so remarkable. Miss may well be proud having Duchesses for Nurses, for she of Devon dandles Her by the Hour, and Her godmother of Ancaster sees Her whenever she is able, poor woman. She is in a sad state. We have had a loss that has affected us grievously. The worthy M^r

---

[1] Archdeacon Coxe.   [2] The Feake family lived in Essex.

Eyre died the 20th of last month. Lady Mary did us the justice to believe we were desirous of giving Her every consolation in our power, that I have seen Her daily, and she came here during the removal of the Corps. I never saw such resignation. Yesterday she was very ill; she had attended all the mournful services of His Church (the Miserere Holy Thursday is said to be very affecting), and she spent above half that day in a dismal Chapel in a dark corner of a Church. We could not interfere; but even the Catholicks said she prayed too much. But knowing the strict sense she has of Her duty, I flattered myself that would support Her. He is a dreadful loss to the Poor, as His charity was unbounded. He is said to have half supported the French Clergy and Bishops who fled here to avoid taking the new Oaths. There certainly cannot be worthier objects than those who have quitted affluence and honours for their Religion.'

The descendant of 'Confessors,' who on account of their religion had twice forsaken home and country, was probably quite unmindful of her family history when she wrote these words. But they were applicable to any age of persecution. The 'blood of the martyrs,' actual or metaphorical, has been fruitful 'seed' upon the bosom of whatever Church it has been shed. It needs but to keep clear of the thorns which would fain grow up to choke it—in the sense of material loss—to profit morally and spiritually by the experience.

Public opinion had been gradually changing in England in respect of the French Revolution. She alone of the nations had welcomed and applauded the sudden outburst of rebellion against the selfishness in France, which had kept her people hidebound under an oppressive system. Free, generous, and equal under the law, the majority of the English nation had at first seen in the French Revolution a counterpart of that of 1688 at home, though Burke was not slow to prophesy the coming of a revolutionary propaganda dangerous to the world's peace and order.[1] The sympathy of England, as outrage after outrage was put upon the royal family, and as massacres and violence began to disgrace the 'wild cats' who fought and intrigued for power in Paris, changed to horror and indignation.[2] For as the terror grew, it gave birth to hate and suspicion; and he who feared to be destroyed, sought first to destroy.

The Emperor Leopold II. died suddenly at a moment when his wise and far-seeing policy was most needful to the European concert.[3] The Archduke Francis, his son, but twenty-two when he found himself in his father's place as King of Hungary and Bohemia, was soon afterwards elected Emperor. Less wary than Leopold, he was eager to meet the growing danger in Europe with force. 'They write from Germany,' the Baroness remarks in a letter from Nice to Madingley, 'that the new King of Hungary shews a vast deal of spirit and a very warlike genius. What a beast was his Father! and yet they do not think the Empress will survive the shock. She is a very worthy woman. I hear you treat our Margravine,' she continues, 'so disrespectfully that she will leave England. Where to go I can't tell. All the Margraviate rejoices in their new Sovereign.[4] The King of Prussia is said to have been quite astonished when he heard of the acclamations with which His Minister was received.'

Baron von Feilitzsch, having retired from the service of the King of Sardinia, was for the first time for many years master of his time and movements, and he and the Baroness now made their promised visit to England, where he was introduced to his wife's many friends and relations. 'With the swallows' they again departed after

[1] Lecky, *History of England*, vi. 4.
[2] *Ibid*, vi.. 14.   [3] 29 February 1792.
[4] Of Bayreuth, in which Weisdorff was situated.

about six months' stay. The next letter we have from Laetitia is dated October the 28th, 1792, and is from Leipsic.

Distrustful of the Empress Catherine and wrangling over Poland, the great German powers still procrastinated and delayed, fearing by engaging in war to leave her free to carry out her plans uncontrolled. Meanwhile the French settled the matter, by themselves taking the initiative, for on the 20th of April 1792 the French National Assembly declared war against the King of Hungary and Bohemia.[1] The expectations of the Coalition of Princes had not been fulfilled, and they began slowly and unwillingly to make preparations to meet and crush an enemy one and all despised. Francis was crowned with all pomp and ceremony at Frankfort, and the King of Prussia leisurely joined his army at Coblentz in preparation for the invasion of France. On the 19th of July the great Conference of the Princes of the Empire took place at Mayence,[2] while Catherine, left to herself, proceeded quietly and unopposed to throw troops into Poland.

The Duke of Brunswick, who had accepted the command of the allied armies most unwillingly, had indeed gauged the difficulties of the task before him, difficulties chiefly due to the procrastination and petty jealousies of the allies; while the vast crowd of French emigrés were a source of friction and annoyance to all. Against the Duke's will, and in consequence of their representations to the Emperor Francis, he was forced to issue a proclamation which proved disastrous to the objects in view of the allies.[3] This manifesto threatened with vengeance any injury to the royal family of France. The result was, that what Louis XVI. had long anticipated took place, for supposing him to be in

---

[1] Von Sybel, *History of the French Revolution*, ii. 23.
[2] *Ibid.*, ii. 41.　　　　[3] *Ibid.*, ii. 46.

league with the enemies of France, his people turned on him with fury. The Tuileries were stormed by the mob, the King and Queen removed by force to the Temple, and all in sympathy with the fugitive emigrés thrown into prison;[1] meanwhile the army of the allies marched across the frontier and entered French territory. Though despised by their trained invaders, the French were undismayed by their first repulses; the enthusiasm of their raw and inexperienced troops soon retrieved their disasters; and so it came to pass that the Republican General Dumouriez triumphantly rolled back the invading host of Germans. Savoy had meanwhile been invaded and occupied by General Montesquieu, while another French army under General Anselme annexed Nice and its surrounding country.[2] The Piedmontese had already listened to the honied words of French emissaries of Revolution, and the population received their supposed liberators from tyranny with enthusiasm.[3]

The Austrian Empire had not joined in the fray; but the French General Custine with a force of 18,000 men, careless of possible disaster, and hailing all as they went with appeals to brotherhood and co-operation in their propaganda of universal liberty and equality, now marched boldly into Western Germany, capturing Spires and Worms, and spreading terror along the Rhine country. Finding no resistance, Custine resolved on a *coup de main*, and successfully subdued Mayence, the Elector retreating hastily. The whole German Empire now stood aghast. Frankfort was next occupied, while neutrality was feverishly proclaimed by the flying and terrified princes, electors, and landgraves. The Landgrave of Hesse-Cassel, who had but now spent a month of

---

[1] Horace Walpole tells how that when the populace broke into the Tuileries they took Princess Elizabeth for the Queen. Some one screamed it was not she; but the Princess cried out, '*Ah! mon Dieu! ne les détrompez pas!*'

[2] August 1792.

[3] Von Sybel, *History of the French Revolution*, vi. 41.

precious time bargaining with the King of Prussia for an
'Electoral Hat' as the price of his 6000 soldiers, took
flight ignominiously;[1] left with 30,000 Prussians only,
by the cowardly retreat of the petty German princes,
Brunswick had no choice but to retreat. Such was the
situation when our Von Feilitzsch couple, who knew
nothing of it, started on their return journey to Dresden. They had gone by way of Holland, and when the
Baroness wrote from Leipsic at the end of October, she
describes their journey as full of adventure. 'Had we
known,' she wrote, 'the turn things have taken, we
should not have left England at least this Winter, tho'
God alone knows where is safety! But my dearest
Sister will be pleased to know we are safe from the
various perils of this long journey. God be praised we
have met with no accident, & are in good health. You
will have known from Mrs Busdieck what a tedious
voyage we had (across the Channel); then the bad
political news which met us quite discomposed my good
Man. But our friends assured us we could not be
inconvenienced by the French; so we went thro' very
heavy roads from Rotterdam, thro' Utrecht, Nimeguen,
Cleves, Cologne to Coblentz; where we heard the
French were besieging Mayence. This made it very
necessary for us to hasten, and indeed we heard some
Cannon. The road was the worst to Königstein I ever
saw! The Baron walked almost a stage to assist the
Servants to hold up the Coach, and help out of holes;
but for Mr Brown's credit[2] nothing broke, & we were
quit for a good shaking.

'At Frankfort they said Mayence was taken, and they
expected the French every Hour; the poor Emigrants
flying for their lives; no Horses to be had at the Post;
but all-powerful gold drew us to Hanau, where all was

---

[1] Von Sybel, *History of the French Revolution*, vi. 43.
[2] The coachbuilder.

preparing for a Siege, and all Horses ordered to be kept for the use of government. We slept there, and the Baron ran miles, and a Man risked hanging to gain 5 times the usual price for 4 horses to Fulda. Much address & persuasion got us thro' the Gates, and glad were we, & with reason, for we hear the French marched in the next day. Wretches! they carry all before them. The Baron says He is ashamed of being a German. Between Vacha & Berga, we met the Landgravine of Hesse-Cassel returning from Berlin. The Baron told Her the bad news and of her husband's flight! She was going to Hanau, & very much shocked. She appears amiable. We were in very bad roads, but she proceeded that stage, and what she heard more I can't tell, but when we were going to bed at Eisenach, she stopt at the Inn & wanted 8 rooms for the night. All was full, & since I have heard no more of Her R.H. We past then thro' Gotha, Weimar, Naumbourg, & this morning arrived here. To-morrow we proceed, & hope the next day to be quiet at Dresden, where we shall be very anxious to hear of you all. We are vastly distrest for our Nice Friends, and particularly the Greens. We could get no authentick intelligence if Nice was Pillaged or what; and indeed what one told us, the rest contradicted, that it was quite teizing. And yet it was impossible not to inquire. Must not England take part now their ally the King of Sardinia is attacked? If somebody does not take his part, He must be annihilated.' The Baroness Laetitia's letter here breaks off, but she presently continues it as follows:—

'Lord Bristol has just interrupted me by a very civil visit, but gave me no intelligence.' (Lord Bristol was an old friend of her father and brothers, and had not yet heard of Laetitia's marriage.) 'He was most diverted with the idea of a grandaughter of Sir John Hynde Cotton's marrying a German Baron! Says had it been an Hanoverean He certainly would have returned to haunt me.' The letter—after messages to home friends, and fears as to badness of the harvest in England and that every necessary will be extremely dear this winter —ends with a quaint message to her late landlady in town: 'Will you be so kind to tell Mrs Busdieck, that I fear we left the black Candlestick, a p^r of Snuffers & Candle knippers behind. I do not wish Mrs Thacker to have them.'

CHAPTER IX

DRESDEN

'War, waste, plague, famine, all malignities.'
TENNYSON, *Harold.*

'DRESDEN, *March* 3rd 1793.

'IT is very long, my Dearest Sister, since I had the pleasure of addressing you personally. But I trust Laetitia received my Letter and presented you my sincere thanks for that you was so good to send me. I am convinced you knew the joy it would be to me to read so good an account of your Son. May the Almighty render your 3 dear Children an increasing fund of blessings & comfort to you for many years. I hope the sea air (as usual) enabled you to brave the fatigue of the Winter, & that you have enjoyed yourselves as much as the melancholy state of political affairs (who could have thought that so many foreign Eyes should weep the death of Lewis the 16th) permits. I believe there never was a time of more anxiety for all Europe. The general safety, it is thought here, depends on the speedy and vigorous exertions of England. God grant it may prove so; it will be glorious for us, and I may be proud to receive the compliments I meet everywhere on my Nation! I want much to know if the Captain has a ship? God send him glory and riches!

'The Electress talked yesterday with Tears of Her Family and Country. Those filthy Devils, not content with pillaging Deux Ponts, broke and destroyed furniture and all else! . . . It is cruelly provoking the post is

ARMS OF THE BARON AND BARONESS VON FEILITZSCH.

now so uncertain; there has been no English mail now 10 days, & the last brought nothing of later date than Feby 2nd. I have been so unlucky as never to receive a letter Edward was so good to write me, & I tremble for my other correspondence.' (Edward Cotton now managed her home business affairs.) 'What a shocking scrape Alexander has brought himself into!¹ But it was no more than might be expected. It appears very odd to us that He should seek refuge in France! I expect He'll find a grave!'²

'Where did my nephew spend His Xmas? His Friend Althorpe I heard of from Rome 2 months since. He was well, but much distrest for want of language. I hope John remembers my advice & studies French. He promised me He would when He returned to College. There is no doing without it, tho' we all declare we are now ashamed to use it. The good O'Dunnes are sadly reduced; obliged to leave off Housekeeping. Giving up a comfortable dwelling for a shabby lodging is always bad, but at past 70 makes every privation still more dreadful. Countess Schall & I wept over one of Her letters, whilst we vainly attempted to unriddle the meaning which it was evident she meant to convey & durst not explain.' (She wrote from Paris.) 'I have not heard of the Greens since I wrote to Laetitia, but hope the ill effects as to their healths at least was past. The expence & loss' (at the taking of Nice) 'must have been very great. I wonder if government will consider Him. I always mistrust His

¹ This young man happened to be on French soil at the outbreak of the war with England. Supposed to be an English spy, he and several others were arrested by the French and kept in close confinement. A letter from Dunkirk (September 1794), at the time of his release, gives a strange picture of the fear and mental apathy produced by long imprisonment. It was eighteen months since he had heard of his family, and he declares that for nineteen he 'only sniff'd the fresh air from an iron grate.' This kidnapping of travellers was repeated by Buonaparte in 1803 on a great scale, when no less than 10,000 unlucky English people paid the penalty of being in France when war was declared.

² Edward and Alexander were Sir Charles Cotton's younger brothers.

noble friends, tho' they promised so very much. He says the Almighty tempers the wind to the shorn Lamb, & He trusts will take care of His little Flock. May it prove so. Lady Mary Eyre is a true friend, & the greatest consolation to them.

'My damsel is everything I wish, for me. For Her I am sorry she leads so dull a life, tho' she seems quite content, embroidering me a dress which received the highest elogium.[1] Mr Smidt, a famous painter & fellow Collegian of the Baron's saw it, & would not go without sketching the pattern & Colors; so I suppose some Canvass Princess will appear in it before me, for it was intended for a Domino for Shrove Tuesday; but all Court Shews were stopt by the cruel murder at Paris.' 'I wish the same fashions reigned at London as here, & that you had the fellow Pelisse to mine. It is in my mind the noblest & most comfortable habit I ever saw, & mine cost very little, for Mr Green gave me a quantity of fine Sable, & I had a rich india-white Sattin; that nobody exceeds me, & most envy me. It served me for mourning, which finishes this day. Should you go into a Furrier's, & think of it, do ask the price of *English Silver-haired Rabbit skins*; for here they set an enormous value on them.'

It would appear that Baron Friedrich had lately sold his estate in Bayreuth, with the intention of purchasing another nearer home. The purchaser of Weisdorff was a member of the Podewils family to whom his only sister Amalia was married. But the Baron was at present fearful of investing the purchase-money in land. Indeed, he soon altogether abandoned his project of so doing, and ultimately invested the money in English securities. 'The Baron thinks the times too perilous,' wrote his wife, 'to engage in a permanent situation

---

[1] The young lady's maid amused herself, unbeknown to her mistress, in a manner that caused her sudden dismissal.

of price, so we are seeking a good House with a pleasant Garden for this Summer in the environs. There are many, but as everywhere else, a *but* to all we have yet seen. The month of May, I believe, we shall pass at Carlsbad; those Waters being highly recommended to establish the Baron's health which, thank God, needs at present little mending; mine, none at all. I hardly remember passing a better Winter! 2 or 3 Colds—for which I was my own Physician—is all, & I have not found the season more severe than in England. It is now quite fine spring, but people seem to fear it is too good to last. Mr Pagett, a nice little soldier, has offered to carry letters, so I hope you will get this safe & free of cost. My love to Mrs Feake, & the best cure for Rhumatick pains—tell her—is to write a little every day to an absent friend, and seal & direct it on a Tuesday. The consciousness of the pleasure with which it will be read will cause a glow in the Heart that will remove all complaints! Most Brotherly affections from mine Spouse. Love to Neices from your affectionate & obliged L. v. F.

'Pray tell me in your next if Mr Egalité's daughter is still in England,[1] & Madame Genlis, etc.'

'DRESDEN, Sepr 8th. 1793

'Since I did myself the pleasure of scribbling to my dearest sister, the accounts of you & yours have been very satisfactory to us, & We sincerely hope your summer has passed as agreably as you expected. Lady Fermanagh is very gay. I always loved Her. Pity the weather spoilt the shooting sight, which I should think the best part of it. I am glad you are not actors, for at least I don't approve of those manœuvres.' (Women in Germany took part with the men in the shooting of game.)[2] The following is how Laetitia greeted the

[1] The Duc d'Orléans' daughter, Pamela, and the famous Madame de Genlis, her *Gouvernante*.
[2] See Moore's *Travels* for a 'hunting' at the Prince von Lichtenstein's. Ed. 1779, ii. 394.

announcement of a lately arrived infant at Madingley—a boy after several girls—but who died after but a brief acquaintance with 'this wicked world.' In those days when a family was supposed to be consumptive (and a single case was sometimes sufficient to brand it), the wiseacres condemned its progeny for evermore to the same fate. It needed several generations to prove the exception to the supposed rule to be the dominant fact. But kind old women and stern fathers alike shook their heads and warned the young ones against such alliances, as 'dear C. C.' was warned against his marriage with Philadelphia Rowley. 'How the Captain could make such a choice always astonishes me,' cried the Baroness Laetitia, '& entail misery on Himself & posterity! *Fate is irreversible.*' It is strange to hear such stuff from so sensible a woman. The sweet face of Philadelphia, Lady Cotton, in Gainsborough's beautiful portrait, is enough to account for C. C.'s choice! Curious to relate, this 'delicate' lady died at the age of ninety-three![1]

The execution of Louis XVI. in January 1793, together with the revolutionary propaganda, which was in full activity in England and Ireland, had finally broken down Pitt's hope of maintaining his policy of neutrality in the war. He dismissed Chauvelin, the French envoy, and soon after the French settled the matter, by declaring war against Great Britain and Holland.

In the opening of the campaign of 1793 the combined forces of the allies—Austrians and Prussians—carried all before them. Sweeping the French from the Austrian Netherlands, town after town surrendered, while the British contingent of 10,000 men commanded by the Duke of York laid siege to Dunkirk. Anarchy was reigning in Paris, rebellion against the Republic at Lyons and Toulon, and civil war in La Vendée. The French were sorely beset from both within and without,

[1] She was the daughter of Sir Joshua Rowley, Bart.

but they met the overwhelming odds with reckless resolution. That their final success was chiefly due to the disintegrating processes of jealousy and division in the camp of their enemies, rather than to their own skill and valour at this time, is more than probable; but suffice it to say that the tide turned in September, when the Duke of York was forced, by a French victory at Hondschoote in the Netherlands, to raise the siege of Dunkirk.

Writing in November to Miss Cotton, the Baroness discourses on the actual situation in Europe from the German point of view. 'We join with you most cordially in wishing the Grand Fleet may do something worthy its name. Every feeling mind must be additionally inveterate against those murderous Wretches. Many lamentations I am grieved to hear from the failure at Dunkirk; and am tempted from your silence to credit what most rational People here assert, that your dear Pitt' (the Cotton family staunchly supported and admired the statesman, however great the abuse he received) 'has all the blame: who, not conceiving the possibility of Lord Hood's great good fortune' (viz. the taking of Toulon by the Mediterranean fleet on the 23rd August[1]), 'and desirous that the English' (troops) 'should do something to excuse the great expenses to Parliament, insisted on H.R.H.' (the Duke of York) 'detaching Himself from the Prince of Saxe Cobourg' (who was in command of the allied forces). 'The gazette restores the Duke and Army to H.S.H.' (Coburg), 'but too late to save the 3000 brave Austrians who' (at Mattignies) 'wanted their assistance the 14th. A Victory is spoke of the 19th. God send it true!'

'As to our moving,' cries the Baroness soon after this, 'I am very sensible of your friendship, but whilst this

1793

[1] On 13 September Captain Buonaparte planned and carried the siege of Toulon, thereby forcing the English garrison and fleet to retire.

diabolical War exists we cannot think of quitting a situation as long as it is safe. Should the contagion spread' (and the French were doing their best through their emissaries to ensure this) 'Heaven only knows where we end our lives! My bravery is to run away from every place that is tainted with French principles. God preserve England, & particularly my dear Relations from all disasters, personal & political, prays your affectionate, etc., L. v. F.'

Hallingbury had been let since 1784 to Lord Mountstuart, eldest son of Lord Bute, the statesman against whose influence so great a jealousy had been aroused in the country in the early years of George III.'s reign. To the family friendship with Lord Mountstuart, who had passed many years in Italy and Spain, Laetitia both before and after her marriage owed many agreeable and useful acquaintance on the Continent. As she expressed it, 'we everywhere fared well that he recommended us.' Lord Bute died in 1792, and Lord Mountstuart succeeded him as fourth earl. The following year was the last of their stay at Hallingbury, the lease of which they had but lately renewed, for their eldest son died suddenly there after a fall from his horse. Through letters of the rector, Mr. Lipyeatt, and others we hear of the great distress of the parents, who with their troop of young people had lived long enough at Hallingbury to make many warm friends there and in the neighbourhood.

1793   'Pray tell me,' wrote the Baroness in November to Charles Cotton, 'what Mr Archer has done; I am out of my wits to know; Maria might have wrote me!' It was nothing creditable; and Maria did well to hold her tongue as to her grandfather's peccadilloes. But apart from that, to those who live long 'out of sight' of dear ones at home, the keeping touch with home news is frequently a problem, for they are but too often 'out of mind' also. 'Maria might have told me' or suchlike plaints deserve sympathy, in that they have behind them the poignant thought of neglect. At how little cost would it be possible for all kind Marias to obviate this pain! But for the rest we propose—like Maria—to defer Mr. Archer's affairs till we have carried to a conclusion the story of our good German couple Von Feilitzsch.

Eighteen months later, and another letter from the Baroness is again dated from Dresden, and the war in Belgium was still at its height. It was May, and she wrote of 'a vast deal of cold rain, very uncomfortable, and terrible hail destroying a district with a long name not far off. But in these environs—the most beautiful of any in the universe—all promises *peace* and *plenty*! Heaven grant it general, but we are not so sanguine to expect all finished this Campaign. What a noble Fellow is the Prince of Saxe Cobourg! Our English gained much glory & I trust will go on so. The Duke of York is extolled as a commander. It pleases me that he is good for something.' H.R.H.'s love of wine and cards was well known on the Riviera.

1795

'What a pretty Novel is the Princes of Prussia's love! How the 2 Princesses' (of Mecklenburg) 'beged Grandmama to take them to Frankfort. How Grañy said, "I wish it with all my heart, but as I have but 3000 Thalers for both your maintenance, I can only buy you muslin dresses & that's not fit!" How Misses wept & coax'd, & that they should die with anxiety to see the King of Prussia, & that they would be quite incog. Granny relented & all packed up. How a Burgomaster who knew them invited them to a Ball, & the moment the Princes' (of Prussia) 'entered, They fell desperately in Love; but that Prince Royal would not speak to the eldest Princess that He might observe Her the more. And how the next morning He threw Himself at the King's feet, & said, as His Majesty had always been so kind to allow Him to speak His mind, He now declared that His whole happiness depended on the Princess of Mecklenburg for a Wife. The K. took Him up, embraced Him, said His first wish was accomplished, which was that His Son's heart might speak. That he highly approved, & would instantly write to the Queen for Her approbation. The Prince went to His Brother: said He was the happiest of Mortals, for His Father had sanctioned His Passion. The young one was sadly alarmed, recollecting that He had noticed only the youngest' (Princess)—'hesitatingly asked which? The eldest! Then, my dearest Brother, you are *not* the happiest of Mortals, for I will marry the youngest! So they hugged; & Papa was as agreeable to this as that. Granny liked to have died with Joy. The Princesses only feared that it would bring on their Father's Jaundice again, who was just recovering. A fine Ball was given, the want of dress was removed, & there's a pretty Tale just as I heard it from a Lady who has come from Frankfort. The King wanted one of *our* Princesses, but George said it must be the Eldest, & she was thought much too old! If that's true our poor Daughters must remain as good Maids as they can.' The eldest of these two little sisters of Mecklenburg Strelitz was afterwards the heroine Luise, Queen of Prussia, who dared to beard Buonaparte in the hour of Prussia's greatest humiliation. Napoleon on this occasion behaved like the *roturier* he was.

A month after the last letter, found the Baron and Baroness in England, where they stayed more than four years. During this period they paid many visits to Laetitia's friends and relations, but resided mainly at Stoke house, near Plymouth, formerly occupied by Laetitia and her mother, and which now belonged to Sir Charles Cotton.[1] A warm affection grew up

[1] Sir Charles Cotton, R.N., succeeded his father as baronet in 1797.

FASHIONABLES 1802.

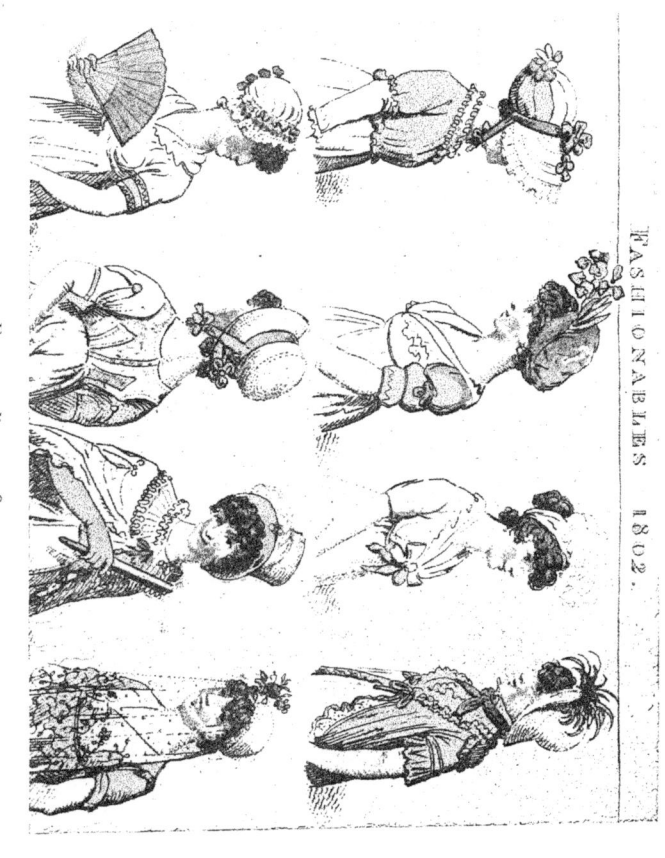

FASHION PLATE, 1802.

DRESDEN

during this time between the Baron and Laetitia's family, especially with respect of young John—now of age—a friendship, which was to last for the life of the elder man, and prove a solace and support in heavy trials in the evening of his life. A letter to Madingley written by the Baroness from Dresden in August 1797, describes their return journey from London through France.

'DRESDEN, *Aug.* 14, 1797.

'According to promise, my dear Cousin shall know by the first post of our safe arrival in 24 days from London; an hideous time spent on the worst of roads. I long for a letter from you, and how you fared at Madingley. I felt much for your first going there, but hope your visit went happily over, and that you left Sir Charles, Lady Cotton & the dear girls quite well, & found M^r & Mrs Oldershaw[1] the same. I found a letter from Maria waiting for me, which was a great joy. She said all were well, & that Her Mother would take them to Chelmsford Race. It pleases me all that compliments Essex! As a grand secret she mentioned the 29th as my dear Nephew's Wedding day. So we drank their healths & I kissed his Picture. I find my Sister gives great part of Her Diamonds, which I am very glad of. I doubt He will get nothing from the rest. The Baron is sure Maria will get an husband at the Races. I wish He may be as true a prophet as He was about Miss Bramston' (John's bride).

'You can have no idea with what joy we were received in France. The Populace thought we brought peace. The Poissardes came two stages from Paris to hug & kiss Baron Jacobi! an honor He would willingly have excused. They were very civil; said good times would return now Travellers began to be seen. We were

[1] *née* Cotton.

4 Carriages, as we smuggled in some Emigrant Ladies & Children, & such a train had not passed since the Revolution. They talk very freely that things can't go on as they are; that they knew not when they were well. The most arbitrary of their Monarchs did not tax them one third so high as their present Rulers. In short all was discontent, & from Calais to the Rhine not a vestige of Religion to be seen. It was shocking. The Churches either quite down (where they could sell the Stones) or standing without a pane of glass or door. All ornaments broken, & a bill "National property to be sold." At Liége the beautiful Cathedral is quite down; and at Cambray the Wretches took up good Fénelon's bones & draged them about the Streets; also those of one who had existed but to do good—I forget his name, but they say they were deceived and are very sorry—But the French told them all Misfortunes came from Priests & Kings. Now they find, had they been wise enough to give their Emperor' (of Austria) 'half the men & money the French have taken, they should now be the happiest instead of the most miserable of People. We were quite enraged when we came near Gueldres. The last time we drove miles thro' an Avenue of such Beeches that we got out of the Carriage to measure them. That Prussian Brute (the King of Prussia) has given up till the peace all His territories there, & the Wretches have cut them all down for firing or what they would sell for. I was astonished in the Westphalian Lands to see numbers of the noblest Oaks I ever beheld. We had time to admire them, as the Wheels cut in almost to the axletrees, & those lousy Prince Bishops take no heed about the Posts, that we went frequently 7 or 8 hours with the same poor Horses. An expeditious way of travelling! & where the roads were full of deep holes and Huge stones ready to overturn our Coach. Our Companions were twice upset &

MARY ANNE BRAMSTON.
m. JOHN₆ ARCHER HOUBLON, ESQ

T

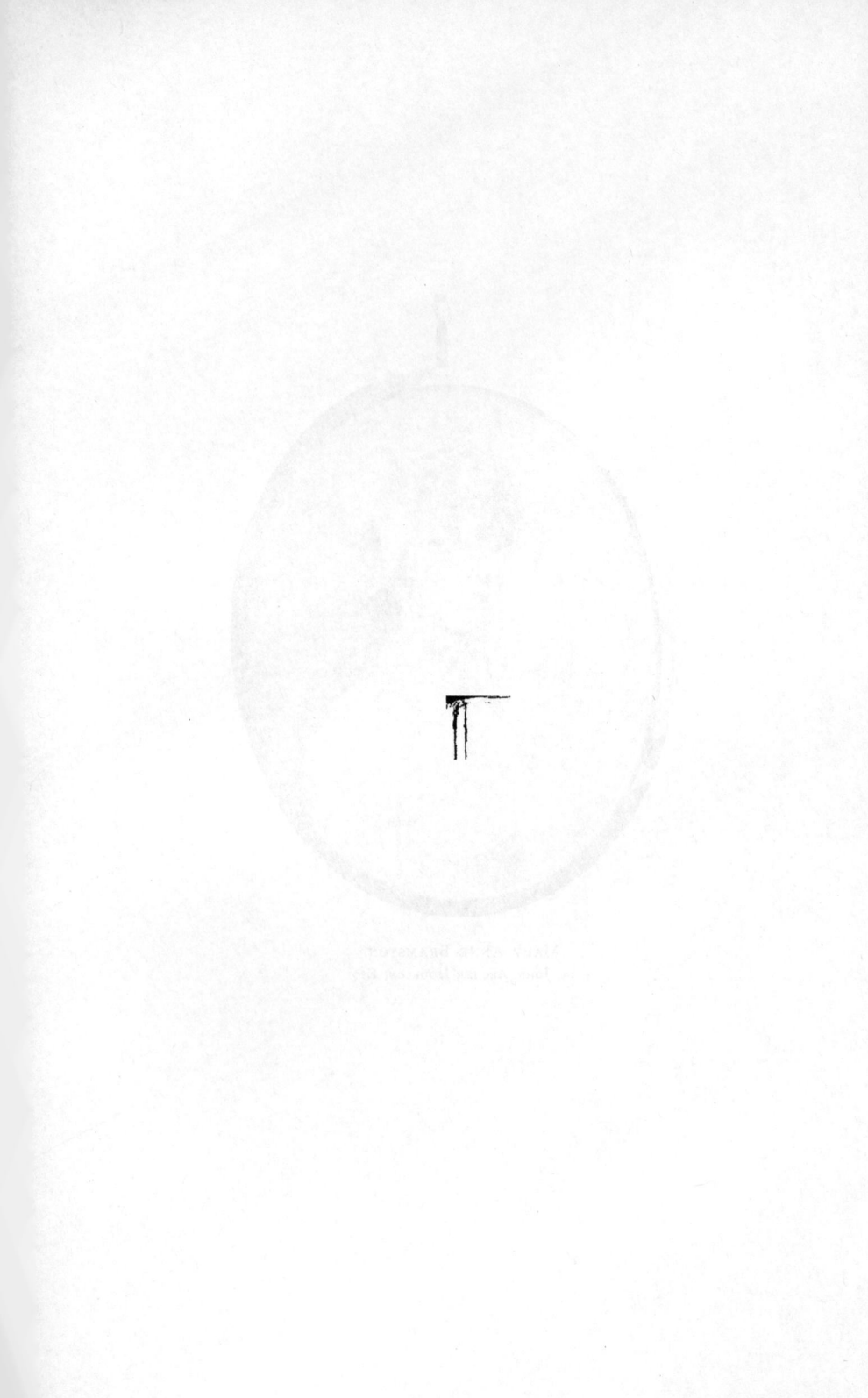

many breakings. My Baron says Brown must have made our Wheels of something stronger than Iron or Timber or they must have broken many times. We got one lay down after we had passed all the bad ways. A fore axletree broke just coming into Eisenach. Providentially a few bruises that red oil soon cured, was all the personal damage, & 2 guineas set us going again the 2nd day. Here' (at Dresden) 'I have a nice little lodging in my brother Feilitzsch's House till my Lord returns. He set out this morn, & we are promised a perfect cure. God grant it. He was better for the journey. My maid is all amaze. She had never hardly been further than Windsor. She behaves very well. Pray wafer your Letters; for this broiling weather melts all the wax together; and favor me with a speedy answer, & tell me all private & Publick news.'

Only two more letters from Dresden have come down to us, and they are both addressed to Miss S. Cotton, who now made her home at 'the Bath.' All other correspondence—notably that with Mrs. Houblon—has disappeared. The letters are few and far between, because the Von Feilitzsch couple from time to time visited England.

'DRESDEN, *Nov*^{r} 4th 1804. 1804

'Your letters, my dear kind Cousin, are & ever must be received with the utmost gratitude. It rejoices me much that all were well at Madingley; for I feared much for that horrid disorder. . . . My Neices had written that yours were much improved, & I am happy that you confirm it; & the dear Boys all that can be wished. I was sure your Godson would be a noble Fellow;. What joy it will be for Sir Charles to find Him so! I doubt He will not be allowed a long stay, & so I will not importune Him with a letter, but beg you to forward a petition from poor Nobe's nephew, who wishes a good word at the Admiralty, to be I believe Master sail maker. He wrote to His Aunt, who, alas! is disabled by a Cancer, which grieves me cruelly. In my reply I recoṁended Him to wait on Sir C. C., who I supposed would put in at Plymouth soon—tell His tale & shew my letter.

'What you say of the Houblons delights me; & I am thankful more are coming. Little John must really be a forward lad;[1] God bless them. I thank you for your Bush Fair Anecdote. It has furnished me with a grateful topick, & have received in return many compliments on the well-judged charity of our nation. I was telling it to a most amiable Woman, the Grande Maitresse to the Electress; who surprised me much by saying, " I know Lady Petre well ; & it was the greatest misfortune to my family She was not my Neice; for Baron (a terrible long name) was so desperately in Love with Her, & His Mother opposing it, He run into such extravagances that He died at 24.

'Thus far had I got 7 days since, when frost & snow came, & we fell a packing for Dresden. Since, I have not had a moment to write, nor are we yet settled. We have taken this House for 2 years, that we may not be necessitated to be every 6 months changing everything. Better acquaintance was not advantageous to our Villa, that we shall not return there unless we can't find a better. One of the Elector's Chamberlains is just dead, & my good attentive Friend the Electress informed me the next day, with the addition: that She had informed the Widow that she insisted on Her not disposing of the Vineyard untill I had refused it; which I am sorry will be the case as it is not consonant to our ideas of comfort.' The Baron had never yet made up his mind to spend his capital—now safely invested in England—upon a 'permanent situation' of price; so they lived in Dresden and passed the summer at a 'Vineyard' in the

[1] John$_6$ Houblon's son, born 1803.

country; this appellation being the usual one for the villas, to which many of the Saxon nobility resorted in the neighbourhood of Dresden, rather than to their own estates at a greater distance.

The Baroness's last letter from Dresden is written in 1805, immediately after the fatal campaign of Austerlitz, and in but little more than two years after that, the Baron von Feilitzsch, broken-hearted at the reiterated blows which had crushed his country and her allies, aged and suffering in body and mind, consented to repair with his wife to England. Whether he meant to return or not we do not know, but it is certain that he never again set foot in Germany.

'*January* 3, 1806.

'The year 1806 shall not be a week old before I address one of my most valued correspondents & kindest Relations. Her most pleasing letter reached me on the 27th of Nov^r., & had I had any good to write a speedy reply would have ensued. But alas! Germany produces no Laurels but what their Emperor blasts directly. Does not your heart ache for the noble Arch Duke Charles, who, after a series of the noblest actions, fought His way back to rescue Vienna; and on summoning the Wretch to retreat or take the consequences of His victorious army in three days, was answered by the Armistice which that mean Booby had signed before His last Victory! So that the Archduke must restore all His Prisoners. This struck Him so, that the Fits which He had been free from near 2 years returned with such Violence, that H.I.H. was lamented as dead for many hours, & is still in a dangerous state, I fear. The excellent Alexander' (the Czar) 'was too brave. He should not have exposed His Person in battle. It had too dangerous effects. His loss would have been a misfortune to the whole World. During his absence Rascals got about the simple Francis, & made Him resolve on Peace; that all the sence of Honor of Alexander could not bring Him back. The French themselves say, had another battle followed they would have been undone, even tho' victorious,—for Russians fight like Tigers, Bless them! The Terms of Peace is unknown here, so supposed to be scandalous for Austria. What the rest will do is equally in the clouds. But truly this is the most charming Place for knowing nothing certain that ever was. My Lord's Sovereign is said to have ruined all by His tardiness. I wish all such Milksop great were shut up at La Trappe from their first proof. B.' (Bonaparte) 'received the Nobles at Vienna in His bedgown, without small Cloaths. True the Room was darkened on account of an inflamation in His Eyes. When they first took possession of Vienna, those Grandees that remained invited the Officers; but they were soon obliged to leave off, as they pocketed the silver spoons & forks! Never were such shabby Wretches; not so much as a uniform; ragged great Coats of all colors, belts over their Arms.

'Now I must finish with a sad love tale. The Princess of Bavaria, the most beautiful girl on the Continent, has long been attached to the Prince of Baden: a mutual passion & settled affair. She gave it as a reason for refusing Beauharnais, on Bonaparte's first coming to Munich. He looked at our Niece Wirtemberg; but she was not worthy: so now He has informed the Princess of B. that if she did not consent directly, He would destroy Her Father, lay waste Her country with fire & sword, & have the Prince of Baden shot. This brisk way of wooing, after dreadful Fits, prevailed, & the hopeless Victim is delivered up to Madame Josephine to be miserable for life. The Viceroy of Italy' (Beauharnais) 'is a fine figure; with the worst of characters & every Vice.

'I wish you could see B.'s account of the battle of

Modes (from Racinet).

Trafalgar published at Vienna! Poor Nelson was entirely beat, the *Victory* taken, the *Royal Sovereign* sunk & so on; Only one of the combined Fleets lost. In the same stile is described the last land battle & as true. He treats the wounded just as He did in Egypt; yet they bear Him through fear, for all say, in every thousand there are not 10 in France but detest Him. I am assured that His project of invasion has already cost the lives of 120,000; & He poisoned Admiral Bruix for saying it was impossible for to do anything with such frail Boats. I was in hopes in his mad fury He would have ordered the Brest fleet out to revenge Villeneuve; then, Cornwallis & *Cotton* would have shown, that Nelson, tho' He could not be surpassed, could be equalled. Indeed it appears there were none but Heroes at Trafalgar. I am proud our Essex Member[1] was so high on the list. Pray tell me why there was none killed or wounded in the *Prince* for Grindall never escaped unwounded before! I wish Harry St. John had been in the fight it would have been a glorious beginning! We are just out of mourning for Lady St. John. What did she die of? The papers say: suddenly.' (Harry St. John was a little midshipman aged eleven! to whom in 1795 the Baron von Feilitzsch had stood godfather at his christening.) '. . . What great things are done at Madingley! We rejoice in the improvements, & still more in what all agree of the dear Family. Houblons, thank God, are flourishing. It is well she was not with child as the shock of losing Her excellent Mother might have been very prejudicial. Good Mr Bramston our hearts ache for Him! . . . Mrs Lutwyche came [here] very well but has not been so of late. He views all on the blackest side. . . . They purpose setting out on their return the 1st of June. It will be a sad loss to me *if* we can remain. My good man is a great sufferer!

---

[1] Admiral Eliab Harvey, commanding the *Téméraire*.

Agitation of spirits added to the unseasonable weather (for December has been much warmer than May) affect Him cruelly. My health is quite sound. . . . Letters from England is our best cordial—adieu.'

Usually, however interested the novel reader may have been in the characters whose careers he has followed, he is content to leave them in the situation to which they have been conducted by the author, content, if it is happy, sad, if tragic. But in either case the first is always 'happy,' the second 'sad.' There is no afterwards to a novel, and if one is written it is generally unwelcome and criticised. 'True people' have an afterwards; and this gives the special interest to their 'remains,' but these are generally sad, and in the case of our good Baron and Baroness it is more so than in most cases of the mortal man who 'groweth up as a flower and withereth as the grass of the field.' From a packet of German letters from Dresden we learn a story of want on the one side, and woe on the other, in which the sun set sadly on the Feilitzsch family. When Baron Friedrich sold Weisdorff, afterwards investing the proceeds in English securities, all the purchase-money was not paid, the balance remaining on mortgage upon the estate. Meanwhile, after his retirement to England, his brother remained in the service of the King of Saxony, his master, at Dresden. We know nothing of him and the sister-in-law whom Laetitia had loved warmly for so many years, except what the few letters above noticed reveal, and which were all written as late as 1826-9, shortly before the death of Friedrich and Laetitia in England; for they died within a year of each other. These letters are inexpressibly sad. War and change had brought in the wake of Napoleon many and great woes. Apart from the great loss of life, the levelling of classes and abrogation of rights had resulted in ruin to many. For while the sweeping changes secured advancement and opportunity to some, neglect and poverty, humiliation and loss, resulted to others. The nobility, shorn of their privileges, were ruined, their sons fallen in battle, their daughters portionless. Baron Wilhelm von Feilitzsch, lieutenant-general and officer at the Court, was likewise ruined. 'There are some expectations of beneficial changes in respect of Lords of the Manor' [*i.e.* of fiefs], he wrote in May 1828. 'God grant it. All payments are greatly decreased. Indeed the nobility is much oppressed. Where indeed is there now no want?' Old, broken, both his sons dead, his fiefs barren of profit, his wife broken-hearted, his King stripped of half his kingdom, no joy, no comfort remained to him, no solace but one; this was Ludwig, the only child of his eldest son.

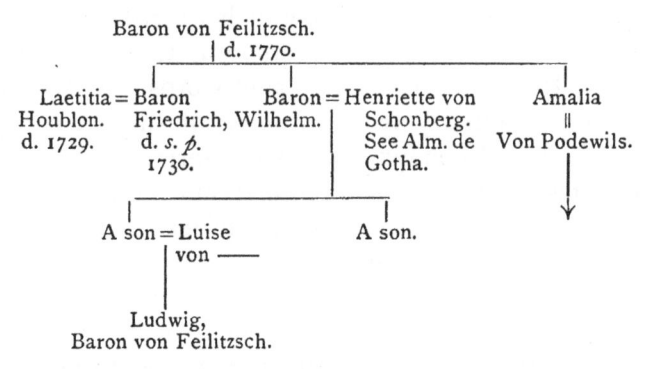

```
                    Baron von Feilitzsch.
                        | d. 1770.
      _____|_____
      |                  |                  |           |
  Laetitia = Baron    Baron = Henriette von         Amalia
  Houblon.  Friedrich, Wilhelm. | Schonberg.           ||
  d. 1729.  d. s. p.            | See Alm. de    Von Podewils.
            1730.               | Gotha.              |
      _____|_____       |                     |
      |                 |       |                     ↓
   A son = Luise          A son.
          | von ——
          |
        Ludwig,
    Baron von Feilitzsch.
```

These German letters have one refrain all through: 'Mein Ludwig' begins them and ends them. Ludwig's mother is nought, the grandparents live and breathe but to cherish and educate their grandson. To this end, in their poverty all is sacrificed—society, friends, even their coach horses. 'I wrote recently to my good sister at Weisdorff in order to enquire after our respective family fiefs; as father and son of the House of Zech, after having become bankrupt, died, one soon after the other, the latter leaving no son, but nine poor unhappy daughters. The surviving Mother is the daughter of Feilitzsch von Heinersgrün. As our family fief is on Trogen, we can demand nothing from there.' . . . 'We live in times when it is not possible for one of us to communicate anything pleasant to the other, but your letter filled us with care and sorrow. Yours is indeed a superfluity of trouble, illness, and cares!'[1]

Riches had vanished for all in Germany, and a dull monotony and gloom had for the time settled down on 'this poor and small country' where but a few years before Dresden had been a centre of life, bustle, and prosperous importance, if not in the eyes of the world, at least in her own. It is some small satisfaction to know that Ludwig turned out 'a good Feilitzsch,' as old Baron Wilhelm fondly boasts to his great-uncle in England. We have the copy of his certificate of proficiency from General von Gersdorff, the commandant of the 'Royal-Saxon-noble-Cadet-Corps' at Dresden, practically a military academy—one of those but lately established by Buonaparte all over Germany.

The last years of his grandparents were comforted by their Anglo-German brother's promise in respect of Ludwig. From the Baron Wilhelm's letters to England we learn that he told them of his intention to make the youth his heir.[2] Doubtless the round sum of £12,000 in solid British securities ultimately served to make him a rich and prosperous man, and helped to set the family once more on its legs in their Saxon home. We believe Von Feilitzsches flourish to this day, though it is uncertain if they descend from Ludwig: two others of the name were at this time living at Dresden; the one Chamberlain to the King, the other 'the grand Ranger of the royal forests.'

[1] Baron Wilhelm von Feilitzsch to his brother in England. Translation.
[2] 'By your generous promises you have enabled my honest husband to look peacefully into the future as regards our darling.'—Baroness von Feilitzsch, *geborn* Henriette von Schönberg, to Baron Friedrich.

Meanwhile the kind 'benefactor' of his kin in Germany had passed and was still passing through a great ordeal. When they settled down in England in 1807 (and Laetitia's old home, Thremhall Priory, received them), although the sorrow and mortification experienced by all good Germans at that time had shaken the Baron's health and aged his hitherto robust frame,—his wife was strong, vigorous, and brilliant as ever. But about two years after their arrival in England her eyes suddenly failed; she was operated on for cataract and recovered. Seven years of tranquil existence now passed by; her Baron became a naturalised English subject, and the Baroness Laetitia was happy, surrounded by her loved ones, old and young. The latest letter written by her that has been preserved, is dated in 1818, but a heavy cloud of silence has till lately hung over her last years. This cloud has been lifted now, by perusal of the German letters lately found; they are the response from Dresden to the Baron's cry for sympathy and encouragement in his 'lonely and desolate fate,' and in his care for his '*arme Laetitia*.' For the brilliant Laetitia's sun had set, long ere she passed from this world, in a clouded mind which, while it continued, could only bring misery upon herself and others. For ten years the faithful Baron watched with grief the gradual settling down of the deep night that made misery for them both; when the last spark was quenched, he was too old and worn with grief to raise his head again. The deep love of two generations of Houblons had become his; and 'pretty Betsy's' daughter Laetitia long since an orphan, had aided him in his task; but he survived but a few months. In the quiet churchyard at Great Hallingbury lie all that was mortal of the Baron and his wife.

CHAPTER X

MRS. HOUBLON NEWTON

'Of these am I—Coila my name;
And this district as mine I claim.'
BURNS, *The Vision*.

SUSANNA ARCHER brought the interests, possessions, and idiosyncrasies of three families beneath the Houblon roof-tree. So far an unbroken line of simple, direct thought had determined impulse and action in the lives of successive generations of Houblons, in whom an attitude almost of stress is observable, even in respect of the two last generations, of squires who may be considered as having enjoyed the so-called 'unearned increment' of land purchased with the proceeds of their ancestors' industry and effort. Be that as it may, prosperity and success attended them, and family affection, friendship, and loyal service accompanied their path through life, while many regretted them when they passed out of sight. They lived guileless lives, for no breath of scandal, selfish extravagance, ill-will, or dishonesty, left its stain behind to be revealed by forgotten papers and documents.

The great property to which Susanna was heiress descended to her long after her husband's death. It is a curious commentary upon *homme propose Dieu dispose* in the matter of rich alliances, that the *mariage de convenance* arranged for Jacob₄ Houblon by his parents in 1770, when he was no longer young, brought him next

ARMS OF MRS. HOUBLON NEWTON.

II

to nothing during his life; nor did his son profit by it, for his mother outlived him many years.

A vast mass of documents of all kinds remain, relating to the business and private affairs of the 'three families' of Susanna, affording material sufficient not only for family history of no little interest, but for the illustration of other matters of importance to students of the period. Although the following detached sketches may be regarded as outside the immediate scope of our Houblon memoirs, the families concerned were so closely connected with the generation with which we are now dealing, that they are not only necessary, but form part of it.

There were several branches of the family of Archer; that one with which Susanna was connected is said to have descended from a certain Simon de Boys, owing its name of Archer to King Henry v., who, when beaten by the knight in a shooting match, dubbed him Archer forthwith. De Boys was a gallant soldier, and fought at Agincourt, where 'he did good service,' for which he received a pension of four marks per annum for his life.[1] Simon's descendant, Henry Archer (who died at Coopersale in Essex in 1615) was the father of Sir John Archer, one of the Judges of the Common Pleas (born in 1598), and author of several thick manuscripts on jurisprudence preserved at Hallingbury.[2]

ARCHER ARMS.

By the annexed table may be observed the connection

[1] Vincent, *History of Essex*. *Memoirs of the Families of Archer*, p. 43. Morant, *Antiquities of Essex*, etc.

[2] The Judge was a Roundhead, but received a free pardon in 1661 and was appointed a Justice of the Bench. Record Office apud *Memoirs of the Archers*, p. 54. Sir John Archer's picture, as one of the Judges of the Court of Judicature who sat on the cases resulting from the Great Fire (1667-73), was painted by Michael Wright and by order 'set up' in the Guildhall. See Walpole's Works: *Anecdotes of Painting*. Other portraits were at Coopersale and Welford.

VOL. II.　　　　　　　　　　　　　　　　　　S

between the families of Archer and Eyre, and how the grandfather of Susanna assumed the former name on his succession to the Archer property through his first marriage.[1] It may be added that the Eyre family of Derbyshire was second to none in that county for ancient and distinguished lineage, and it may also be observed how it happened that through the failure of heirs-male in three generations—Susanna, the third of her Christian name, came to unite in her person not only the name and lands of Eyre and Archer, but those of Newton also. This later inheritance was also the signal for a change of name, assumed, as is expressed in the *Gazette* recording the fact, 'out of affectionate respect to the said family of Newton.'[2]

1819

Mrs. Houblon Newton, as she was now called, was justly proud of her Newton ancestors. A grand old pedigree roll (drawn for Frances Newton, Lady Cobham, in 1584), a precious heirloom in the Newton family, was now continued down the generations, till in Susanna herself we have the representative of the long and illustrious line.[3]

FROM PEDIGREE ROLL, 1584.

Sir John Newton = Margaret, d. of
alias Cradog, Kt. | Sir Anthony Pointz, Kt.

Wyllyam, = Frauncys,	Sir Henry = Katrin, d. to	Nazareth.
Lord Cobham d. to Sir John	Newton Sir Thos.	‖
now Lyvynge. Newton now	now Lyvynge. Paston, Kt.	The Lord
Lyvynge.		Pagett.

---

[1] See table of Mrs. Houblon Newton's descent, at end of volume.
[2] Dated Whitehall, 29 June 1819.
[3] The roll, which is finely emblazoned, was doubtless bequeathed to her brother, Sir Henry Newton, by Lady Cobham. In it the earlier generations are designated as Caradoc or Kradog, lords of Newton and Nangel in Wales.

SIR JOHN NEWTON, THIRD BART.

MRS. HOUBLON NEWTON

About 1540 Leland, when on his *Itinerary*, visited   1540
Barre's Court at Hanham in Gloucestershire. 'At this
Hannam,' he writes, 'in a fayre old Manner place of
stone, dwellyth one Sir John Newton, whose very
proper name is Caradoc. ...
The Forest of Kyngeswodd
cummyth just onto Barre's
Court, Master Newton's
house.'[1] In the *History of
Bitton*, in Gloucestershire,[2]
we have an interesting account of this house, which
was pulled down about 1770
by the last baronet of the
name. Round it was a moat,
with a drawbridge and gate-
house, and the place was
adorned with many gigantic
leaden statues. All that
now remains of the ancient
glories of Barre's Court, the
home of the Newtons for   ARMS OF CARADOC, *als* NEWTON.[3]
many generations after they
left their native Wales, is a coat of arms 'beautifully
wrought in stone,' emblazoning the arms and many
quarterings of the family.[4] Their ancient pedigree tells
us it was to Kradog, King of South Wales, ancestor of
the Caradocs or Newtons, that they owed the simple
beauty of the Newton arms proper; who, having
'banished all y⁰ Forreners out of his Kingdom, ... toke
to his selfe ye present coate in token of his fruitfull
Countrey.' This was three golden sheaves—or garbs,

---

[1] Leland, *Itinerary*, vii. 37.
[2] *History of Bitton*, part i. p. 102. Privately printed for Rev. H. T. Ellacombe, rector of Bitton, 1881.
[3] From the ancient pedigree roll.
[4] As a Confirmation of Arms granted in 1567. *History of Bitton.*

as is the heraldic term—on a field azure which compose it.[1]

When Susanna Houblon Newton succeeded to it, Barre's Court was no longer the chief seat of the Newtons. The old direct line had died out, the last of them (on being created a baronet by Charles II.) having secured the reversion of his honours to a distant kinsman, by a special limitation to the patent. Although Sir John Newton likewise bequeathed to him the Barre's Court estate, the second baronet (born in 1626) already owned a fine property in Lincolnshire. He was the great-grandson of Sir John Newton of Westby in Basingthorpe, co. Lincoln, knight, and was descended from a branch presumably of the old stock settled in the County Palatine of Lancaster.[2] The wife of this baronet was an Eyre, and was greatly loved by her numerous children, as their letters show. Her eldest son, John, was an aristocrat of the pre-Revolution type of France—handsome, *mondain*, and restless. He was twice married, and his only child by his first wife was named Cary after her grandmother, Lady Mary Cary, whose heiress she became at the age of sixteen.[3] The correspondence relating to the second marriage of Cary's father is in existence. The bride (who was the sister and heir of Sir Michael Warton, Bart. of Beverley, co. York) was a young widow,[4] and was the first of three ladies of the name of Susanna. J. B. Langton, the steward, writes from Newton Park, 16 April 1689, to his master, 'Ye young Lady is now in London where Mr. Newton y^r sonn may have oportunity to see her. . . . Morris gives a faire character of ye young Lady.' Two children, viz.

[1] The Caradoc pedigree comprises other lines of descent, notably that of Tudor to Queen Elizabeth—all tracing their origin from the same ancestor, viz. Rhodry the Great, King of all Wales.
[2] See pedigree.
[3] Lady Mary Cary (by marriage Heveningham) was daughter and heir to John, second Earl of Dover. Cary Newton married Edward Coke of Holkham, co. Norfolk, Esq. They were ancestors to the Earls of Leicester.
[4] Of Sir John Bright of Badsworth, co. York, Bart.

SIR I^sAAC NEWTON (AS A YOUTH).

Michael and Susanna, were the issue of this marriage of John Newton, who succeeded his father in 1699 as third baronet. Marriage probably did not greatly improve this 'man of the world'; we have come across his name included in a key to the actual persons figuring under fictitious names in the famous *New Atlantis* of Mrs. Manley.[1] Sir John and his wife travelled about to their various estates almost as frequently as did Mr. John Archer (their grandson) and Lady Mary his wife.

1699

The second baronet sat for the town of Grantham for five successive Parliaments, and possessed a large house in Soho Square, at that period a very fashionable locality. Here Sir Isaac Newton must often have visited Sir John, his son, and Lady Newton and his young 'cousins' Mick and Sue, with all of whom he seems to have been on terms of friendship, if not affection.[2] When the great philosopher was knighted by Queen Anne in 1705, it became necessary for him to deposit his pedigree at the College of Arms, and he accordingly did so, after taking infinite pains to render it correct. To this we owe the knowledge of his kinship with the Lincolnshire branch of the Newton family, and that they were descended from a common ancestor.[3] Besides his own declaration as to his lineage, delivered at the Heralds' College, to which his signature is appended, is one signed by Sir John Newton acknowledging the relationship between himself and his illustrious namesake. Indeed, the proud and worldly baronet was very sensible of the honour of this kinship with so great a man as Sir Isaac; while the latter would also appear not to have been without some pride of race.[4] A portrait, said to be of Sir Isaac as a young man (now at

1705

[1] It appeared early in the eighteenth century and resulted in her imprisonment for libel.
[2] Turnour, *History of Grantham*, pp. 85-6, and other evidence.
[3] See pedigree at Heralds' College, which has been printed.
[4] The present representative of the Newton family in the female line is fourth cousin five times removed from Sir Isaac Newton.

Hallingbury), was possibly given by him to Sir John, or purchased by the latter at the sale of Sir Isaac's effects after his death in 1727. The baronet survived him some years, and was represented at the funeral by his son Sir Michael (Knight of the Bath in his father's lifetime), who acted as chief mourner on the occasion.[1] It is said that Sir Isaac was sufficiently superior to prevailing fashion as to wear no wig, and his flowing hair *au naturel*, as we see him in his portrait in the National Portrait Gallery, must have looked strange amongst the curly perukes of his colleagues at the Bank and Mint in the early days of the Revolution. As a young man, however, he had not yet risen above fashion's thraldom, for in the portrait above mentioned he wears one. They were just come into vogue, as Pepys tells us—with the growing grey of the King (Charles II.).

If Sir John Newton, the second baronet, entered into close negotiations when arranging the second marriage of his son, the third baronet was no less particular as to the prospects of his only son Michael. A diamond necklace worth £2000 was one item in this settlement on the part of the bride's father-in-law. To the great grief of Sir Michael and his wife, Lady Coningsby,[2] they lost their only son.[3] A fine old stone house, they caused the family home, Culverthorpe, to be beautifully decorated by the famous Grinling Gibbons, the eighteenth-century carver, who was himself a Lincolnshire man.

---

[1] Poulson, *History of Beverley*. Many articles were purchased at the sale by members of the Newton family. See Catalogue, Sotheby.

[2] Margaret, Countess of Coningsby, succeeded to her father's honours in 1617.

[3] The child died in London; but a strange story was afterwards invented of how, during the absence of its parents from Culverthorpe, a tame ape carried it to the roof of the house and threw it down. (*Herald and Genealogist*, ii. 124. Ed. John Gough Nicholas, F.S.A.) Local tradition still repeats this myth. For many years Sir Michael Newton sat in the House of Commons, first as member for Beverley and later for Grantham. The same year that he was created Knight of the Bath (1725) he succeeded, through right of his mother, to the 'great estate' of his uncle Sir Michael Warton of Beverley, Bart.

SALOON AT CULVERTHORPE.

MRS. HOUBLON NEWTON

On Sir Michael's death in 1743 he was succeeded by his only sister Susanna$_2$, and the Newton family in the male line came to an end. Of Susanna—little 'Sue,' the friend of Sir Isaac Newton, and later 'Madam Archer'— we have already heard something, and of the able manner in which she administered not only her own but her husband's properties.[1] She enjoyed the Newton estates for more than twenty years, but after her death they passed consecutively through the hands of three of her children (all of whom died childless); and finally devolved upon the daughters of her eldest son, John Archer of Coopersale and Welford, in default of male issue.[2] Thus it was that Susanna, the third of her name (poor Charlotte was but lately deceased), succeeded at last to the name and lands of the third and greatest of 'her families.' The sale of Barre's Court in 1819 closed a chapter of family history, but it probably cost Susanna, Mrs. Houblon Newton, but little regret; indeed, as there was no longer a mansion-house upon the estate, she may never have been there.

After Mr. Archer's death in 1800, Mrs. Houblon and

---

[1] See pp. 158-9.
[2] See table at end of volume. 'Madam Archer's' second son Michael assumed the name of Newton. He died s.p., leaving his personal estate, including many family portraits, papers, and documents, to his wife Anne Bagshawe. They are now in possession of William H. Graves Bagshawe, Esq., of Ford Hall, co. Derby. Early in the nineteenth century the representative of the family solicitor died, and his effects were sold. Failing the claim of the family to their ownership a large mass of valuable documents and private letters of the Newton and Archer families were thus dispersed. Some were acquired by the British Museum, including an interesting set of letters from Dr. Josiah Woodward (who acted as bailiff to the Archer estates of Welford and Coopersale) to members of that family. They extend over a long period, Charles II.—1695. Other papers were purchased by Lord Monson. A large number are in the Cottonian Library at Plymouth, others are in the Bristol public library; others again were purchased by the present head of the Houblon family from Mr. H. T. Ellacombe, rector of Bitton. A very interesting collection of Archer papers was presented in 1852 to the Smithsonian Institute at Washington by Mr. J. Orchard Halliwell, F.R.S., who originally purchased them for the purpose of illustrating the history of prices. Of the value of these papers Mr. Halliwell thought very highly. We have come across a memorandum of the sending of a 'Trunk of old writings,' and again 'two boxes of writings,' for security by Mrs. Archer to Lincoln's Inn in 1747.

her daughters went to live at Coopersale House. Shut up by its eccentric owner in his grief after Lady Mary's death, this house had been for five-and-twenty to thirty years unvisited even by a caretaker. Needless to say, all Essex flocked to see the strange sight when 'the surveyor sent by the elegant M[rs] Houblon' came to visit and inspect it, and bars and bolts and iron plates erected to baffle prying eyes and fingers, were thrown down and the place entered. A curious account in a newspaper describes the wilderness of 'tall weeds in the courtyard,' while inside, 'rooks and jackdaws had built their nests in the chimneys, owls had taken possession of the principal drawing-room, and pigeons had long made their home among the books in the library,'[1] finding their way in and out by a broken window-pane. So long had they lived here undisturbed 'that several loads of dung cumbered the floor.' 'Never before were cobwebs seen so beautiful or such an amazing size. They extended the whole length of one room, and from the ceiling to the floor.'

The old lath-and-plaster house of Coopersale was now modernised and painted from top to bottom. The panelled gallery shared the fate of that of Hallingbury, though a part remains of fine Elizabethan work bearing the Archer arms.[2] The two sisters sold their father's Derbyshire estates of Highlow and Holme in order to pay the heavy debts he left behind him. Long ago the Baroness Laetitia wrote from Dresden: 'I'm mad to know what has M[r] Archer done?'[3] It was an unprofitable story; only a foolish old man in the hands of a designing woman. Miserable, half-blind, tortured with eczema and estranged from his children, he lived at Bristol, and, except by his steward or man of business, was seen and

---

[1] A curious old theological library of the anti-popish type.
[2] A chimney-piece and overmantel of this work was found some years ago thrown aside in the stable loft.
[3] See *ante*, p. 258.

Sir Michael Newton, G.C.B., Bart.

communicated with by no one. During many years Charlotte, his younger daughter, lived alone at Welford, in sad contrast to the happy days when kind—if vulgar—Parson Abdy sung the praises of 'the divine Charlotte' at the Welford wedding! In a lonely middle age of dull monotony, it is perhaps not wonderful that Miss Archer made a foolish marriage. Mr. Gillery Pigott, having quarrelled with his family, was employed by her father in respect of his Berkshire property. This gentleman began by ingratiating himself in the lady's good graces. In her youth she had loved riding on horseback; Mr. Pigott now took her 'airings, riding double,' viz. on a pillion. Thus began an ascendency over her mind, and he finally married her, to the furious indignation of her father. Pigott had no means of his own, neither had Charlotte. The pair were shortly reduced to wellnigh destitution, and to the intervention of Mr. Black, Mr. Archer's steward, was due a meagre subsistence being allowed his daughter by her angry parent. As to Charlotte herself, she quickly found out her mistake. Mr. Pigott, however, was not disappointed of his expectations; for though separated from his wife, after Mr. Archer's death his claims in respect of her inheritance were only settled by the payment of £50,000. Such was the outcome of the law as to married women and their property in those days.

CHAPTER XI

THE SIXTH JOHN

'Should you ask me whence these stories
. . . . .
I should answer, I should tell you,
I repeat them as I heard them.'—LONGFELLOW.

JOHN$_6$ HOUBLON was an amiable and well-meaning young man, but of a negative personality, and in his earlier manhood (partly through an obstinate bashfulness) apparently slightly stupid. The Baroness von Feilitzsch writes from her German home earnestly pleading for some of those interests and accomplishments with which his father's and grandfather's minds had been plentifully stored; she urges him to study French, to read; strives to rouse his mind beyond the level of the country squire *pur et simple*, but apparently without much success. The feeble efforts of Mrs. Houblon were equally futile, for the Court of Chancery refused to provide funds to enable him to travel—her sole panacea for improvement. The only person not disappointed was John himself; he hunted instead.

To Mrs. Houblon the education of her daughters was a simpler matter; the day of the educated woman was over, and a few petty accomplishments were all that was considered necessary; but the young ladies were agreeable and popular. 'My Mother's morning levées have began,' wrote young Laetitia to her aunt and namesake, 'and consequently I see many.' It is clear that of the two, Laetitia$_2$ was the more amiable, and in consequence the best loved. 'Tell nobody, my dearest of all

Laetitias,' wrote the Baroness, 'but I wish you to know I have left *you* my pearls,' and she adds the request she would bequeath them to John's daughter, 'the lovely Susanna-Laetitia.'

John's₆ father had died at a moment of great political and financial stress, extending from every department of the state into private concerns of each and every class, and under these conditions the youth's early years were spent; but it is to be doubted if he ever listened to the sermons of his guardian on the need for economy. John was only twenty-four when he met his future wife, and it is curious to note that out of ten generations of the Houblon family, all but two or three wives (in the direct line) have borne the name of Mary. With John's bride a new series of names, mostly composite, came into the family. Mary-Annes, Annes, and Anne-Marias abounded; so many of them crowded the years that it must have puzzled their relatives to distinguish one from the other. John's aunt, writing from Germany, triumphantly recalls her Baron's prediction of the match between her nephew and Miss Mary-Anne Bramston.[1] The Baron was an inveterate matchmaker, and some months before, the blooming daughter of Essex's tory member had delighted the German uncle, accustomed to what his English wife called, the 'shapeless inelegance of the German female.' The young couple after their marriage settled at Walbury Dells, a house belonging to the squire, and here they continued to live, till in 1802 they removed to Hallingbury Place, which hitherto had been let.

BRAMSTON ARMS.

The year 1798 was one of great national anxiety as to invasion by Bonaparte, and great efforts were made

[1] Mary-Anne, born 6 January 1777, daughter of Thomas Berney Bramston, Esq. of Skreens Park, Essex. Knight of the Shire for Essex.

to meet the danger. John Houblon did his part by the raising of a troop of 'Essex Gentlemen and Yeomanry,' and was appointed to its command.[1] In 1800, on the death of his grandfather Mr. Archer, he assumed, in accordance with a family settlement, the name of Archer in addition to Houblon.

The open-handed generosity and hospitality of his forefathers were to be found in John, but curiously blended with the reserve and obstinacy characteristic of some of his Archer relations. When in society, his rather slow mind took refuge in taciturnity, for he was both proud and shy; but, nevertheless, he was not backward in all that related to the duties of his position. Before the Reform Bill of 1832, though Essex returned eight members, the county itself was represented by two only, the other six being returned by the boroughs, and between 1734-63 two tory members sat continuously, as representing the great county. But in the year 1763 on a bye-election, and under the excitement of the Wilkes riots, a Whig was elected. It may be remembered that at the election of 1768, in the hope of winning back the seat, Jacob$_4$ Houblon, junior, came forward as tory candidate and was beaten, two Whigs being returned; again in 1774 he was invited to contest the county, but declined doing so. The fact was that the former election had been, what this later one again proved to be—*ruinous*. 'Both sides stood aghast at the cost.' The result was a compromise; a 'family compact,' as it was called, by which the representation of the county of Essex was afterwards divided between a Whig and a Tory. This lasted for thirty or forty years, and while Colonel Bullock of Faulkbourne Hall was the whig, Mr. Bramston of Skreens was the tory member.[2]

---

[1] The Essex Gentlemen and Yeomanry was later called the 1st Essex Volunteer Cavalry, and in 1815 John$_6$ Archer Houblon was promoted Lieutenant-Colonel in command.

[2] See 'A Century of Essex Politics,' *Chelmsford Chronicle*.

THE SIXTH JOHN

When in 1810 a vacancy of the whig seat occurred by the death of Colonel Bullock, Mr. Montague Burgoyne, a 'radical,' came forward, John₆ Archer Houblon being run by the Tories for the same seat. A great fight followed, the poll being kept open for the full fifteen days allowed by law. John Houblon's oratory not being his strong point, he had the good sense not to talk much. His opponent, on the contrary, talked incessantly; moreover, he indulged in many philippics at the expense of the young tory squire who, in spite of his lame performance, headed the poll at the start, increasing his majority day by day. But when, towards the end of the long unnecessary contest, Mr. Burgoyne descended to personal insult, the shy squire stiffened at once, his pent-up indignation giving eloquence to his tongue and authority to his hot and determined words. As might be expected a duel was talked of. An amusing pamphlet written by the defeated Whig tells the story of the fight, but exhibits himself in no very amiable light. At the close of the poll Archer Houblon had polled 2519, Mr. Burgoyne 811.[1]

A second contest in 1812 awaited our squire, said to be as annoying and expensive as the one of 1810, but after that, Burgoyne considered he had sufficiently worried the 'family compact,' and six years succeeded during which two Tories sat in uninterrupted peace until in 1820 Mr. Houblon retired. The enormous expense attending these elections was such as seriously to embarrass the squire, but this was indeed but the beginning of the great struggle upon which the landowners of England had embarked against the tide of

---

[1] The following is the first verse of a song sung by Essex Tories on this occasion :—

'Good Bullock is dead your Member so dear,
But we'll find another as good, never fear;
And though he was faithful, he's now dead and gone,
And we'll fill up his place with brave Archer HOUBLON.

'*Chorus*—Success to brave Houblon, etc. etc.
Huzza and Huzza.'

reform which had set in, a struggle as futile as that of Canute, when he bade the inflowing tide not invade his sacred feet on the seashore! Many a mortgaged estate tells how its owners fought a losing fight in the effort to stay the supposed impending ruin.[1]

Family history repeats itself almost *ad nauseam* in the generations, and is only interesting as exhibiting changes in thought and custom. The first few years of the married life of John₆ and Mary-Anne Houblon had been clouded by much trouble in respect of the many 'olive branches' with which they were blessed. No less than four died soon after birth. An old nurse —probably her own—ruled Mary-Anne's nursery, and the fears and weird management of this woman (whose name was Mrs. Boggis) were apparently disastrous. When she had gained her own experience Mary-Anne did better, and a troop of strong, healthy boys and girls followed the sickly first-comers. It was a day when people were proud of adding largely to the population, and Mrs. Houblon in after years boasted of having borne thirteen children to her lord. All grew up except the four first, and one other, who fulfilled the old nurse's prophecy that he would never stand school life.[2]

A family legend recalls the great punctuality of her father. Mr. Bramston was a pompous old gentleman conscious of many years of parliamentary and magisterial importance and unaccustomed to contradiction, and the young members of the Houblon family stood in much awe of him. When he visited his daughter at Hallingbury he expected due consideration to his idiosyncrasies. Dinner was at six, and all assembled in good time, but apparently the staff of servants at the Place were accustomed to the easy-going ways of the master of the

---

[1] In 1817 a sum of £22,000 was raised on Hallingbury by mortgage, and later another considerable sum, most of which was spent during these stormy years.

[2] Jacob, born 10 February 1805.

HALLINGBURY PLACE, ESSEX.
From an engraving. 1832.

house, and were not always perfectly exact. 'My Mother used to fidget,' her youngest daughter related in after-life, 'if the Jacob-Houblon clock began to strike before dinner was announced; because you see it would not be content with striking, but played its tunes as well!' Before this consummation, the company should have been seated at the dinner-table. Acquaintance with the clock in question explains this necessity:[1] 'God save the King' and 'Britons Strike Home,' reiterated persistently for a minute together, would be apt to be trying to the nerves of an old gentleman just going to his dinner and port.

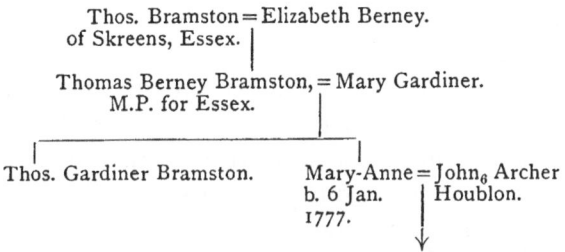

```
      Thos. Bramston = Elizabeth Berney.
      of Skreens, Essex. |
                         |
        Thomas Berney Bramston, = Mary Gardiner.
            M.P. for Essex.           |
      _____
      |                                 |
Thos. Gardiner Bramston.    Mary-Anne = John₆ Archer
                            b. 6 Jan. |  Houblon.
                              1777.   ↓
```

An amusing correspondence between the headmaster of Harrow and Mr. Houblon, shows the eldest son of the latter to have been backward and idle, and in a moment of irritation the master wrote advising his removal to another school. The outcome of this communication was such as to make the good man repent his suggestion, which he hastens to explain away. At the same time the cause of the disturbance wrote a boyish epistle to his sister, wholly unconscious of failure in anything so unimportant as lessons! This large little family grew up in much joyousness in spite of adverse circumstances inseparably connected with the educational process; for the motherly Mary-Anne had been brought up in a strict school herself, and both she and the squire thought it their duty to be severe.

[1] See page 88.

Indeed it was considered right and proper in those days to demonstrate to the letter Solomon's injunction not to spare the rod, and whippings were frequent. Soon a governess came into the life of the three daughters of the house, and loomed large in it for many years. Crimes increased with the enactment of new laws, and a training in genteel manners began, which sought to stamp out all that was supposed to be 'inelegant' in the young ladies. The long-necked, short-waisted Susanna-Laetitia, with sweet lovely face and pliant will, bent easily to the governess's firm hand, while Mary-Anne$_2$ was 'always good,' and schooled her temper and taste to the 'rights of authority';[1] but 'little Harrot'—and thus they pronounced the name of Harriet—fought hard against the thraldom, rebelled against the discreet walk, and envied girls who wore long white trousers frilled round the ankles—simply for the reason that 'their frocks were not so long as ours, that we were made to walk that our ancles might not show.'

The Hallingbury governess was given a free hand and uncontrolled authority, and in the education of the children there never was and never could be, the child's side of the story. 'Little Harrot' in her old age was the sweetest and humblest of old maids, and in confidential moments recalled memories of her childhood at once amusing and pitiful. The governess stayed like a limpet on the family rock long after she was no longer wanted, and Harriet was not allowed to 'grow up.' Old letters and journals speak of her as of too little account for family councils; yet her diaries reveal a charming fresh nature, somewhat slow, it is true, but full of life and fun, and sympathy with the brothers and their interests and pursuits, which probably accounted for the governess's chronic disapproval of her youngest pupil.

[1] Mary-Anne$_2$ was tenth child, and remembered being told she was to be paid to the clergyman for tithe.

What her pupils learned they probably learned elsewhere than from her; Harriet at any rate learned nothing, and regretted it. Learning by rote was an easy task to *set*; and 'it was all I was ever given to do; so I learnt nothing, for I could never learn by rote,' said little Harrot.

At Hallingbury the old traditions of open and generous hospitality were maintained, but already a far greater luxury prevailed than in the last two generations of simple dignity and comfort, and this change pervaded all departments of life. The great war was the dominant factor in both domestic and political existence in England during the earlier years of the century, and the strain on her resources complicated all the ordinary issues of life to such an extent as to deceive nearly all as to their real status and condition. Especially did the artificial demands upon agricultural produce induce an inflated prosperity, and the incomes of landowners and farmers are said to have doubled during these years.[1] To John$_6$ Houblon, in spite of his mortgaged acres, money came pouring in. He was naturally open-handed and kind, and numerous evidences of his generosity are to be found amongst his papers. Although at the end of the war a great shrinkage in people's incomes was the result of the reaction, accompanied by an immense amount of misery and distress amongst all classes,[2] it was long before either he or many of his class accepted the inevitable, or reduced their expenditure, and for many years a large establishment was kept up at Hallingbury as well as in London during the parliamentary season.[3]

1815

---

[1] Lecky's *History*, VI. xxiii. 172.   [2] *Ibid.*
[3] In 1813 John$_6$ Archer Houblon bought the pack of the Essex foxhounds; but Mr. H. J. Conyers acted as Master. A story is told of a famous run this same year. On the 3rd of November, the huntsman having had a bad fall, Mr. Conyers hunted the hounds himself 'through the Roothings, by Skreens Park, to Witney Wood. There the fox was headed and returned to Canfield Hart, where the hounds ran into him. Mr. Houblon and Mr. Conyers had with them two companions only when the fox was killed.' See the *Essex Fox Hounds*, p. 72, by R. T. Ball and Tresham Gilbey, 1896.

1813

Asked if she remembered her mother's dress and appearance when she was a child, Harriet—who was born in 1812—related a circumstance faintly remembered as having struck her imagination. 'In London once—when she and my father were dining out—she wore a silk turban, and it had to be twisted round her head. It was made of a long scarf of soft silk, and she *would* do it herself. It was dreadful! She could not get it right, and got hot and flurried, while my father was fussed, coming in and out of the room! Turbans were twisted on the head then, not as they were later,' she explained, 'ready-made to put on. But I scarcely remember my Mother without a *front*. I fancy her hair began to turn grey early; and it was always considered necessary to hide grey hair.' A front was a narrow wig parted in the middle with tight floss-silk curls on either side; it was worn under a cap and held in place by a narrow velvet ribbon across the forehead. There are many who still remember these flaxen monstrosities, and the sweet old faces marred by them; but in earlier days it was not only old faces which were thus disfigured. However, the æsthetic sense was still dormant, and doubtless no one suffered at all from its being outraged.

It was a day of much wine. While the wine-loving Cottons had consumed their oceans of claret, they were able to 'carry it' cheerfully, and it is said to have done them but little harm, but port did not agree with their descendants so well. Gout became a potent factor in John₆ Archer Houblon's life, as also indirectly in those of his children. In a large old house with many ins and outs, strange things sometimes tell the story of its old inmates, and in some old houses the lumber-rooms are never quite explored. At Hallingbury an inquisitive new mistress long ago found relics of a past, telling their tale of hopes and fears, pain and grief, youth and age. Among these, 'gouty leg-rests,'

THE SIXTH JOHN

hidden away in cupboards and turrets, witnessed by their number to the fact that one was kept ready for use in each room visited by the testy, tender-footed master of the house. When very old, 'little Harriet' was heard once to say, that the memories of her early youth were inextricably mingled with thoughts of the Gout; and of the fact that whenever a pleasure was projected or an expedition planned, a 'fit of the Gout' supervened to prevent its taking place. But if to his children and nephews and nieces John Houblon was gruff and severe (and doubtless his sufferings were not accounted as an excuse with them), his wife's passionate devotion led her to subordinate all else to him and him only.

Bad times and a heavily burdened estate brought Mr. Archer Houblon at last to see the necessity for a narrower horizon of expenditure, so Hallingbury was let, and the family removed to Welford, where he died in 1831. Though he was only fifty-eight, he was an old man in habit and suffering, and the sad part of the matter was, that except for the good and faithful Mary-Anne, who 'was prostrated with grief,' nobody seemed to care much, least of all Mrs. Houblon Newton, his mother.

JOHN$_6$ ARCHER HOUBLON.

1831

CHAPTER XII

EARLY VICTORIA

'And well we love the Squire.'
LOCKER LAMPSON.

WHEN the Pater Bursae was gathered to his fathers at the ripe age of ninety, and good Bishop Burnet was preaching his funeral sermon, six stalwart sons sat listening to his eulogiums on the old father they had all loved. But when the preacher would have said something of those who were left he paused: 'For,' as he said, 'that belongs too much to the living to be insisted on by me.'[1] In like manner, though what remains to be told in these Memoirs refers to a generation now passed out of sight, it still 'belongs too much to the living to be much insisted on' by ourselves.

1800   Seven years after Mrs. Houblon Newton went to live at Coopersale, her elder daughter Maria married her cousin Alexander Cotton and went to Girton, one of his livings, near Cambridge.[2] Her second daughter Laetitia$_2$ died in 1818, and from that time till her death Mrs. Houblon Newton lived all alone at Coopersale House. A pile of red morocco pocket-books, each representing a year in the lady's calendar of life, remain to testify to its monotony,—but meanwhile her riches increased.

1837   When she died in 1837 came a surprise. For thirty years Mrs. Alexander Cotton had regarded herself—except in respect of the settled estates—as her mother's

---

[1] See vol. i. p. 164.   [2] He had four.

CULVERTHORPE, LINCOLNSHIRE. NORTH FRONT.

sole heir, and so certain was she of this that everybody else believed it also. The younger members of the family were all informed many times and with much warmth of the shocking plot which 'disinherited' her; but so it was. Controlled and directed the greater part of her life by her masterful daughter, the ancient lady quietly took her measures, and with the assistance of her lawyer made the will which divided her inheritance between thirteen grandchildren.[1]

When Mr. Archer Houblon died in 1831 his second son Charles, as heir of entail to the Archer property of Welford, assumed the name of Eyre. This was in accordance with the will of his grandfather, Mr. Archer.[2] At the same time his elder brother John, succeeded to Hallingbury Place, and after the death of his grandmother, the Lincolnshire property of the Newton family descended to him, likewise Coopersale in Essex. But while the two owners of land had to wait long before fat years of agricultural prosperity redeemed some of their burdens,[3] their brothers and sisters and cousins rejoiced at once in an affluence which filled full the measure of their content. Of 'Little Harrot,' always merry and light-hearted, her sister wrote: 'She has just been begging me to tell you that now she means *always* to wash her hands with lavender water, and that we shall have the boards scrubbed with *sweet* soap! We like the thought of living at Coopersale, and trust nothing may prevent the scheme.'

John and Charles were already married, and both young wives were pretty. Their unconventionality and high spirits brought new conditions into the stiff procedure of

---

[1] Viz. eight children of her son, and five of her daughter, Mrs. Cotton. To Mrs. Cotton herself she left £20,000.

[2] See table at end of volume, showing Mr. Archer's original patronymic to have been Eyre.

[3] Mrs. Houblon died worth about a million. Mere money she despised in comparison with land, yet it did not occur to her to pay off any of the burdens her family had laid upon their ancestral acres.

the family circle, and none appreciated it more than old Mrs. Houblon, who 'delighted in both.' They were once described by a friend as a great contrast at a party: John's wife as a vision of pink, ringlets, and diamonds; Charles's, as snow-white, arms, neck, and all—and with a crimson camelia in her hair.

In the letters and journals of the Miss Houblons we have various references to their neighbours in Berkshire, the Pophams of Littlecote, and to the lovely Mary-Anne, who afterwards became Charles's wife. Everybody knows about the ancient house and its many eerie associations. It was probably Sir Walter Scott's famous note to Rokeby[1] which excited interest in the old story of Wild Dayrell, and turned curious eyes upon Littlecote. Before those early days it had been worth no one's while closely to examine the haunted room, the scene of the tragedy; but it is a fact that the particulars described in the Rokeby note (and they are but little altered now) all existed in the youth of Mary-Anne Popham, even

MRS. ARCHER HOUBLON (*née* BRAMSTON).

[1] Note X., 'Littlecote Hall.'

to the curtains out of which the patch was cut and re-sewn. Unfortunately, so great was the interest manifested in these, that General Leyborne Popham, the owner of Littlecote,[1] finally caused them to be burnt.

About 1834 Charles Eyre's mother and sisters were living with him at Welford, which is about seven miles from Littlecote. The young squire was 'very busy settling his yeomanry business, besides being now a Magistrate.'[2] 'Mama, Charles, and I,' wrote his sister, 'dined at General Popham's on Saturday. . . . It is one of the pleasantest houses to go to. . . . Wednesday they came here, the whole party, at 3 o'clock, and stayed dinner. Miss Popham we have longed to see more of. Her brother stayed to sleep, and go with Charles and Fred to an archery meeting 12 miles off, and Charles went to Littlecote with him afterwards and stays there till Monday.'[3]

1834

ARMS OF POPHAM.

[1] General Edward W. Leyborne Popham, born 1764, died 1843.
[2] He was captain of a troop, viz. the 'Welford and Yeomanry Cavalry.' Their colours still exist.
[3] Francis L. Popham, Esq., born 1809, died 1880. He won the Derby in 1855 with 'Wild Dayrell,' a horse bred at Littlecote, home-trained and ridden by his stable-boy. The original Wild Dayrell has given rise to much folklore, but he was probably more sinned against than sinning. The fact that Judge Popham (who was said to have got Littlecote as the price of Dayrell's acquittal of the murder) was not a judge at the time, shows that story to have been legendary. This was in the days of Elizabeth. A myth still clinging to Littlecote (though for long it was forgotten) is that when the heir dies, Wild Dayrell drives his coach to the door. About 1861 a child in the line of succession was 'sick to death' in a chamber overlooking the entrance, which is enclosed by tall iron gates. The nurse sent an express for the parents, who were absent; and the next night, as she sat by the child, she heard the gates flung open and a coach drive to the door; then the peal of a bell. When the parents did not come to the room, she rose and threw open the casement, but all was still beneath the moonlight. When the next day they arrived the child was dead, and the nurse mentioned what she had heard, but it struck no chord of association with the past. However, when many years later Mr. Francis Popham, the child's father, came upon a document relating to the legend, he remembered the nurse's story. A box of Cromwell's letters were formerly at Littlecote, but during a time of neglect and ignorance they were lost. The buff jerkins and mail of a troop of Ironsides still hang on the walls of the great hall.

Of the five sons of Mr. and Mrs. Archer Houblon, Charles Eyre most resembled his forebears, the two

```
    General Leyborne  = Eliz., d. of
    Popham of Little-   Archdeacon
    cote, b. 1764, d. 1843.  Andrew.
                    |
         ┌──────────┴──────────┐
       Francis,           Mary-Anne = Charles Eyre,
    b. 1809, d. 1880.     married 1835.  b. 1806, d. 1886.
```

Jacobs, in his tastes and talents. Though it is clear that his father was willing to facilitate the wishes of his son for self-culture, it was further made possible by his marriage with his brilliant wife, who shared interests and aspirations not always easy of fulfilment in a most prosaic age. Charles's early journals, when travelling 1829 in France and Switzerland, show an enthusiastic love of nature rare in those days; and, like his ancestor Jacob₄ on the Grand Tour, he bought books everywhere. He became a good linguist, and soon filled the empty shelves of the Welford Library with well-chosen volumes, including many French, German, and Italian. He also became a great gardener and horticulturist.[1] In later years his wife's delicate health induced them frequently to 1851-5 winter in Italy either at Florence or Rome, and a collection of pictures of the Italian school, purchased in days when it was possible to procure genuine specimens of good masters, remains as the evidence of sound advice and their own good taste. At a time long before the pre-Raphaelite craze, Mrs. Eyre employed Marionecci—later a famous copyist of last century, but then unknown—to make water-colour drawings of portions of her favourite pictures and frescoes.[2]

We have many records of Mary-Anne Eyre, including her journals kept in Italy, where her beauty and wit

[1] The name of Charles Ross (gardener at Welford Park since 1860) is famous among horticulturists.
[2] These exquisite sketches greatly surpass the formal drawings made by Marionecci for the Arundel Society reproductions of old masters.

Mary Anne Eyre.

attrac...
sc...
...
...
streng... ...
...sionally co...
... her devo...
temper... ... will r...
mined'; ... ...
less forebo...
remember the...
supposed) at V...
danger was she. ...
sympathetic rel...
port them, and ...
fragile frame ha...
never recovered, ...
few months later ...

Old Mrs. Archer H...
in-law many years; a...
companion till the las...
dead, and when her s...
one said, 'How will ...
Harrot?' Harriet ne...
have done so; her o...
and she confessed it ...
once an aspirant for ...
and Papa refused; la...
elder brother was told ...
to accept, but John...
she would not leave ...
Coopersale was her ...
years, and as young ...
was when she was ...

'Ann is so merry ...

it was at Rome that th...
purity of her pro...
his own request. A ...
...bining elements of ...
for those she love...
Having lost three ...
... softened and ...
... very deter-
... by ground-
... scarcely
... as was

1852

... ...'s

... ...
...
...

...
was
...
...
...

...
...
...

... had w...hed
... ... later
... ... years
... died full of ...
... in heart as ...
... by the govern...

... valuable add...

attracted many around her. It was at Rome that the sculptor Gibson, struck by the purity of her profile, executed a medallion of her at his own request. A woman of vivid personality, combining elements of strength and brilliance, anxious cares for those she loved occasionally cost her much misery. Having lost three boys, her devotion to 'little George' softened and tempered a will regarded by her family as 'very determined'; but her happiness in him was marred by groundless forebodings. He and his two sisters scarcely remember their mother; she contracted malaria (as was supposed) at Wiesbaden in the year 1854, and in such danger was she, that many of her own and her husband's sympathetic relations flew to the spot to help and support them, and bring them home! But Mary-Anne's fragile frame had received a shock from which she never recovered, and she passed away at Brighton a few months later in the following year.

Old Mrs. Archer Houblon survived both her daughters-in-law many years; and 'Little Harrot' was her faithful companion till the last. When Susanna-Laetitia was dead, and when her sister Mary-Anne$_2$ married, every one said, 'How will the Mother do with only Little Harrot?' Harriet never married, though she might have done so; her one beauty was her rippling hair, and she confessed it had been admired. More than once an aspirant for her hand was told to 'ask Papa' and Papa refused; later it was 'speak to John,' and the elder brother was told to decline. Once she had wished to accept, but John$_7$ thought 'better not'; and later she would not leave her mother. For thirty more years Coopersale was her home, till in 1896 she died full of years, and as young in mind and guileless in heart as she was when she was bullied in her youth by the governess.

'Ann is so merry she will be a valuable addition to

our party,'[1] wrote her sister-in-law from Welford in the midst of the Chartist riots. 'Fred and Richard came home Wednesday, both sorry the riots here are over; for they should have enjoyed the fun of them.' But Charles meanwhile had had his hands full, both as a magistrate and as captain of his yeomanry troop.

1837   John₇ and Ann Houblon found their financial concerns sufficiently prosperous in 1837 to admit of their taking up their abode at Hallingbury Place. Unlike his tall, good-looking brothers, John was short and plain; he apparently resembled his grandfather Mr. Bramston. During his long residence of more than half a century at the family home, the squire endeared himself to a wide range of acquaintance of every class and condition, though it must be confessed that his hot temper and dominating will were occasionally the cause of friction. Yet his tenderness of conscience and real humility would lead him to make *amendes honorables* if by chance he became aware of having offended. Those who knew him well, remember his favourite exclamation. In his early life he occasionally sought relief in strong language, but latterly he had so schooled himself, that 'My Wig' in various degrees of accentuation generally expressed his feelings suitably and adequately, whether in sunshine or storm. A most devoted husband, the vivacious Ann received the squire's chivalrous homage, though occasionally even she would set a torch to the vehement passion which scarcely burnt out, till in the last flicker of patient age he mastered it for good and all.

184–   A story was told by the youngest member of a large party assembled at Hallingbury in the early forties, which was scarcely whispered for many years, but which was nevertheless true. Ann's boudoir, on the first floor at Hallingbury, was arranged and rearranged

[1] Ann, daughter of Sir James Whitby Deans Dundas, G.C.B., of Barton Court, co. Berks, married John₇ Archer Houblon, Esq., 1829.

our party,'[1] wrote her sister-in-law from Welford in the midst of the Chartist riots. 'Fred and Richard came home Wednesday, both sorry the riots here are over; for they should have enjoyed the fun of them.' But Charles meanwhile had had his hands full, both as a magistrate and as captain of his yeomanry troop.

1837   John₇ and Ann Houblon found their financial concerns sufficiently prosperous in 1837 to admit of their taking up their abode at Hallingbury Place. Unlike his tall, good-looking brothers, John was short and plain; he apparently resembled his grandfather Mr. Bramston. During his long residence of more than half a century at the family home, the squire endeared himself to a wide range of acquaintance of every class and condition, though it must be confessed that his hot temper and dominating will were occasionally the cause of friction. Yet his tenderness of conscience and real humility would lead him to make *amendes honorables* if by chance he became aware of having offended. Those who knew him well, remember his favourite exclamation. In his early life he occasionally sought relief in strong language, but latterly he had so schooled himself, that ' My Wig ' in various degrees of accentuation generally expressed his feelings suitably and adequately, whether in sunshine or storm. A most devoted husband, the vivacious Ann received the squire's chivalrous homage, though occasionally even she would set a torch to the vehement passion which scarcely burnt out, till in the last flicker of patient age he mastered it for good and all.

1840   A story was told by the youngest member of a large party assembled at Hallingbury in the early forties, which was scarcely whispered for many years, but which was nevertheless true. Ann's boudoir, on the first floor at Hallingbury, was arranged and rearranged

[1] Ann, daughter of Sir James Whitby Deans Dundas, G.C.B., of Barton Court, co. Berks, married John₇ Archer Houblon, Esq., 1829.

"Little Harrot" æt. 80.

in a manner which was then a great innovation on the heretofore stiff distribution of tables and chairs in a seemly order against the walls of the apartment.[1] A new 'Empire' sofa had its place near the door. Unaccustomed to navigate a room as modern squires are well trained to do, John, Archer Houblon twice tumbled over this sofa. The second time he swore loudly, and warned his spouse she had better remove it, for if the same fate again overtook him he would throw it out of the window. To Ann, secure in her John's devotion, the threat was not worth consideration; but when one evening he came in late from shooting, before dressing for dinner, he once more tumbled over the sofa. That dinner waited long, and the guests waxed hungry before the squire appeared, very warm and bearing marks of agitation. 'Mrs. Archer Houblon,' he said, 'begged to be excused, she was indisposed and was lying down.' The next day the story leaked out, and it was simply the sequel to the part already told. *The sofa was thrown out* of the window in spite of tears and entreaties of the lady, and perhaps the fit of hysterics which followed was sufficient punishment to the squire. How the fragments of the sofa were gathered up, and what was said by way of explanation, we were not told, but doubtless this was the way the guests learned the truth.

Poor Ann died the victim of an operation, and the squire was inconsolable; but Ann's best friend married the 'best of squires' the following year, to everybody's surprise.[2] Both his wives being Scotswomen the squire went frequently to Scotland, and it was when he and Ann were on a visit at Floors Castle, and

1847

---

[1] An early Victorian drawing-room was not complete without a large round table around which the ladies sat at their work. This was the 'circle.' The custom was probably introduced from Germany.

[2] He married secondly Georgina Anne, daughter of Sir John Oswald, G.C.B., of Dunnikier, Fife.

·Mary-Anne₂ Houblon was with them, that she met her future husband, William Forbes, and this marriage further cemented the family link with Scotland. At the time of her marriage Alexander Forbes (afterwards Bishop of Brechin) stayed at Hallingbury, and in a long letter from there, described the large family of young men and women of his brother's future relations, and of the strange fact of their all being rich and independent.

According to the received tradition of those days, a fat family living must needs be occupied by a member of the family. Nevertheless, that one of the Houblon brothers[1] who in 1832 entered the Church, chose his profession with real enthusiasm. The Oxford movement likewise swept Thomas Houblon along with it, and he accepted Dr. Pusey and his leading in all matters ecclesiastical. His saintly wife came of a stock as wholly devoted to the Church as himself, and their children followed in their footsteps. But though their only son has become a distinguished church dignitary at Oxford, it is to be doubted if, in the eyes of many of his old friends, the honour of having rowed stroke in the 'Varsity boat race in the early seventies, does not entitle him to at least as much human appreciation as the services he had rendered to that Church which sent him back to his own old College.[2]

Of two other sons of the family—Frederick and Richard—the former had a sad fate. Owing to a blow on the head received as a boy at Harrow, he ultimately developed symptoms which resulted in his being unable to manage his own affairs. Richard, who was extremely handsome, even as an old man, joined the 17th Lancers in 1837. He married late in life Anne-Maria, the

---

[1] Rev. Thomas Archer Houblon, Rector of Peasemore, Berks, born 1808, died December 1874. Married Eleanor, daughter of the Rev. John Deedes, Rector of Willingale Doe, Essex.

[2] Rev. T. Henry Archer Houblon, Vicar of Wantage, 1881-1903; Canon of Christchurch and Archdeacon of Oxford, 1903.

daughter of his aunt, Mrs. Alexander Cotton. Through this marriage a great many interesting family papers, miniatures, and other relics ultimately returned (by his will) to Hallingbury Place after an interval of a hundred years—by reason of their removal by Jacob$_4$ Houblon's widow, afterwards Mrs. Houblon Newton, in 1783.

1783

```
        Jacob₄ Houblon = Susanna Archer
                        (Mrs. Houblon Newton).
                    |
        ┌───────────┴───────────┐
  John₆ Archer Houblon.    Maria₁ = Rev. Alexander
        |                           Cotton.
        |                           |
                Richard₁ = Anne-Maria Cotton.
                d. s. p.
```

This generation of Houblons lived to a great age; they came of a hardy stock hardily reared, and to the last they kept up their hardy, active habits. Their friends would laugh at what they called 'the Houblon necessity' for exercise. The Squire of Hallingbury was born in the year 1803, and it is a singular coincidence, that four other Johns, all *habitués* of Hallingbury, were born the same year, and all lived to between eighty and ninety. The author remembers with amusement once singing to four of these ancient Johns as they played whist on a winter's night at Welford, and the sudden outbursts of somewhat discordant song that came from the whist-table as she sang their favourite Scottish airs!

But little remains to be told of John$_7$ Archer Houblon's honest and uneventful career. Rich and prosperous, he had a keen power of enjoyment which gave zest to all he did, whether of business or pleasure, and if he never spared himself in the former, he did not stint himself in the latter. He hunted[1] and shot at home,[2] and for many

[1] In 1838 he bought the Puckeridge Pack. For an award given in 1854 *re* Hatfield (or Takely) Forest, see *The Essex Foxhounds* (Ball and Gilbey.)

[2] It is a tradition at Hallingbury that when a storm was brewing in the squire's mind he would flourish his pocket-handkerchief. When they saw this the keepers would keep out of his way.

years rented a moor and salmon river in Scotland together with his old friend Mr. Bruce of Kennet.[1] Of all that the squire accomplished for his pleasure or for the advantage of his estate, that which related to the forest of Hatfield Broad-Oak was the most important. It will perhaps be remembered how Miss Laetitia in the eighteenth century alluded to the 'splashings in our forest,' and it appears to have been practically impassable in the winter. In the first half of last century, when deep draining had become almost a religion, the forest came to be regarded by the squire as calling for such treatment. Many thousands were spent by the landlords of England in those days in deep draining, and it is to be questioned if they would have so spent their substance or charged their estates for the purpose, if they could have foreseen the latter-day results of 'Cobdenism'! The squire not only drained much arable land, but he undertook in 1854 the draining of his forest, and it cost him a large sum of money; but before he embarked on this work he purchased the manorial rights from the representatives of the old Barrington family, and later, the forest was enclosed.[2]

1854

1858   In 1858 the Broad Oak (or Doodle Oak) of Hatfield forest last showed green leaves. Frederick Locker in one of his London Lyrics sang of the old tree and how,

> '. . . the country side
> Lamented when the Giant died.
> Who struck a thousand roots in fame,
> Who gave the district half its name.'

Though the huge trunk of the old tree now lies on its side:

> 'No forester had dared to fell
> What time has felled at last.'

---

[1] Father of the present Lord Balfour of Burleigh.
[2] By Act of Parliament.

As to the great age of the Doodle Oak, the poet declares with perhaps some irony:

> 'The Squire affirms with gravest look
> His oak goes up to Domesday Book,
>   And some say even higher!
> We rode last week to see the ruin,
> We love the fair domain it grew in,
>   And well we love the Squire!'[1]

Another pleasure of Mr. Houblon's was the taste for bric-a-brac, of which he collected a vast amount, and he was regarded as a connoisseur, as also of engraved gems; but he had no children, a great loss to a man with a yearning desire to love and be loved. Many of the finest instincts of a generous nature thus found no vent, and turned in upon itself in wilfulness and tyrannies sometimes hard to be digested by those at issue with him. He lavished upon his second wife the same devotion as he had bestowed on his first, though Mrs. Archer Houblon—except, perhaps, in the matter of ringlets—was not in the least like poor Ann.

One of the squire's idiosyncrasies was his dislike of dissent. A Tory of the Tories, and high and dry churchman of the old school, he was loyal always to the powers that be. He rebuilt the ancient white-washed church of Great Hallingbury, and spacious schools, in accordance with the then new conditions of ecclesiastical and educational requirements; while he would tolerate no tenant on his estates but that he was a churchman. But in spite of his intolerance of all encroachments upon his ideal, 'The Squire'—and all Essex gave him this distinctive title as he grew hoary with age and dignity—was humble and tender as a child in his efforts to break his faults and school his life to the standard of duty he held above himself; for he had, as his friend the poet wrote of him,

[1] See Frederick Locker Lampson, *London Lyrics*: 'The Old Oak Tree at Hatfield Broad-Oak, Hallingbury. April 1859.'

> 'A nature, loyally controll'd
> And fashioned in the righteous mould
> Of English gentleman!'[1]

He would bare his grey head to wind and rain if the name of God crossed his lips or those of his companion; and there are those who remember the zeal, if not beauty, of his singing in church. His last walk was along the 'straight path' he made of stone across his park, so he might walk dry-shod there, for the doing of his duty in worship according to the light he had. And so, in a green old age, this chivalrous squire of a past that is gone, slept with his fathers, and his brother's son reigned in his stead.

1891

[1] See Frederick Locker Lampson, *London Lyrics*: 'The Old Oak Tree at Hatfield Broad-Oak, Hallingbury. April 1859.'

TABLE SHOWING DESCENT OF MRS. HOUBLON NEWTON

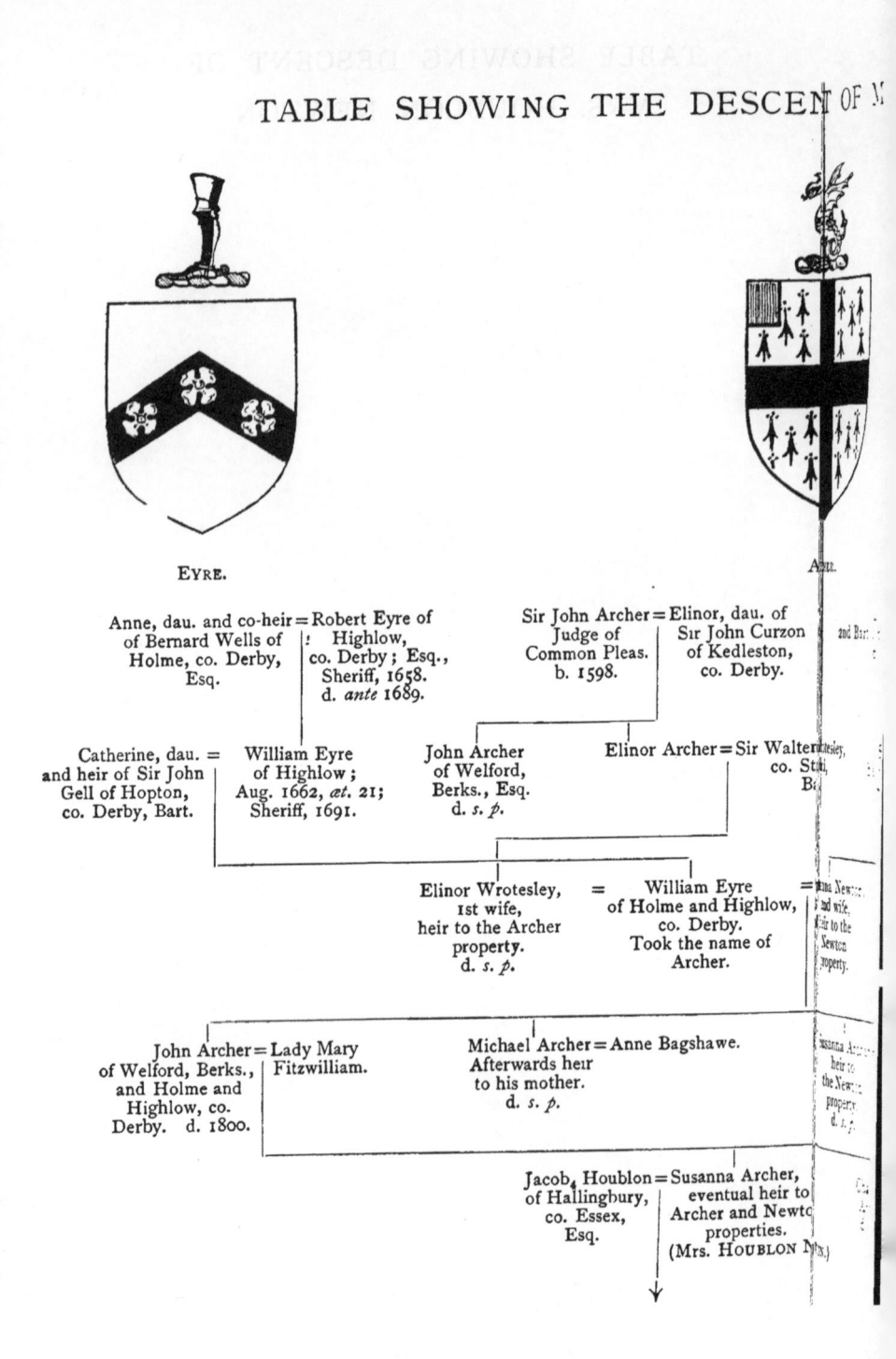

TABLE SHOWING THE DESCENT OF M[...]

EYRE.

Anne, dau. and co-heir of Bernard Wells of Holme, co. Derby, Esq. = Robert Eyre of Highlow, co. Derby; Esq., Sheriff, 1658. d. ante 1689.

Sir John Archer, Judge of Common Pleas. b. 1598. = Elinor, dau. of Sir John Curzon of Kedleston, co. Derby.

Catherine, dau. and heir of Sir John Gell of Hopton, co. Derby, Bart. = William Eyre of Highlow; Aug. 1662, æt. 21; Sheriff, 1691.

John Archer of Welford, Berks., Esq. d. s. p.

Elinor Archer = Sir Walter [Wrotesley], co. St[aff], B[art].

Elinor Wrotesley, 1st wife, heir to the Archer property. d. s. p. = William Eyre of Holme and Highlow, co. Derby. Took the name of Archer. = [...]na Newt[on], [...]nd wife, [he]ir to the Newton [p]roperty.

John Archer of Welford, Berks., and Holme and Highlow, co. Derby. d. 1800. = Lady Mary Fitzwilliam.

Michael Archer = Anne Bagshawe. Afterwards heir to his mother. d. s. p.

[Susa]nna A[rcher], heir to the New[ton] property. d. s. [p].

Jacob Houblon, of Hallingbury, co. Essex, Esq. = Susanna Archer, eventual heir to Archer and Newton properties. (Mrs. HOUBLON N[...].)

DESCENT OF MRS. HOUBLON NEWTON

EYRE.   NEWTON.

Sir John Newton = Mary, dau. of
2nd Bart., of Barre's Court,   Sir Gervase Eyre, Kt.
co. Derby, and   slain at Newark
Culverthorpe Line.   (Charles I.) 1643.
b. 1626.

Susanna Warton = Sir John Newton = Abigale, dau. of   Sir Isaac Newton.
heir to her brother,   3rd Bart.   Will. Heveningham, Esq.,
Sir Michael, of   by Lady Mary Cary,
Beverley.   dau. of Earl of Dover.
2nd wife.   1st wife.

Anna Newton,   Sir Michael Newton, = Margaret,   Cary Newton = Edward Coke of
2nd wife,   G.C.B.,   Countess of   heir to her   Holkham, Esq.
heir to the   4th Bart.   Coningsby.   grandfather,   (Earls of
Newton   d. s. p.   Earl of Dover. Leicester).
property.   d. 1707.

Susanna Archer = Edward, 4th Earl   Catherine = Philip   John Newton,
heir to   of Oxford.   heir to   Blundell, Esq.   Viscount
the Newton   the Newton   Coningsby.
property.   property.   d. young.
d. s. p.   d. s. p.

Charlotte = Gillery Pigott, Esq.
Archer.
d. s. p.

PARAGRAPH PEDIGREE OF THE HOUBLON FAMILY

(*Continued from Vol. I.*)

VIII. Jacob₃ Houblon, of Hallingbury, co. Essex, only son of Charles₁ Houblon, merchant of London, and Mary Bate. Born in London, the 31st of July 1710. Educated at Harrow and Corpus Christi, Cambridge, where he graduated M.A. in 1729. On coming of age—being the last heir-male of his family—took possession of estates in Herts and Essex, which, in accordance with the will of the late Sir Richard₁ Houblon, Kt., had been purchased with trust funds. In 1735 was returned burgess for Colchester in the tory or 'Country' interest. In 1741 was elected Knight of the Shire for Herts, which county he represented till 1768; comprising thirty-three years' parliamentary service. A member of the Cocoa Tree and Royston Clubs. J.P. for Herts and for Essex. High Sheriff for Hertfordshire in 1757. Major, and in 1761 Lieut.-Colonel in command, of Herts Regiment of Militia (embodied during the Seven Years' War). Died at Hallingbury, the 15th of February 1770, aged 60, having married, the 31st of July 1735, Mary, only daughter of Sir John Hynde Cotton of Madingley, co. Cambs, 4th Baronet. She was born the 22nd of March

1716, and died the 19th of May 1779. The issue of the marriage was :—

   i. Jacob$_4$ Houblon. See below, IX.

   ii. Mary, born the 3rd of May 1738. Died young.

   iii. John$_5$ Houblon, second son of Jacob$_3$ Houblon and Mary Hynde Cotton. Born at Hallingbury, the 30th of June 1740. Educated at Harrow and Trinity Hall, Cambridge. Called to the Bar 1766. Joined the Herts Militia in 1761, and served as Senior Captain during its embodiment, 1778-82. Died at Hallingbury, the 13th of July 1783.

   iv. Laetitia$_1$, only surviving daughter of Jacob$_3$ Houblon and Mary Hynde Cotton. Born at Hallingbury, the 6th of July 1742. Married, the 24th of November 1789, Friedrich Ludwig, Baron von Feilitzsch of Saxony, then Captain in the Piedmontese Regiment of the King of Sardinia. After the war the Baron (having sold his estates in Germany) took out letters of naturalisation as a British subject and settled in England. The Baroness died *s.p.* the 20th of December 1828; and the Baron the 30th of June 1830.

   v. Charles$_2$ Houblon, third son of Jacob$_3$ Houblon and Mary Hynde Cotton. Born at Hallingbury, the 8th of September 1744, and died the 6th of November 1759.

IX. Jacob$_4$ Houblon, of Hallingbury, co. Essex, eldest son of Jacob$_3$ Houblon and Mary Hynde Cotton. Born at Hallingbury, the 9th of August 1736. Educated at Harrow and St. John's College, Cambridge. In 1758 entered at the Academia Reale at Turin for six months, after which he made the 'Grand Tour.' Having been refused permission to serve in the allied armies, returned home in 1761, and joined the Herts Militia, then embodied under the command of his father. After the close of the Seven Years' War he travelled in the Holy Land. At the general election 1768 stood for Essex county (tory) and was defeated. Declined to stand at

PARAGRAPH PEDIGREE

next general election. A member of the Cocoa Tree and Royston Clubs. In 1771-3 he partly rebuilt Hallingbury Place in the Georgian style. Served as Senior Major in the Herts Militia during its embodiment, 1778-82. He died the year following, after a short illness, on the 14th of October 1783, three months after his brother's death, having married, the 18th of September 1770, Susanna, elder daughter and eventually heir of John Archer, of Welford, Berks, and Coopersale, Essex, etc., and Lady Mary Archer, *née* Fitzwilliam. She was born the 17th of May 1753, and succeeded to her father's estates in 1800. As heir of entail to the Newton estates of her grandmother, Mrs. Archer, Susanna Houblon assumed in 1819, by Royal Sign Manual, the additional name of Newton. Mrs. Houblon Newton died at Coopersale in Essex, the 14th of February 1837. The children of the marriage were:—

    iii. John$_6$ Houblon. See below, X.

    i. Maria$_1$, elder daughter of Jacob$_4$ Houblon and Susanna Archer. Born the 5th of July 1771. Married, August 1809, her cousin the Rev. Alexander Ambrose Cotton, brother of Rear-Admiral Sir Charles Cotton, R.N., of Madingley, co. Cambs, 5th Baronet. She died at Girton, Cambs, March 1860. The children of the marriage were:—

        1. Alexander. Married first Marianne, daughter of Sir Charles Watson, Bart.
        2. Susanna. Married John, eldest son of Sir John Gibbons, Bart.
        3. Anne-Maria. Married her cousin, Richard$_2$ Archer Houblon late of 17th Lancers, of Bartlow, co. Cambs.
        4. John Hynde.

    ii. Laetitia$_2$, second daughter of Jacob$_4$ Houblon and Susanna Archer. Born the 10th of August 1772, and died the 4th of January 1818.

X. John$_6$ Houblon, of Hallingbury, co. Essex, and Welford, Berks (afterwards Archer Houblon), only son of Jacob$_4$ Houblon and Susanna Archer. Born the

1st of December 1773. Educated at Charterhouse and Emanuel College, Cambridge. During the scare of invasion in 1798 raised and commanded a troop of 'Essex Gentlemen and Yeomanry,' afterwards called the 'Essex Volunteer Cavalry.' In accordance with a family settlement, on the death of his grandfather, Mr. Archer (1800), he assumed the additional name of Archer. On a vacancy in the representation of the county of Essex occurring in 1810 he contested the seat in the tory interest and was returned, and again in 1812. He retired in 1820. In 1813 Mr. Archer Houblon bought the pack of the Essex foxhounds. In 1815 was promoted Lieut.-Colonel in command of the Essex Volunteer Cavalry. Died at Welford, the 11th of June 1831, having married, the 29th of July 1797, Mary-Anne, elder daughter of Thomas Berney Bramston, of Skreens, Essex, Knight of the Shire for Essex during twenty-six years. She was born the 6th of January 1777, and died at Coopersale, Essex, the 4th of April 1865, aged 88, having survived her husband thirty-four years. The children of the marriage were :—

i.-iv. Four sons died in infancy.

v. John$_7$ Archer Houblon of Hallingbury, co. Essex, and Culverthorpe, co. Lincoln, eldest surviving son of John$_6$ Archer Houblon and Mary-Anne Bramston. Born the 29th of September 1803. Educated at Harrow and at Christ Church, Oxford. J.P. for Herts and Essex. At one time Colonel of the Essex Militia, and Chairman of Petty Sessions (Herts). High Sheriff of Essex in 1841. Bought the Puckeridge hounds in 1838. Died *s.p.* at Hallingbury, the 6th of October 1891, having married first in 1829 Ann, daughter of Sir James Whitley Deans Dundas, G.C.B., of Barton Court, Berks. She died in 1847, and Mr. Archer Houblon married secondly in 1849 Georgiana Anne, daughter of General Sir John Oswald, G.C.B., of Dunnikier, Fife. She died the 19th of April 1896.

PARAGRAPH PEDIGREE

vi. Jacob$_5$ Archer Houblon, born the 10th of February 1805, and died the 19th of December 1819.

vii. Charles$_3$ Archer Houblon. See below, XI.

viii. Thomas Archer Houblon, third surviving son of John$_6$ Archer Houblon and Mary-Anne Bramston. Born the 4th of January 1808. Educated at Harrow and Oriel, Oxford; M.A. in 1834. Ordained 1831. Rector of Peasemore, Berks, 1837. Died the 21st of December 1874, having married, the 19th of July 1839, Eleanor, daughter of the Rev. John Deedes, Rector of Willingdale Doe, Essex. She died the 11th of June 1815. The children of the marriage were:—

1. Eleanor.
2. Sophia. (Sister of Mercy.)
3. Louisa. (Sister of Mercy.)
4. T. Henry$_2$ Archer Houblon, only son. Born the 9th of October 1849. Educated at Christ Church, Oxford; Ordained in 1873; M.A. in 1875; D.D. in 1903. Rector of Peasemore, Berks, 1875-81. Vicar of Wantage, 1881-1903. Canon of Christ Church and Archdeacon of Oxford, 1903.
5. Maria$_2$.

ix. Susanna-Laetitia, eldest daughter of John$_6$ Archer Houblon and Mary-Anne Bramston. Born the 24th of December 1809. Died the 26th of March 1846.

x. Mary-Anne$_2$, second daughter of John$_6$ Archer Houblon and Mary-Anne Bramston. Born the 21st of October 1811. Married, 21st of December 1842, William Forbes of Medwyn, N.B. She died the 23rd of May 1896. The children of the marriage were:—

1. Mary Forbes. Married Walter, 11th Earl of Mar and 13th of Kellie.
2. Louisa Forbes. Married Sir James Fergusson, Bart. of Spitalhaugh, and had issue, Louis Forbes Fergusson.
3. Harriet Forbes. Married the Hon. Augustus Erskine.
4. Helen Forbes.
5. Elizabeth Forbes.
6. John Houblon Forbes. Married the Hon. Katrine Fraser, daughter of the 17th Baron Saltoun.

xi. Harriet, third daughter of John$_6$ Archer Houblon and Mary-Anne Bramston. Born the 28th of December

1812, and died the 29th of July 1896, after a residence of sixty years at Coopersale House, Essex.

xii. Richard$_2$ Archer Houblon of Bartlow, Cambs, fourth surviving son of John$_6$ Archer Houblon and Mary-Anne Bramston. Born the 26th of October 1814. Joined the 17th Lancers in 1837. J.P. and D.L. for Cambridgeshire. High Sheriff in 1870. Died *s. p.* at Bartlow, the 27th of November 1894, having married, the 26th of July 1853, his cousin, Anne-Maria Cotton, daughter of the Rev. Alexander Cotton and Maria$_1$ Houblon. She died the 3rd of May 1888.

xiii. Frederick Archer Houblon, fifth surviving son. Born the 30th of September 1816, and died the 27th January 1891.

XI. Charles$_3$ Archer Houblon (afterwards Eyre of Welford Park, Berks), second surviving son of John$_6$ Archer Houblon and Mary-Anne Bramston. Born at Hallingbury, the 13th of October 1806. Educated at Harrow and Christ Church, Oxford. Assumed, the 27th of September 1831, by Royal Licence—in compliance with the settlement of his great-grandfather Mr. Archer, and on succeeding to his Berkshire estate—the name and arms of Eyre. J.P. and D.L. for Berks. High Sheriff in 1834. Mr. Eyre died at Welford the 22nd of July 1886, having married first, the 12th of May 1835, Mary-Anne, daughter of General Leyborne Popham, of Littlecote, co. Wilts. She was born the 20th of August 1814, and died the 12th of March 1855. He married secondly, on the 14th of January 1858, Louisa Charlotte, daughter of the Rev. Thomas Randolph, Rector of Great Hadham and Prebendary of St. Paul's. By his first wife Mr. Eyre had issue :—

i.-iii. Three sons died young.

iv. George Bramston Eyre. See below, XII.

v. Isabella Mary Eyre. Born the 31st of January 1845. Married, the 15th of July 1865, Captain Archibald Hamilton Dunbar, 66th Foot, now Sir Archibald Dunbar of Duffus, co. Elgin, Baronet.

vi. Annie Georgiana Eyre. Born the 12th of July 1849. Married, the 25th of February 1884, the Hon. William Borlase Warren Vernon, second son of the 5th Lord Vernon, and has had issue :—

1. May Warren Vernon.
2. Arnold, R.N. Died 1906.

XII. George Bramston Eyre, of Welford, co. Berks (afterwards Archer Houblon), only surviving son of Charles$_3$ Eyre and Mary-Anne Popham. Born at Welford, the 26th June 1843. Educated at Harrow and Christ Church, Oxford. Joined the 3rd Battalion of the Royal Berks Regiment in 1871. Lieut.-Colonel in command 1887-93. Succeeded his father to the Welford estate in 1886. On the death of his uncle, John$_7$ Archer Houblon, of Hallingbury, *s. p.*, succeeded to the family estates in Essex, Herts, and Lincolnshire, under the family settlement, and at the same time resumed the patronymic of Archer Houblon by Royal Licence (see *London Gazette*, 25th December 1891). Married, the 17th of April 1872, Lady Alice Lindsay, eldest daughter of Alexander, 24th Earl of Crawford and 9th of Balcarres. Colonel Archer Houblon is J.P. for Berks, Essex, and Herts. Was High Sheriff for Essex in 1898. Is Chairman of Petty Sessions, Bishop's Stortford, Herts. And has issue :—

i. Margaret Mary-Anne.
ii. Henry$_3$ Lindsay. See below, XIII.
iii. John$_3$ Newton.
iv. Francis.
v. Sybil Harriet.
vi. Alice (Elsie).

vii. Richard$_3$, Royal Field Artillery.
viii. Robert Eyre.

XIII. Henry$_3$ Lindsay Archer Houblon. Born at Villa Palmieri, Florence, the 31st of January 1877. Educated at Winchester and Christ Church, Oxford. Captain 2nd Battalion The Buffs (East Kent Regiment). Served in South Africa, 1900-2.

SKELETON PEDIGREE TO VOL. II.

1. HOUBLON.
2. ARCHER.
3. EYRE,
   brings in :
4. PADLEY.
5. WELLS.
6. GELL.

7. NEWTON,
   brings in :
8. NEWTON.
9. WARTON.
10. HANSBY.
11. MALTBY.
12. HOUBLON.

IX. JAC
   of

X. JOHN₆ AR
   of H

John₇ Archer Houblon = 1st. Ann Dundas.   Mary Anne = XI. CHARLES₂ ARCHER HOUBL
   of Hallingbury.   2nd. Georgina Oswald.   Popham.   afterwards Eyre of Welford,
   d. s. p.   Berks.

   XII. GEORGE BRAMSTON = Lady Alice   Isabella Eyre = Sir Archibald   Anni
        EYRE, afterwards   Lindsay.   Dunbar, Bart.
        ARCHER HOUBLON.

                              XIII. HENRY₂ LINDSAY,   John₈ Ne
                                    Captain 2nd Buffs.   Francis.

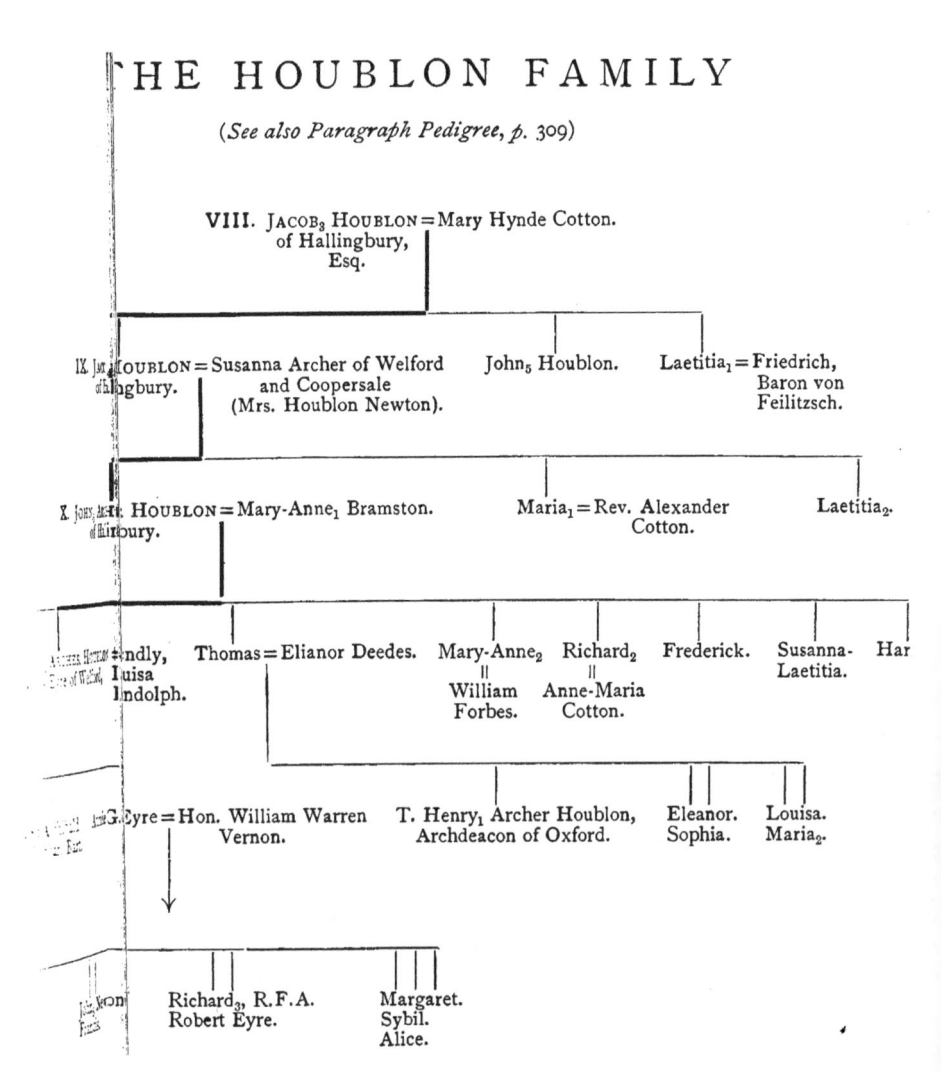

THE HOUBLON FAMILY

(See also Paragraph Pedigree, p. 309)

VIII. JACOB₃ HOUBLON = Mary Hynde Cotton.
of Hallingbury,
Esq.

IX. J.. HOUBLON = Susanna Archer of Welford   John₅ Houblon.   Laetitia₁ = Friedrich,
of Hallingbury.   and Coopersale   Baron von
                   (Mrs. Houblon Newton).   Feilitzsch.

X. JOHN ARCH. HOUBLON = Mary-Anne₁ Bramston.   Maria₁ = Rev. Alexander   Laetitia₂.
of Hallingbury.   Cotton.

... Hendly,   Thomas = Elianor Deedes.   Mary-Anne₂   Richard₂   Frederick.   Susanna-   Har—
Louisa   ‖   ‖   Laetitia.
Randolph.   William   Anne-Maria
                                         Forbes.   Cotton.

...G. Eyre = Hon. William Warren   T. Henry₁ Archer Houblon,   Eleanor.   Louisa.
                 Vernon.   Archdeacon of Oxford.   Sophia.   Maria₂.

Richard₃, R.F.A.   Margaret.
Robert Eyre.   Sybil.
                     Alice.

TABLE OF ALLIANCES TO VOL. II.

TABLE OF ALLIA

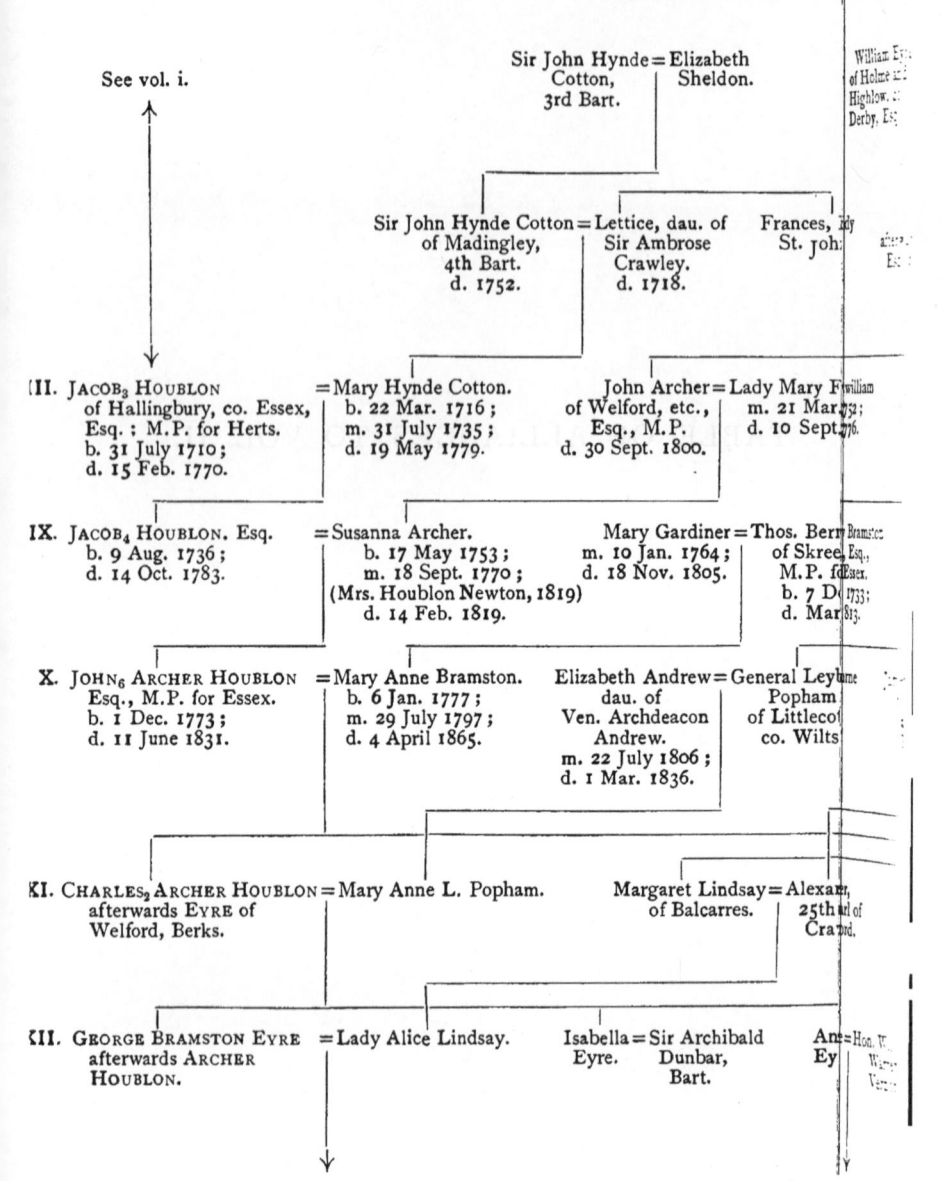

```
                            Sir John Hynde = Elizabeth              William E...
See vol. i.                    Cotton,       Sheldon.               of Holme ...
    ↑                          3rd Bart.                            Highlow, ...
    |                                                                Derby, E...
    |                                  |
    |              ┌───────────────────┴──────────┐
    |              |                              |
    |     Sir John Hynde Cotton = Lettice, dau. of   Frances,  ...
    |        of Madingley,        Sir Ambrose         St. John  ...
    |          4th Bart.           Crawley.                      E...
    |          d. 1752.            d. 1718.
    |                                  |
    |         ┌────────────────────────┴─────────────┐
    |         |                                      |
VIII. JACOB₃ HOUBLON = Mary Hynde Cotton.    John Archer = Lady Mary F... William
   of Hallingbury, co. Essex,  b. 22 Mar. 1716;   of Welford, etc.,  m. 21 Mar. 1752;
   Esq.; M.P. for Herts.       m. 31 July 1735;   Esq., M.P.          d. 10 Sept.1776.
   b. 31 July 1710;            d. 19 May 1779.    d. 30 Sept. 1800.
   d. 15 Feb. 1770.
         |                                          |
IX. JACOB₄ HOUBLON. Esq. = Susanna Archer.    Mary Gardiner = Thos. Berry Bramston
   b. 9 Aug. 1736;          b. 17 May 1753;    m. 10 Jan. 1764;  of Skreens, Esq.,
   d. 14 Oct. 1783.         m. 18 Sept. 1770;  d. 18 Nov. 1805.  M.P. for Essex.
                            (Mrs. Houblon Newton, 1819)          b. 7 D... 1733;
                            d. 14 Feb. 1819.                     d. Mar. 1813.
         |
X. JOHN₆ ARCHER HOUBLON = Mary Anne Bramston.  Elizabeth Andrew = General Leyborne
   Esq., M.P. for Essex.    b. 6 Jan. 1777;       dau. of            Popham
   b. 1 Dec. 1773;          m. 29 July 1797;      Ven. Archdeacon    of Littlecot,
   d. 11 June 1831.         d. 4 April 1865.      Andrew.            co. Wilts
                                                  m. 22 July 1806;
                                                  d. 1 Mar. 1836.
         |
XI. CHARLES₂ ARCHER HOUBLON = Mary Anne L. Popham.    Margaret Lindsay = Alexander,
   afterwards EYRE of                                  of Balcarres.    25th Earl of
   Welford, Berks.                                                      Crawford.
         |
XII. GEORGE BRAMSTON EYRE = Lady Alice Lindsay.   Isabella = Sir Archibald   Ann = Hon. ...
   afterwards ARCHER                               Eyre.     Dunbar,         Ey...
   HOUBLON.                                                  Bart.
         ↓                                                                    ↓
```

LLIANCES

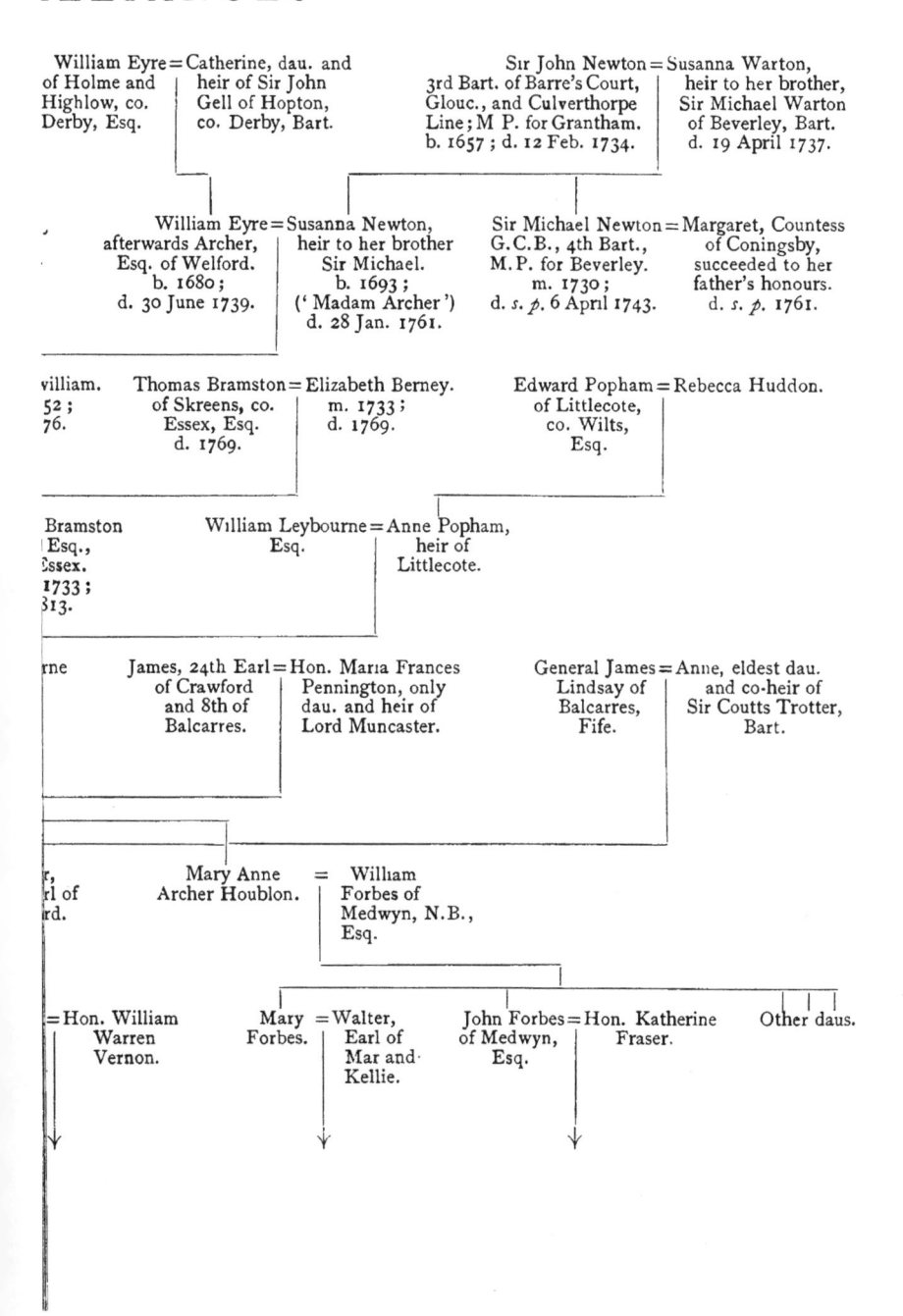

William Eyre = Catherine, dau. and
of Holme and | heir of Sir John
Highlow, co. | Gell of Hopton,
Derby, Esq. | co. Derby, Bart.

Sir John Newton = Susanna Warton,
3rd Bart. of Barre's Court, | heir to her brother,
Glouc., and Culverthorpe | Sir Michael Warton
Line; M P. for Grantham. | of Beverley, Bart.
b. 1657; d. 12 Feb. 1734. | d. 19 April 1737.

William Eyre = Susanna Newton,
afterwards Archer, | heir to her brother
Esq. of Welford. | Sir Michael.
b. 1680; | b. 1693;
d. 30 June 1739. | ('Madam Archer')
| d. 28 Jan. 1761.

Sir Michael Newton = Margaret, Countess
G.C.B., 4th Bart., | of Coningsby,
M.P. for Beverley. | succeeded to her
m. 1730; | father's honours.
d. *s. p.* 6 April 1743. | d. *s. p.* 1761.

villiam.   Thomas Bramston = Elizabeth Berney.
52;   of Skreens, co. | m. 1733;
76.   Essex, Esq. | d. 1769.
          d. 1769.

Edward Popham = Rebecca Huddon.
of Littlecote,
co. Wilts,
Esq.

Bramston   William Leybourne = Anne Popham,
Esq.,   Esq. | heir of
Essex. | Littlecote.
1733;
313.

rne   James, 24th Earl = Hon. Maria Frances
      of Crawford | Pennington, only
      and 8th of | dau. and heir of
      Balcarres. | Lord Muncaster.

General James = Anne, eldest dau.
Lindsay of | and co-heir of
Balcarres, | Sir Coutts Trotter,
Fife. | Bart.

r,   Mary Anne   = William
rl of   Archer Houblon. | Forbes of
rd. | Medwyn, N.B.,
                             | Esq.

= Hon. William   Mary = Walter,   John Forbes = Hon. Katherine   Other daus.
  Warren   Forbes. | Earl of   of Medwyn, | Fraser.
  Vernon. | Mar and· Esq.
                       | Kellie.

INDEX

ABDY, Sir Anthony, Bart., 118.
—— Sir John, Bart., 143.
—— Sir Robert, Bart., 40.
—— the Rev. Stotherd, his Journal of the 'Welford Wedding,' 118-52; exertions to amuse, 125; sacerdotal habiliments, 127; the 'orifice of his stomach,' 127; buries 'a corpse,' 128; the 'Day of days,' 128; the 'Undresses,' 129; 'Full dresses,' 130-131; his Frock, 130; wedding feast, 131; Minuet, 132; doggerel, 135; leaves Welford, 137.
—— Sir Thomas, Bart., 25.
Academy, the Royal (Turin), 65; 67.
Agriculture, Arthur Young on, 46; prosperity of, 29; 102-3; the Mercantilists and, 46-7.
Alexander, the Czar, 265-6.
Amoretti, the Abbé, geographer and naturalist, 203; 204-5; 210, 210 note.
Ancaster, Duchess of, 192; 243.
Archer, John, of Coopersale, Esq., 73; 114; 118; his daughters, 123; 124; daughter's wedding, 118 et seq.; his 'coach and six,' 132; 155; and Charlotte, 157; his hounds, 157; 159-60; marriage, 165; wardrobe, 166; 'what has he done?' 258-9; estranged, 280; will, 293.
—— Charlotte, the 'fair,' 123; 129; 130; the 'divine,' 132; 136; 144; 'just mad,' 156; 165; 168-9; 'riding double,' 200, 235-6; lonely middle age, 281; marriage, 281.
—— Lady Mary, 114; 119; dressing-room, 121; 123; 'Mr. Archer handed,' 129; 130; 'corns,' 144;

147; health, 157; her character, 157; sisters, 158; death, 158.
Archer, Susanna: disposition, 124; 'her apparel,' 129; journal of her wedding, 118-52; married Jacob₄ Houblon, 149, 274. See Houblon, Susanna, and Houblon Newton.
—— 'Madam,' née Newton, 158; 279, 279 note.
—— Papers, 273; 279 note.
Artois, Comte d', 227; 240; at Dresden, 242.

BADEN, the Prince of: palace of, 233; a 'sad love tale,' 266.
Bavaria, the Princess of: love story of, 266; 'dreadful fits,' 266.
Bank of England, the, 176.
'Baron, Saxon,' account of the, 189; 194; 221.
'—— My,' 217 et seq.; 219.
Bastille, fall of the, 226; 228.
Beauharnais, and the Princess of Bavaria, 266; character of, 266.
'Beggars, the beautiful,' 196.
Bon ami, title of, 189 note; 'my,' 188.
Bonaparte, 266-7; the 'Wretch,' 265; 'B.', 266-7; invasion by, 283.
Bramston, Mary-Anne (wife of John Archer Houblon), 261; 267; marriage of, 283. See Houblon, Mary-Anne.
—— Thomas Berney, Esq., 267; 283 note; pomposity of, 286.
Bristol, Lord, 65; 220; 250.

CAROLINE, the Lady, 81; 82-3; surname unknown, 117.

VOL. II.   2 A

Carte, Thomas, 36.
Catherine of Russia, 240-1 ; 247.
Cavaliere servente, custom as to, 189-190; 'mean nothing, ways of,' 219. See *Bon ami*.
Charles, Prince, 54 ; hopes for, 57.
City, the, 'thought scorn,' 28 ; the 'darling of,' 45 ; in 'the '45,' 55.
Cobham, Lady, *née* Newton : her pedigree roll, 274.
Cole, William, antiquary, 36 ; on Cotton family, 37 ; 38 note.
Coningsby, Margaret, Countess of, 278 ; wife of Sir Michael Newton, 278.
Coopersale House, opening of, 279-280.
Cotton, Sir John Hynde, third baronet, 31 ; 34 ; Jacobite leader, 35 ; appearance of, 38 ; descent, 38 note ; great talents of, 51 ; career, 51 note ; active Jacobite, 52-5 ; in the Tower, 55 ; 113 ; 172 ; grand-daughter of, 250.
—— fourth baronet, 93, 157 ; his son Charles, 163 ; dilatory, 164 ; letter of, 231.
—— Mary Hynde, marriage, 35. See Houblon, Mary.
—— Captain Charles, R.N., 163 ; 166-167 ; 'Receiver,' 179, 182 ; 'C. C.,' 191 ; 237 ; 241 ; 256 ; Sir Charles, 260-1 ; 263.
—— Alexander, 253 note ; wife of, 292-3.
'Country, Town and,' 27.
Coventry, Lady, *née* St. John, 72 ; 229 ; Lord, 237.
Cranborne, Lord, Colonel of Herts Militia, 169 ; 173 ; 174 ; Earl of Salisbury, 177.
—— Lady, 169 ; 170 ; her dress, 174.
Craven, Captain, 126, 139 ; 150.
—— Lady, 'playing the D.,' 235-6.
—— Lord, 150 ; 235-6.

DAYRELL, Wild, of Littlecote, 294 ; won the Derby, 295.

D'Estaing, Count, 167.
Doodle Oak, Hatfield forest, 107 ; 114 ; last green leaves, 302 ; poem on, 202-3.
Dresden, great Masque ball at, 242 ; 252 *et seq*.

EDEN, Mr. (Sir F. Morton), and Lady Elizabeth, 237, 238.
Elizabeth, Queen, visited Hallingbury, 15.
Essex, politics of, 284-6.
Eyre, Mr. and Lady Mary, 243-5 ; 254.
—— family of, 274 ; name of, 293.
—— Charles, of Welford, Berks, 293-4, 295 ; wife, 296 ; 298. See Archer Houblon, Charles.
—— Mary-Anne, *née* Popham, 296-7. See Popham.

FARO, 195 ; stakes at, 197 ; George III. and, 198-9.
Fashions (dress), 83 ; Joshua Gee on, 83 ; gold, 84 note ; 85, 193-4, 208, 226. See Modes.
Feilitzsch, Baron von, 'portrait' of, 189-90 ; 'If he loves,' 195 ; 196 ; 205 ; 216 ; 'The Baron,' 218 ; parting, 219-20 ; career of, 221 ; 222 ; engagement of, 228 ; marriage, 232-4 ; 236-7 ; 241 ; 'ran miles,' 249 ; sold estates, 254 ; 265 ; 'Baron Jacobi,' 261 ; 'sufferer,' 267-8 ; 'Friedrich's' end, 268-71.
—— Baroness von, marriage, 233 ; dress of, 235 ; at Dresden, 236 ; at Pillnitz, 239-42 ; adventurous journey of, 249-51 ; letters of, 252-68 ; last days of, 271 ; a 'deep night,' 271 ; her pearls, 282. See Houblon, Laetitia.
—— Baron Wilhelm von, 221 ; 'brother Feilitzsch,' 237, 243 ; ruin of, 269-70 ; letters of, 269-70 ; 'Mein Ludwig,' 269-70.
—— Baroness Wilhelm von, *geborn* Henriette von Schönburg, 236-7 ; letter of, 270 note.

INDEX

Feilitzsch family, history of, 221; 229; 268.
Foxhounds, the Essex, 71; 73; 75; 79; 112; Mr. Archer's, 156; 162; Jacob₁ Houblon's 'little,' 163; a 'good day,' 163; a 'famous run,' 289 note; bought the, 301 note.
Francis, Archduke, 'pretty man,' 242; Emperor, 246-7; 'the simple,' 265.

GALVANI, discoveries of, 203-4.
Game, deficiency of, 120-1; 141.
Gascoyne, Mr. Bamber, 155; 157.
Gay, his *Beggar's Opera*, 45.
George II., 43; 63; mourning for, 80.
George III., his 'friends,' 101; crowning stupidity of, 102; 258.
Georgian manners, etc., 43-5; 93-4.
Gilbey, Daniel, 115; perquisites, 116.
—— Sir Walter, Bart., 115.
Godolphin, Lady, *née* Fitzwilliam, diamonds of, 158; 205.
Gordon, Lord George, riots, 175-6.
Green, Mr., English Consul, Nice, 190; 194; 199; 200; 206; 211; 'all rapture,' 215-16; 219; Mrs., 220; 228; 233; 'The Greens,' 250; 254; daughter Laetitia, 271.

HALLINGBURY, Great, church 'deformed,' 14; estate, 11-12; pronounced Hollingbury, 11 note; 18.
—— Place, or Morley, 12, 15; 17; house, 31; festivities at, 39-41; 'old Hallingbury,' 56; 'Evidence room,' 56; 89; shut up, 117; partly rebuilt, 117, 155; velvet bed, 160; let to Lord Mountstuart, 182; large establishment at, 289; 298; 301.
Hatfield, Forest of, 16; royal demesne, 17; 70-1; depredations on, 86; search for deeds on, 86 note; lake made, 103; history of, 104-10; the Cottage, 110; grotto, 111; visits to, 111; Doodle Oak of, 114 (see Doodle); Lodge, 115.
Hesse-Cassel, Landgrave of, 248; Landgravine, 250.

Hogarth, election scenes, 34.
Houblon, Ann Archer, wife of John₇ Archer Houblon, Esq., 'so merry,' 297-8; story of, 198-9; her death, 199.
Houblon, Charles₁, son of Jacob₁, a merchant, 1; marriage and children, 2, 3; death, 2.
—— Charles₂ Archer, second surviving son of John₆ Archer Houblon, Esq. of Hallingbury, 293; assumed name of Eyre, 293; life at Welford, Berks, 295; 298; marriage, 296-7. See Eyre.
—— family, last remaining members of, 5; future of, 26; letters and accounts of, 47; welcome the Peace, 89; character of, 89; generations of, 110; the guileless lives of, 272.
—— Harriet Archer, daughter of John₆ Archer Houblon, Esq., 288; character, 288-9; memories, 291; her fortune, 293; 'admirers,' 297; life, and death, 297.
—— Jacob₁, Fellow of Peterhouse, 1. See vol. i.
—— Jacob₂, Rev., Rector of Bubbingworth, Essex, 1; guardian to his brother's son, 3-7; correspondence with Lord Palmerston, 7-8, 10, 11, 20; 21; work for the Trust, 22-3, 29; unselfishness, 23; godfather, 25; death, 25; 'Dr. Houblon,' 41.
—— Jacob₃, Esq., of Hallingbury, aged six, 2; an orphan, 3; only heir-male, 4, 5; school life, 8; illness, 9; came of age, 11; 20-1; his uncle, 25; education of, 27; 29; M.A. in 1729, 29; whig principles of ancestors of, 29; tory influences, 30; Parliamentary career, 30; a 'man of parts,' 31; the Cotton family and, 31; election at Colchester, 31-4; marriage, 34-5; birth of son, 39; 40; happiness of, 38; London house, 42; 49; children of, 45; estate of, 46; 48-9; politics of, 50; 52; M.P. for county of Herts,

52; a Bluebook of, 56; his independent 'toryism,' 58; High Sheriff, 59-60; joins Militia on embodiment, 1757, 62; letters of, 72-3; 86; in camp, 86-7; commands Herts Militia, 88; frequent journeys, 89; his library, 94-8; member Cocoa Tree Club, 99; D. L. for Herts, 100; favourite horse, 102; venison book, 109; his 'good neighbours,' 111-14; account book of, 116; illness and death of, 116-17.

Houblon, Jacob$_4$, Esq. of Hallingbury, elder son of Jacob$_3$ Houblon : birth, 24; goes to Harrow, 59; Paris, etc., 59; sent abroad, 61; journey to Turin, 62-5; admitted Royal Academy, 65; 67; society, 68; wardrobe, 69; at Court, 69; letters home; 69-71; 74; 75; travels of, 74; 76; at Siena, 75; more money, 76; a galley, 77-8; friends of, 78-80; a 'black regiment,' 80; good temper, 81; illness at Stuttgart, 81-2; received by the King, 82; flowers for Lady Caroline, 81-2; his clothes, 83-5; request refused, 87; Herts Militia, 87-8; goes to Holy Land, 88; his books, 94; stood for Essex county, 100-1; treaty of marriage, 117; at Welford, 118; future bride, 119; his age, 123; wedding day, 128-30; dress, 153; Mr. Abdy and, 143; 144; 145; letter from his mother, 151-2; rebuilds Hallingbury, 153-5; children, 155-6; horses and hounds, 162-3; his watch, 162; 168; in camp, 168; business set aside, 170; at Hertford, 172; encamped in Hyde Park, 175-6; brother officers, 177; death of his brother, 178; own good health and death, 178; will, 179; his 'mariage de convenance,' 272; relics of, 301.

—— John$_5$, second son of Jacob$_3$ Houblon, Esq., sent to Trinity Hall, Cambridge, 60; 'Jack,' 71; called to the Bar, 89; his tastes, 100; 'devoured physic,' 100; at the 'Welford Wedding,' 121; anxiety, 124; on horseback, 132; Captain of Herts Militia, 176; failing health, 177; idiosyncrasies, 177-8; death, 178.

Houblon, John$_6$, Esq., afterwards Archer Houblon, only son of Jacob Houblon of Hallingbury: his birth, 155; advent of, 156; 'little heir,' 179; good advice to, 206; birthday, 218; leaves Charterhouse, 236; advice to learn French, 253; wedding-day, 261; character, 282, 284; his bride, 283; Captain of Essex Gentlemen and Yeomanry, 284; assumed additional name of *Archer*, 284; two contested elections, 285; his mortgaged acres, 287; a 'famous run,' 289 note; gout, 290; gruffness, 290; goes to Welford, 291; death, 291; 293.

—— John$_7$ Archer, Esq. of Hallingbury, co. Essex, and Culverthorpe, Lincolnshire, eldest surviving son of John$_6$ Archer Houblon, Esq.; 'Little John,' 264; idle at Harrow, 287; succeeds to Hallingbury, 293; married, 293; character and appearance, 298; a story of, 298-9; second marriage, 299; career, 301; and deep draining, 302; encloses forest, 302; bric-à-brac, 303; 'the Squire,' 303; his last walk, 304.

—— Laetitia$_1$, only daughter of Jacob$_3$ Houblon, Esq., 45; 57; 59; letter to, 75; personality and appearance, 91-3; at Welford, 120-1; anxiety of, 124; brother's wedding, 129-30; 134-5; a 'song,' 134; at Thremhall Priory, 171; happiness marred, 178; her warm affections, 181; 'Laetitia,' 181 *et seq.*; goes abroad, 182; diary and letters, 183; 202; cleverness, 184-5; dress, 193-4; Baron von Feilitzsch, 195; gaming, 197-9; jonquils, 200-1; at Venice and Milan, 202-3; science and art, 205; the 'best society,' 207; Turin, 211; at Court, 213-4; a stag-hunt-

INDEX

ing, 214-5 ; return to Nice, 216 ; ' My Baron,' 217 *et seq.* ; a party, 218 ; 'mean-nothing ways,' 219; a parting, 220 ; is bled, 220 ; Paris in 1789, 225-8 ; a secret, 228 ; perilous voyage, 229-31 ; engagement, 231 ; difficult journey, 252-3 ; marriage at Turin, 234 ; her pearls, 282-3 ; 301. See Von Feilitzsch.

Houblon, Laetitia$_2$, second daughter of Jacob$_4$ Houblon, Esq.: début, 201-2 ; amiable, 282 ; death, 292.

—— Maria, eldest child of Jacob$_4$ Houblon, Esq.: birth, 155 ; letters of, 173 ; début, 201 ; 'Maria might have wrote me,' 258-9 ; marriage, 292 ; a 'shocking plot,' 293.

—— Mary-Anne$_1$ Archer, *née* Bramston, wife of John$_6$ Houblon, 283 ; her 'olive branches,' 286 ; her father, 287 ; her 'front,' 290 ; grief of, 291 ; her daughters-in-law, 294 ; 297 ; her sons, 296.

—— Mary-Anne$_2$ Archer, 'always good,' 288 ; married, 297.

—— Mary, *née* Hynde Cotton, marriage, 34-5 ; family, 37 ; life, 49 ; a Jacobite, 50 ; 57 ; character, 90-1 ; on horseback, 102 ; letter on her son's wedding, 151-2 ; and her nephews, 164 ; death, 171-2 ; her *bonbonnière*, 172. See Cotton, Mary Hynde.

—— Sir Richard$_1$, plan of Trust, 4-5 ; death and will, 7 ; 18 ; 21 ; legacy to Lady Palmerston, 19 ; severs old ties, 27 ; a pioneer, 29.

—— Richard$_2$ Archer, Esq., 298 ; of 17th Lancers, 300 ; marriage, 200-1.

—— Susanna, *née* Archer (Mrs. Houblon-Newton), marriage, 129 ; 'looked enchantingly,' 130 ; 136 ; her coach, 144 ; 149 ; her commonplace book, 155 ; her 'Godolphin diamonds,' 158 ; 160 ; 168 ; at Cocksheath, 169 ; account of a ball, 173-5 ; widowhood, 179 ; Laetitia's letters to, 187-90, 194 ; 'presents' her daughters, 201 ; 205 ; 216 ; letters to, 219 ; 229 ; 234 ; 'Cousin Eyre's,' 243-5 ; letters to, 252-5 ; her 'three families,' 272 *et seq.* ; takes additional name of Newton, 274 ; at Coopersale, 279 ; 292 ; deserted house, 280 ; her son, 282. See Archer, Susanna, and Newton, Mrs. Houblon.

JACOBITES, 35 ; intrigue, 36 ; 50 ; the 'Rising of the '45,' 54-7 ; loyalty of, 57 ; nest of, 112 ; waiting of, 113.
Joseph II., Emperor, 209 ; 235 note.

KING, Dr. William, 36.
Kradog, King of South Wales, 275 ; arms of, 275.

LANDAFF, Lord and Lady, 195, 220.
Lang, Mr. Andrew, and the Wogans, 112.
Leland, his Itinerary, 275.
Leopold II., Emperor, 'The King of Bohemia's daughters,' 235 ; 235 note ; 239 ; at Pillnitz, 239 ; his sister Marie Antoinette, 240 ; arrives at Dresden, 241-2 ; death of, 246.
Library, the, at Hallingbury, 94-100 ; the Squire's, 94-99 ; lists, 96-7 ; books on religion in, 98.
Lipyeatt, Rev. Thomas, 59, 114 ; 157, 180.
—— Jonathan, accompanies Jacob$_4$ Houblon abroad, 62 ; 66, 258 ; 'The Lipyeatts,' 237.
Littlecote Hall, Rokeby note on, 294 ; haunted room, 294-5 ; and Wild Dayrell, 295 note.
Louis XVI. described, 227 ; 239 ; 'kingly instinct of,' 240 ; at the Temple, 247-8 ; 'foreign eyes weep for,' 252.
Lovat, Simon, Lord, trial of, 56 ; execution, 56 ; Jacob$_3$ Houblon's Bluebook on, 56.

MACKENZIE, Mr. Stewart and Lady Betty, 68 ; 73 ; 79.

Madingley, seat of Cotton family, 31; 34, 36, 37; library at, 38; 71; Christmas at, 73; 205; 261; 263.

Maintenon, Madame de, 'influence monacale,' 91.

Malta, Knights of, galley of, 77-8.

Manège, the, at Turin, 67; Siena, 76.

Marie Antoinette, headgear of, 193-4; majestic, 227; brother of, 240.

Maynard, Lord and Lady, 73; Lord, his 'gold coat,' 197; his 'lady,' 197; Lady, 218-19.

Mecklenburg Strelitz, the Princesses of, at Frankfort, 259-60.

Mercantilists and wheat, 47.

Militia, reorganised, 62; 88; George III. and, 63; the Herts, 86-7; disembodied, 89; 'Gentlemen of the,' 153 *et seq.*; 'called out,' 168; in Hyde Park, 175-6; disembodied, 177; expenses of, 179.

Mode, the French, 167; *à l'Américaine*, 193. See Fashions.

Monteagle, Lord and Lady, 15-16.

Morley, Lords de, 13; descent, 13-16; Lady Alice de, 14-15; 17; Lord, a 'Malignant,' 16; lawsuit of, 16; royalist Lord, 106.

—— Pond, 17-18.

Mountstuart, Lord, Hallingbury let to, 182; at Spa, 211 note; Lady, 213; 237; succeeded as fourth Earl of Bute, 238; death of son, 258.

NAPOLEON, and Queen Luise of Prussia, 260.

Newbury, Pelican at, 118; wedding party at, 133.

Newton or Caradoc family, 275; pedigree roll of, 274-5.

—— Sir John, Knight of Westby, Lincolnshire, 276.

—— Sir John, second baronet, his wife an Eyre, 276; 278.

—— Sir John, third baronet, 158; his marriages, 276-7; character, 276-7; 'Mick and Sue,' 277; cousin of Sir Isaac, 277; settlements, 278.

Newton, Sir Michael, fourth baronet, Knight of the Bath, 'Mick,' 277, 278; died *s.p.* 279.

—— Sir Isaac, his cousins, 277; knighted, 277; portrait when young, 277; his wig, 278; Sir John's children and, 279.

—— Frances, Lady Cobham. See Cobham.

—— Mrs. Houblon, 277 *et seq.*; assumed name, 274, 279; at Coopersale, 292; will of, 292-3; riches of, 293 note. See Houblon, Susanna, and Archer, Susanna.

Nice, town of, 187; 289; annexed by the French, 248; 250.

O'BRYNE, Mr., 223; *vin de grave* of, 226.

O'Dunne, Mr. and Mrs., 226; Count, 226 and note; sadly reduced, 253.

Oxford, Edward Harley, fourth Earl of, letter of, 171.

PALMERSTON, Henry Temple, first Viscount, and Houblon Trust, 6; marriage, 8; chagrin of, 9; 9 note; letters on Trust, 7; 8; 10-11; 18 note; 21; marriage settlement of, 18-19; and fellow-trustee, 21; death of, 21; whig principles of, 29; favour at Court, 29.

—— Anne, Viscountess, *née* Houblon, 6; 7; beauty destroyed, 9; fortune of, 18 note; 21; will, 19-20; death, 19; Lady-in-Waiting to Queen Caroline, 29 note; 42; of the 'Court set,' 42. See Houblon, Anne.

—— Viscount (the statesman), his mother, 20.

Pillnitz Conference, 239-42; preceded the Coalition, 241 note; 'royalty at,' 242.

Pitt, William, independence of, 53; in power, 62-3; King's dislike of, 63; the patriot, 93; fruitful rule, 217; 'Mr. Pitt,' 223-4; and Regency Bill, 225; policy, 256; 'your dear Pitt,' 257.

INDEX

Pope, the, blessing and cursing of, 80.
Pophams of Littlecote, 294-5.
Popham, Mary-Anne, daughter of General Leyborne Popham, 295. See Eyre, Mary-Anne.
—— Francis L., Esq., won the Derby, 295 note; a tradition, 295 note. See Littlecote.
Prior, Matthew, at Down Hall, Essex, 114.
Prussia, King of, 240; at Pillnitz, 242; 246; 247; bargain with, 248; his sons, 259-60; 'That Prussian Brute,' 262.
—— the Princes of, story of their 'love,' 259-60.
—— Queen Luise of, story of, 260; and Napoleon, 260.

RANELAGH, 50.
Revolution, the French, 225; 'ripe for riot,' 226; 'makes crowned heads ache,' 228; 245.
Rising, Jacobite, of the '45, 54-7.
Rivers, Lady, 187; 188; 196; 223-4.
Rochfort, Lord, 15; 18.

St. GILLES, Countess of, 66; 212; 214.
St. John of Bletsoe, Alice, Lady (De Morley), pious gift of, 14-15.
—— Lady, of Bletsoe, 'Aunt Fanny,' 72; 219; 229; mourning for, 267.
Sancroft, Archbishop, niece of, 112; 191.
Sardinia, King of, and Faro, 198; Court at Moncaliere, 215-6; his army, 220-1; Court, 234; 241; 246; 'take his part,' 250.
Saxon nobles ruined, 265.
Saxony, Elector of, 221; 240; the 'crowns fly,' 242; King of, 168-9.
—— the Electress of, 237-8; 239; tears of, 252; her Grande Maitresse, 264.
Schall, Count and Countess, 238; wept, 253.
Schonburg, Henriette von. See Von Feilitzsch.

Society, London, 43; so-called 'best,' 94.
Squire, the, 26 *et seq.*; 'Country Squires,' 27; views on, 27-8; training of, 44; 48; opinions of, 50; 'the Squire,' 303.
Stuart, the royal, 36; house of, 37; name a power, 54.
Swift, Dean, letter to Lord Palmerston, 19 note; and Gay, 45.

TAKELEY (or Hatfield) Forest, 12; 120 note.
Thremhall Priory, 'nest of Jacobites,' 112; 160; 171; 181-2; 191; 229; 271.
Tour, the Grand, 58 *et seq.*, 'Brown's estimate' on, 61.
Trust, a Family, 1 *et seq.*; terms of, 5; 8; work of, 10; nature of, 11; 18 note; 19-20; closed, 21; 'the Trust had provided . . .,' 46.
Turner, Sir Edward, Speaker, 12-13.

VERSAILLES, Court at, 226-9; 239.
Volta, Professor of Physics, 203; experiments of, 203-4; discoveries, 204 note.

York, Duke of, his debts, 242; siege of Dunkirk, 256-7; 'good for something,' 259.
Young, Arthur, on Essex, 46.

WALLBURY Dells, 12.
Walpole, Sir Robert, administration, 29; Excise Bill of, 32; 35; and the Georges, 43; hated, 44; 58; wisdom of, 50.
—— Horace, and bric-à-brac, 37; on the Bastille, 228; and 'crowned heads,' 239.
Watson, Miss Betsy, 182; 'fears' of, 186; 'belle Angloise,' 188; 'person and manners,' 190; 205; danced, 192; 'painful state,' 197; a parting, 202; proposals to, 204-5; 'frequently weeps,' 211; at Court (Turin), 212-13; wedding, 215. See Green.

'War, the Great,' 289 ; strain of, 289.
Waverley, first reading of, 57.
Welford, Berkshire home of the Archers, 94; the 'Welford Wedding,' 118 *et seq.*; three weeks at, 124 ; the Welford family, 133 ; 'Welford Frolic,' 135 ; estate of, 279 ; 279 note ; 281 ; 293 ; 295.
Wigs in eighteenth century, 48-9 ; of boys, 40 ; 49.
Wine, quantity drunk, 39-41 ; port, 287 ; oceans of claret, 290 ; port and gout, 290-1.

Wogan, Jack, 'lean as,' 73 ; 81 ; fate of, 73-4 ; 'went under in the Cause,' 112-13.
——— John, Esq., family of, 112 ; and South Sea Bubble, 112.
Wogans, the, race of Cavaliers and Jacobites : their ill luck, 112.
Wogan, Mrs., 'the Empress,' 112 ; 'generous,' 191 ; letter of, 191-2.
Wraxall, Sir Nathaniel, Bart., 163-4 ; 185.
Wurtemberg, Duke of, kindness of, 41 ; 82 ; his coach-horses, 82.

Printed by T. and A. Con8table, Printers to His Majesty
at the Edinburgh University Press

```
DA          Houblon, (Lady) Alice
301           Frances (Lindsay) Archer
 .1              The Houblon family
H7H6
v.2
```

PLEASE DO NOT REMOVE
CARDS OR SLIPS FROM THIS POCKET

UNIVERSITY OF TORONTO LIBRARY

SD - #0048 - 091224 - C0 - 229/152/22 - PB - 9781331011231 - Gloss Lamination